ON MY OWN

BOOKS BY ELEANOR ROOSEVELT

THIS IS MY STORY

THIS I REMEMBER

INDIA AND THE AWAKENING EAST

ON MY OWN

UN: *Today and Tomorrow*
(with William DeWitt)

ON MY OWN

BY ELEANOR ROOSEVELT

HARPER & BROTHERS PUBLISHERS

NEW YORK

Now that I near the end of my active life, I would like to dedicate this book to all those who have worked with me, one of whom is no longer living, except as she lives in my memory. I am grateful to them and to my children for allowing me to live freely, and to my close friends. I list them here below in the hope that this book will bring them a few interesting hours:

Malvina Thompson

Maureen Corr

Anna Roosevelt Halsted

James Roosevelt

Elliott Roosevelt

Franklin D. Roosevelt, Jr.

John A. Roosevelt

David and Edna Gurewitsch

Joe and Trude Lash

I wish to express deep appreciation to Joe Alex Morris. His patient help in the preparation of the manuscript and his suggestions for material to be included in these memoirs were of great value to me.

Also I wish to thank those who helped in minor ways: Mr. John P. Humphrey and Mr. Egon Schweb, who read part of the manuscript, and Miss Lorena Hickok for some research in the Hyde Park Memorial Library.

E.R.

CONTENTS

ILLUSTRATIONS

*The following, grouped as a separate section,
will be found after page 82.*

ON MY OWN

I

AN END AND A BEGINNING

I rode down in the old cagelike White House elevator that April morning of 1945 with a feeling of melancholy and, I suppose, something of uncertainty because I was saying good-by to an unforgettable era and I really had given very little thought to the fact that from this day forward I would be on my own.

I realized that in the future there would be many important changes in my way of living but I had long since realized that life is made up of a series of adjustments. If you have been married for forty years and if your husband has been President of the United States for a dozen years, you have made personal readjustments many times, some superficial, some fundamental. My husband and I had come through the years with an acceptance of each other's faults and foibles, a deep understanding, warm affection and agreement on essential values. We depended on each other. Because Franklin could not walk, I was accustomed to doing things that most wives would expect their husbands to do; the planning of the routine of living centered around his needs and he was so busy that I was obliged to meet the children's needs as well.

Some of these things were in my mind as I said my farewells to the staff that Head Usher Howell G. Crim had gathered in the diplomatic reception room and in the hall near the front door of the old mansion. Then, going out past the big columns of the White House to the waiting automobile, I had to face the future as countless other women have faced it without their husbands. I realized that no more children would be living at home. In the last years in Washington we had my daughter, Anna, her husband and their youngest boy with us. But now the readjustment to being alone, without someone else as the center of life and with no children about, would be difficult. Having Miss Malvina Thompson with me made it easier at first, for "Tommy," as she was called in the family, had long been my secretary and she made coming home to wherever it might be worth while. But there was a big vacuum which nothing, not even the passage of years, would fill.

I had few definite plans but I knew there were certain things I did *not* want to do. I did not want to run an elaborate household again. I did not want to cease trying to be useful in some way. I did not want to feel old—and I seldom have. In the years since 1945 I have known the various phases of loneliness that are bound to occur when people no longer have a busy family life. But, without particularly planning it, I have made the necessary adjustments to a different way of living, and I have enjoyed almost every minute of it and almost everything about it.

It was not always easy. At first there was seemingly a greater readjustment to be made in my outer way of life than in my inner life. Ever since my husband had become President in 1933, I had lived in the White House, which meant a public existence. In earlier days he had held various public positions such as state senator and Assistant Secretary of the Navy but somehow our public and private lives had meshed more easily. Then came the years of his disabling illness. Later, beginning with the governorship of New York, we were back in public life on a changed basis. There was less of a family private life. Franklin was very busy and there was at all times a public life that had to be planned and arranged with care.

As I look back now, I think these latter-day readjustments in life have been made easier for me by the fact that I had become used to changes ever since Franklin's illness. He had to rely on many people to keep his own life going the way he wished and to take care of his daily needs. He had to have a good man to help him get ready for the day and to get ready for bed at night. He had to have secretaries— Margaret LeHand and Grace Tully and others; above everyone else

Louis Howe filled a very particular niche. Louis developed a personal interest in his hobbies, his stamps, naval prints, ship models, books and letters. Louis could go to auctions for him and pick up unexpected treasures, for he was as good a bargainer as Franklin himself had been. (I, on the other hand, never was any good at dickering, and Franklin used to discourage me from accompanying him to auctions, saying that I always gave in too quickly.) Some time after Louis's death, when Harry Hopkins's second wife died, he and his little girl came to live with us and, in many ways, he filled the gap left by Louis's death. Harry and Diana (and after he had married again his wife Louise) meant much joy in Franklin's life. Many of my old friends also visited us, such as Nancy Cook and Marion Dickerman, and my younger friends, as well as the children, were in and out a good deal.

Looking back now, I think I had long been preparing for the personal adjustments that came with Franklin's death. I had always been a pretty good organizer and I could make decisions. In the long night's trip from Warm Springs, Georgia, before my husband's funeral in the White House, I had made certain definite decisions. I wanted to leave the White House as soon as possible, although President Truman had urged me to take as long a time as I desired before moving. I did not want to live in the big house on the Roosevelt estate at Hyde Park. These things I decided as the train wheels jolted on during the night. But what would the children feel? They loved the Hyde Park house. Their grandmother had made them feel it was their permanent home. How would it seem to have it swept out of their lives?

For myself, I knew I would live in the cottage that I had made out of my furniture factory on Val-Kill Creek, two miles back from the big house at Hyde Park. Tommy already had an apartment there. The land was my husband's but he had given a life interest in a small acreage to me and my friends Nancy Cook and Marion Dickerman, and he had taken a great interest in our experiment in making reproductions of Early American furniture. After this experiment ended and Miss Cook and Miss Dickerman moved to Connecticut, I bought out their life interest, and did over the factory without benefit of architect, but with the help of a practical engineer, Henry Osthagen. This became my cottage, while the nearby original stone cottage that my husband and Henry Toombs had designed was taken over as his home by my son John. My own cottage has a small apartment for a couple who work for me, two living rooms, a dining room, seven bedrooms, a dormitory for young guests, two large porches downstairs and a sleeping porch upstairs. We built a swimming pool and Franklin came there when he wanted to swim. The cottage was an adjunct of our life at Hyde Park but it was mine and I felt freer there than in the big house.

My decision to make the cottage my future Hyde Park home was reached before the train got into Washington on April 14. Then, for two days, time stood still for me. Three daughters-in-law had arrived when I reached the White House and Bernard Baruch had flown back from England for the funeral. To my joy, he brought my son Elliott, then a brigadier general in the Army Air Force flying reconnaissance missions over Germany. Elliott was the only boy to get home for the funeral. Franklin, Jr., was commanding a destroyer escort in the Pacific war zone, and John was on an aircraft carrier in the same area. James, then assistant chief of staff and intelligence officer of Amphibious Group 13 in Philippine waters, arrived home the day his father was buried in the rose garden at Hyde Park and joined us on the train returning to Washington. I was grateful that Anna was in the house and she, with Tommy and Mrs. Helm, made all the necessary arrangements, and Mrs. Nesbitt kept our complicated household running smoothly.

The will was read when we were back at the White House but it was not until the next day that James discovered in a safe some papers addressed to him by his father, including a letter of directions about arrangements for his funeral. We had not done exactly what he wanted. I fear I had followed my own inclinations, bolstering them by some casual remarks I had heard my husband make. For instance, I was surprised after the letter was found to be told that Franklin would have had his coffin go to the Capitol in Washington, where he would lie in state. I had a horror of lying in state and had been confident that he agreed with me, so his coffin was not taken to the Capitol. When I was told of the contents of the letter I felt guilty and sad, but the funeral was over. It was not until a dozen years later that I myself read the letter or memorandum he had written, and then I discovered that he did bar lying in state and merely wished the closed coffin to go to the Capitol for another service. So my sense of guilt was finally alleviated.

In his will, Franklin left the place at Hyde Park to me and to our children through our lives if we desired to live there. At our deaths a certain acreage including the big house was to go to the government. But he also left a private letter to me saying that he did not think we could afford to run the place and advising me to urge the children to give the house to the government at once. He wrote that his experience with the homes of other Presidents had made it clear that visitors would make private life difficult. Characteristically, he remarked that he would hate to think of us taking refuge in the attic or the cellar in search of privacy.

I was very happy when the children joined with me in deciding to turn the big house over to the government as soon as it could be arranged. I also soon found that I had better liquidate the farm at Hyde Park, since it was being run with doubtful efficiency. While I had my own daughter and three daughters-in-law and two sons with me, I arranged for the division of jewelry and furs, including all that had been designated for me from Franklin's mother's estate and everything else that I felt I would not need in my new way of life. Under the will, I had first choice of silver, pictures, furniture, linen, china and other things, but I decided that I would take very little. I wanted a few things for sentiment—the Turner water colors my husband had given me, some of the linen and other objects that we had used for a long time. There were some things I would need that belonged to me. But, somehow, possessions seemed of little importance, and they have grown less important with the years.

My feeling that it is a mistake to hoard possessions was confirmed when I discovered under the eaves of the Hyde Park attic some bolts of Chinese silk. They probably had belonged to Mrs. Paul Forbes, my mother-in-law's sister, and had been literally "put under the plank," as she called it, many years earlier. When I found them hidden away under the eaves, however, the beautiful silk had been hopelessly ruined by rain water.

After all the urgent matters had been taken care of as well as possible and I had left the White House for the last time, I went to New York, where I had taken an apartment on Washington Square a year earlier. I had thought it would be just the right place for my husband and me when he left the Presidency. He had been there only once— a very stormy day in the 1944 campaign when he drove about New York in a pouring rain and then came to the apartment to change his clothes and get warm before attending a dinner. When I arrived there without him at ten o'clock on the evening of April 20, Lorena Hickok, a newspaperwoman and long-time friend, was arranging boxes of flowers and carefully gathering up the cards so we would know whom to thank.

Tommy was there, too, having traveled with me from Washington. The fact that she stayed on after Franklin's death made it seem at first as though he were on one of his trips and we were living the kind of life we would have lived in any case. That first summer of 1945 I did much physical work, clearing out cupboards in the big house at Hyde Park, unpacking boxes and barrels that had come from Washington. I had a great deal to do, and I would have felt the lack of more secretarial help if President Truman had not realized how heavy the burden must be and lent us Dorothy Dow. She worked with Tommy throughout the summer, reading all the letters that came at the time of my husband's death and helping us to answer as many as we could. Nine cases of these letters are now in the library at Hyde Park. Some of them actually give the life histories of the people who wrote them and document the value of various New Deal projects that saved so many people from utter despair in the early days of Franklin's Presidency.

President Truman also sent to Hyde Park a chauffeur and automobile to help us through the first month. Having a White House car helped us to solve the difficult problem of wartime gasoline rationing and I was grateful for the President's thoughtfulness. After the chauffeur left in the middle of May, I discovered for the first time what the shortage of gasoline and automobiles meant to people generally. I had no car except the little Ford fitted with hand controls which my husband used to drive around Hyde Park. It was an open car and all right for summer. But when winter came we still had nothing else except a small work truck, and Tommy and I must often have been an odd sight when, wrapped in all the rugs we could find in order to keep ourselves from freezing, we drove between Hyde Park and New York City.

I quickly adjusted to living with a small household; it seemed easy to manage after all the big establishments I had had to run. I never missed the services of a personal maid, though I often missed, as a person, Mabel Webster, who had been with me for several years at the White House, where one needed to be well looked after.

There were in the summer of 1945 a number of kind friends who worried about me. One day my long-time friend Major Henry Hooker,

who had been close to Franklin, telephoned to ask if he and John
Golden, the theatrical producer, could call at my apartment in New
York. When they arrived they were very serious-faced and they asked
me about my plans for the future.

"I've had a number of offers of various jobs that might interest me,"
I said.

"Now, Mrs. Roosevelt, we have come here to offer you our services,"
Mr. Golden said. "We have appointed ourselves as a kind of committee to help you. We would like to have you consult us in connection
with the various things you have been asked or will be asked to do.
Then we could pass on whether such proposals are a good idea. In
other words, we would be a committee to consider how your life is to
be planned."

Miss Thompson was sitting nearby and as he talked her mouth
dropped open and she gave them an unbelieving stare.

"Did I hear you correctly?" she asked. "You want to plan her life?"

"Exactly," Mr. Golden replied. "As old friends of the family, we
feel she should be careful to do only things that count. Now our idea
is that I will provide whatever showmanship is necessary and Major
Hooker will pass legal judgment. . . ."

I had either to interrupt them or to burst into laughter. "Look, my
dears," I said, "I love both of you dearly. But you can't run my life. I
would probably not like it at all."

They departed, still warmhearted, still a little worried and perhaps
a little sad. "Remember," Major Hooker said, "we are still a committee
and if you need us we'll always be ready to help."

As time went on, the fact that I kept myself well occupied made
my loneliness less acute. I am not sure whether this was due to my
own planning or simply to circumstances. But my philosophy has been
that if you have work to do and do it to the best of your ability you
will not have so much time to think about yourself.

The first year after my husband's death was a busy one. Many
persons—Princess Juliana of the Netherlands, Madame Chiang Kai-
shek, Ambassador and Madame Andrei Gromyko of Russia, General
and Mrs. Eisenhower—came to call at Hyde Park. And, particularly
in the summer, my children and grandchildren, nieces, great nephews
and others were often there. Among other activities, as summer turned
to autumn, I had a great deal of Christmas shopping to do. In addition
to five children, I had thirteen grandchildren (now I have nineteen

and nine great-grandchildren). It has long been my custom to shop for Christmas presents throughout the entire year. Otherwise, I am sure I would never get it all done, although I am quick about it and sometimes when I have had an hour free in New York I have gone to one of the big stores and bought a dozen presents or more before the hour was up.

Wherever I may be in January or June or November I always seem to be picking up some small gift that I think might please a member of the family or a friend on the following December 25. These packages I stow away in "the Christmas closet" for safekeeping. The closet is likely to become pretty crowded as the year-end approaches, although occasionally I cannot resist opening it ahead of time to give one of the children a present that is particularly appropriate for some other day or for a special event like a trip abroad. Since 1935, I have kept a Christmas Book, a journal in which I list what I have given to relatives and friends each Christmas over the years. In this way, I can avoid giving them the same things again, or if it is a present that should be duplicated, I don't forget. The book is now about two inches thick and, including friends and persons who have worked for us in the past, it contains more than two hundred names. Of course, many of these gifts are mere tokens (usually fruit or maple sugar or honey or, in recent years, a special Christmas card) which I send to persons who have done thoughtful things for me—Madame Pandit and Prime Minister Nehru of India, the Trumans, Queen Elizabeth, King Olaf, Queen Wilhelmina, Marshal Tito and his wife, a state trooper who was helpful to Franklin in New York, a telephone operator at the White House, and many others.

For the thirty-four members of the family listed in the book I usually have more than one present although nothing that anyone would be likely to regard as elaborate. Looking back at one page, for example, I see that in 1936 I gave my daughter, Anna, six handkerchiefs, a book, a wrapper of some kind and half a box of oranges and grapefruit. That was the year that Bernard Baruch—and quite a few others—received from me a token gift of honey.

Christmas in 1945 probably would have been a difficult time had not Elliott and his wife decided to live in the Top Cottage, which Franklin had built on a hill about two miles from the big house at Hyde Park. Elliott was going to try to farm—he soon discovered this was impractical at Hyde Park unless you worked the land yourself—

but it was his companionship and that of his wife and children that made the first Christmas a natural, happy family reunion. Without Elliott it would have been a very sad time and I shall always be grateful to him and to his wife for the help they gave me that autumn and winter. During that first summer I also found myself, when in New York City, spending considerable time with two young friends who were having babies. One was Mrs. Joseph P. Lash, whose husband was still in the Army. The other was my cousin, Mrs. W. Forbes Morgan, Jr., whose husband was in the Philippines. He had asked me to watch over her and I went to the hospital with her when her son, William Forbes Morgan, was born, as I had done with Mrs. Lash a few weeks earlier.

The real point at which outer readjustment seemed to culminate was on April 12, 1946, when we turned the big house over to the United States Government at a ceremony attended by President Truman. In my speech I told how Franklin had pictured the estate, under federal auspices, as a place to which the people of our own country and even of the world might come to find rest and peace and strength, as he had. I said I had no regrets in turning it over to the government for safekeeping. For one thing, my children and grandchildren might now learn about their illustrious ancestor in a way that would have been impossible had they lived on in the house. Then, too, it was better to pass on the house with its contents just as it had been left by my husband so that it might not take on any of the personality of those who might have made the house their home after his death. "His spirit," I added, "will always live in this house, in the library and in the rose garden where he wished his grave to be."

Readjustments in one's inner life have to go on forever, I think, but my main decisions probably were made by the end of the first year. It was Fala, my husband's little dog, who never really readjusted. Once, in 1945, when General Eisenhower came to lay a wreath on Franklin's grave, the gates of the regular driveway were opened and his automobile approached the house accompanied by the wailing of the sirens of a police escort. When Fala heard the sirens, his legs straightened out, his ears pricked up and I knew that he expected to see his master coming down the drive as he had come so many times.

Later, when we were living in the cottage, Fala always lay near the dining-room door where he could watch both entrances just as he did when his master was there. Franklin would often decide suddenly to go somewhere and Fala had to watch both entrances in order to be ready to spring up and join the party on short notice. Fala accepted me after my husband's death, but I was just someone to put up with until the master should return. Many dogs eventually forget. I felt that Fala never really forgot. Whenever he heard the sirens he became alert and felt again that he was an important being, as he had felt when he was traveling with Franklin. Fala is buried now in the rose garden at Hyde Park and I hope he is no longer troubled with the need for any readjustments.

II

"NOT MANY QUIET MINUTES"

I have led a busy life for many years and it has not seemed less busy since the death of my husband. In the years since 1945, my life has been complicated in some ways because my working hours are long, I travel a great deal and see many people. But in another way I live very simply—so simply that not a few visitors, especially those from some distant countries where servants are plentiful as well as inexpensive, are often surprised to find that I plan the meals, do part of the daily shopping and serve dinner for a dozen guests with a "staff" consisting of a couple in the country, one maid in town.

In the years immediately after Franklin's death I discovered that financial matters could be rather nightmarish because I was not a trained businesswoman. At first I focused mainly on cutting down expenses and earning enough money to meet my regular bills. Franklin had been too busy during the last years to settle his mother's estate, which meant that now both estates had to be settled, and this took a long time. In 1933, when we first went into the White House, I had stopped sharing many of the expenses I had previously carried jointly with my husband. This had left me free to use most of my inherited income—about $8,000 a year—for clothes, which in Washington, and for almost the first time as far as I was concerned, were an important item. Then whatever I earned by writing and speaking could be used for my personal interests and charities.

But from the day of my husband's death it was clear that I would have to meet all the daily expenses of the apartment in New York and, for a short time, of the big place at Hyde Park, which had a considerable payroll. Luckily, my husband had left me two life insurance policies. I used their proceeds while awaiting settlement of the estate, which amounted to approximately a million dollars. Then I had to make another decision. I could live on what my husband had left me and stop working. Or I could continue to work and pay most of what I earned to the government in taxes. I don't suppose that there was really much of a decision to make because, of course, I wanted to go on working. In my new position, however, because of the tax laws I could no longer give my earnings to people or organizations in which I was interested. I had to establish a charity fund into which I put all earnings from lectures, which amounts to about twenty to thirty per cent of my income. The laws permit me to give that much to tax-exempt charities, educational institutions, hospitals and churches.

I found in time that I could live on what I earned by writing, appearing on radio or television and reading manuscripts at $100 a month for the Junior Literary Guild. Actually, these earnings total somewhat more than I spend on living expenses and it is a good thing they do because all the income from my inheritances and more besides is required to pay my annual tax bills.

In the autumn of 1945 I had been offered a job as chairman of the National Citizens' Political Action Committee. Some instinct made me refuse because I did not feel I could control the committee's policies and I did not think the people there and I would share the same views in general.

When I am in New York, I live alone in a four-room apartment in the East Sixties, having given up my Washington Square apartment a few years after Franklin's death. There were originally two bedrooms on the second floor but one of them I converted into my office and the other one I had divided into two small bedrooms so that I could have an occasional overnight guest. On the first floor there is a kitchen and a very small space supposed to serve as both entrance hall and dining area. Actually, the living room does double duty as living and dining room, although it is not large enough to accommodate a dining-room table as well as other furniture. Since I usually have luncheon or dinner guests four or five times a week when I am in New York, I solve the dining problem by setting up a folding table in the living room or, if necessary, several smaller tables that can be easily removed after the meal. It is sometimes a little crowded because I have served as many as eighteen persons at dinner there, but fortunately we can overflow in pleasant weather into my small garden, where we are shaded by a neighbor's tree that leans over the high brick wall in friendly fashion.

My apartment decorations and furniture are of no particular period or style. Indeed, they are of many periods and styles and the only criterion is that they are things I like to have around me. There are a couple of my favorite pictures of Franklin, an oil painting of my son John's house and the pool at Hyde Park (presented to me by John Golden), a water color of Washington Square and several water colors of Venice, which were a wedding present from Charles Forbes, a cousin of my mother-in-law. Whenever I look at the pictures of Venice I think of the three Forbes sisters who as very young ladies were sent by sailing ship to Europe on a kind of educational and sightseeing journey. The trip across the Atlantic Ocean was so rough and they were so seasick that, once they were safely in Paris, they vowed that they would never again venture on the ocean. And they never did, but lived in Paris the rest of their lives, and since one of them married the Count de Choiseul we still have many cousins in France.

I also have on the wall a black-and-white illustration that was done for the cover of a book called *A Christmas Story* that I wrote long ago, two pictures of Japanese kabuki dancers I bought in Japan and two panels my father brought from Japan when he was only twenty years old. These last, unhappily, are in danger of falling apart any day now.

The damask hangings in the living room I purchased in Hong Kong, the small tables came from our Val-Kill factory for Early American reproductions at Hyde Park, the carved elephant table was given me by a boy from Nigeria who was then a student in this country but now is finance minister in his own land, the tiny chair my mother-in-law had in her living room for several generations of babies, and the books are those I have bought over the years for myself or been given.

The dominant object in my living room is, I suppose, a large Japanese screen about five feet tall and ten feet long, and divided into eight sections so that it can be folded together. It has an unusual history that I know about and doubtless a far stranger history that I do not know. I visited Japan in 1953 as one of a group of exchange people invited in an effort to improve understanding between our two countries. While I was there I gave many talks, especially to Japanese women. Just before I left Tokyo there arrived for me a large wooden case which obviously contained a screen. It was from a Japanese lady whom I did not remember and perhaps had never even met.

The screen was so perfectly packed that I did not open it but had it shipped to my apartment in New York. When I eventually opened the case I found that the screen, when unfolded, was one great scene —a village done in simple and delicate strokes, mountains, a road, fields, a river with rushing rapids, a bridge, many small Japanese figures glimpsed through a dominant design of clouds painted boldly and flatly in gold. I had no idea what the scene could be and I still do not, but I know it is lovely and fascinating to study in detail. Every time I study it I find something that I have not seen before. Some time later the Japanese representative at the United Nations and the leader of a Japanese political party visited my apartment. They could not tell me anything about the screen except to express the opinion that it was so old and of such excellent workmanship that it must have come from some medieval home in Japan. Eventually, I had an expert examine it but he could say only that it was valuable.

Although I have said that I live very simply, I do not mean that my life is always quiet or that things always go smoothly. It isn't and they don't. There was one day in 1957, for example, when I had a rather busy schedule but I firmly announced that I was reserving "a few quiet minutes" before dinner for a chat with an old friend, Lady Reading, who had just arrived from England. The day was not far along, however, before another old friend, former Governor Adlai Stevenson of Illinois, called me on the telephone. He had just returned from a trip to Africa.

"I wondered if it would be all right if I dropped by and had just a few minutes' quiet talk with you before dinner," he said.

Of course, I told him I should be delighted to see him and he and Lady Reading arrived about the same time. We had hardly settled down in the living room when the doorbell rang. The maid went to answer it. I noticed that she remained at the door an unusually long time but I thought nothing of it until I heard a rather confused babble of voices. Finally, I could stand it no longer and went to see what was wrong.

There were two young men in the hallway. One of them was wearing a bathrobe—and obviously nothing else! When I asked what was the matter, the other, a young colored man, who was fully clothed, explained that his companion in the bathrobe was staying in the apartment above mine while the owner was away and that he had accidentally been locked out of the apartment.

"He can't speak any English," he added. "He talks only French and the maid can't understand much he's trying to say."

When I spoke in French the man explained almost tearfully that he had been getting ready to take a bath when the ground-floor door-bell rang. He was expecting his friend and, after pushing the buzzer to let him in the front door, he opened the door to his apartment, walked out into the hall and leaned over the banister to be sure that his friend got in.

"And then," he added, "the wind blew the apartment door shut and I was locked out. We thought, madame, that perhaps you would permit us to go through your apartment to your balcony and from there we could perhaps climb up on the wall and then get into the window of my apartment."

I said I would certainly not permit it because it would not be possible and anyway I was not going to have two young men risking their necks in my garden. I sent the maid to find the janitor so he could use his pass key to open the apartment but she came back saying that the janitor was on his vacation. Then, suddenly, the French boy cried:

"Oh, madame! I forgot! I left the water running in the bathtub and it will overflow and flood the floor."

Yes, I thought, and it will all come down through my apartment ceiling!

At that moment, Governor Stevenson came to the door, saying that he could no longer stand the suspense and wanted to know what was wrong. When I explained, he rose to the emergency by dashing down into the basement and turning all the knobs he could find, in an effort to shut off the water for the entire building. Meantime, I sent around the corner to get a locksmith. By the time he arrived, Governor Stevenson had acknowledged a certain lack of success as a plumber, but the locksmith was able to open the door of the boy's apartment before we were flooded out. It was all rather amusing, but it did interfere with my "few quiet minutes" with my guests. In fact, by the time we sat down again it was so late that Dore Schary had arrived to be my guest at dinner and to read for all of us the new play he had written about Franklin's illness at Campobello.

I don't normally have many quiet minutes in the day.* I get up around seven-thirty o'clock most mornings and take a couple of vitamin pills. I also take three garlic pills which were recommended to me by Dr. David Gurewitsch as helping to improve the memory. They are chocolate coated, have no other smell or taste and, I hope, have a beneficial effect on my memory, which is nothing to brag about either with or without pills. At breakfast, I read the newspapers. Then I work out the menus for the day and write instructions in "the cook's book." Occasionally, I like to shop in New York and I have found half a dozen little stores where I think I can get the best cheeses or vegetables or cakes. But usually the maid does the shopping after reading what I have written in "the cook's book," which is a day-by-day journal in which I jot down instructions. A typical page looks like this:

> *Saturday, August 3:*
> *Nellie [my maid] do not come in until 4. Get Little Anna P. to help. 7:15—dinner for 8. Coffee, leftover ham, melon, spaghetti, salad, dessert. I will arrive about 6. I do not stay tonight. I ordered a cake and cookies for Sat. night. Pick them up. Store is going to be closed until after Labor Day.*

By nine o'clock my secretary, Maureen Corr, has arrived to start work with me on my daily newspaper column. I have three secretaries, but not all in the same place!

---

* Take, just for example, my engagement pad for December 9, 1957, which notes the principal events on my schedule:

10 A.M.—Saw a man who had written to ask for appointment.

11 A.M.—To my office at American Association for United Nations.

Noon—Spoke at Carnegie Endowment for International Peace to a college group.

1 P.M.—Home for luncheon with my literary agent, but my son James had called and wanted to come to luncheon so we had to hurry through our business and then talk politics with James.

2 P.M.—An emergency call asking if I would go to the United Nations later and sit with Lady Munro and the three Moroccan princesses during the speech of King Mohammed V before the Assembly, and act as interpreter. The princesses speak French but little English.

2:30 P.M.—Appointment with a television agent on business matters.

3:30 P.M.—To United Nations hurriedly. Interpreted for Lady Munro and

After my years of work with the UN, I became a volunteer in charge of organization work for the American Association for the United Nations. My secretary there is Patricia Baillargeon, who accompanies me when I travel for that organization. When I am at Hyde Park, I have someone there. On my lecture tours and other journeys, Miss Corr often goes along because I must find time to do my column and a monthly page for a magazine. I dictate the column, which Miss Corr takes down on the typewriter. Then I correct it and she puts it in final shape for the messenger who comes each day before two o'clock.

I usually try to arrive at my office at the A.A.U.N. by ten o'clock. In the early 1950's when I was a member of the United States delegation to the United Nations, I often had to be present for a meeting as early as nine o'clock. That proved so difficult that I gave up my apartment on Washington Square and, for a while, moved into a hotel apartment in order to give myself sufficient free time. At the A.A.U.N. office there now is always some routine work in connection with organizing new chapters—we had thirty when I took the job in late 1953 but by 1957 we had about two hundred—and sometimes there is a meeting that I must attend in the afternoon.

I try to get back to my apartment for luncheon, if possible, and then in the afternoon I usually have engagements or errands to run or friends to see or perhaps a meeting of the board of some organization in which I am active. But, if not, I start work on the mail. I receive an average of about a hundred letters a day from relatives, friends and—mostly—from strangers. Virtually all of them are answered but

princesses, all of whom said, "How do you do?" and nothing else because the King began speaking immediately. I had invited the King and his daughters to tea that afternoon but he was so exhausted that it was decided to cancel our 6 P.M. date.

4:30 P.M.—Back to my apartment for tea. It was raining. Archbishop Makarios, Mr. Pendar, an American living in Morocco, and two others arrived.

6:30 P.M.—Doorbell again. I was upstairs dressing. Put on a wrapper and went to door. There were two news photographers, two policemen and the head of the King's household, who had failed to discover that the party was called off. "What do I do then?" he asked, shaking the rain off his hat. I replied: "I guess you go home, but will you come back tomorrow for tea?"

7:30 P.M.—To a dinner and went to the Silberman Gallery and saw art exhibit for benefit of A.A.U.N.

11:15 P.M.—Home again to work on my correspondence.

1:30 A.M., December 10, 1957.—To bed.

obviously that is a task that requires good organization. Miss Corr opens all except my personal letters and is able to draft answers to most of them because she is familiar with what I would say.

I have been forced to make certain rules in regard to these letters, many of which are requests for help of one kind or another. For example, there are always a number of requests for autographs. I can provide an autograph merely by answering the letter. But others ask for a photograph, which I rarely send now. Still others want some kind of contribution. "My church is having a fair. Would you send some little gift we can sell?" Or "We wish you would please send an autographed copy of your book for our club to auction." Or "I am trying to collect clothes for a needy family of ten whose house burned down. Can you help?" To all these I point out that I receive so many requests of this nature that I would have to hire a large staff just to wrap and mail packages if I responded. So I send nothing. Of course I am asked to loan or give money to individuals or groups and for many purposes, but I explain that I have no staff to investigate so only give to tax-exempt organizations.

Then there are other letters, asking for advice. Perhaps a woman writes that her husband is in jail and she wants me to recommend a lawyer. Or I am asked for advice in regard to handling disobedient children or for the name of a good doctor. Of course, I could never give such advice or make such recommendations, but I always try to point out to these correspondents the various reputable organizations to which they can go for assistance or guidance. Youngsters who want information for papers they are writing I try to refer to books that might be helpful.

By the time my secretaries have drafted answers to these letters there are probably only a dozen or fifteen left for me to read and answer. I go through them at odd times, whenever I have the opportunity, and scribble a note indicating my reply. Then, usually in the late evenings, when all the answers have been typed, I read all of them and sign them all. Many times, especially if I have guests or go out during the evening, I am still signing at one o'clock in the morning. I don't have to stamp the letters that are going to towns or cities in the United States because all wives of former Presidents have the franking privilege, but I do have to buy stamps for the large number of letters that I send abroad.

Occasionally, I do something on radio or television. One radio broadcast across the Atlantic I remember very clearly. It was with Lise Meitner, who had helped to give us the secret of the atom bomb. She had worked on uranium research in Germany in the 1930's but had been expelled from that country under the Nazi regime because of her Jewish blood. In 1945, she was in Sweden and I, in New York, was asked to speak to her on a transatlantic broadcast. It was a strange experience. While I was in the National Broadcasting Company studio prior to the start of the program, the technicians hooked us up by telephone to the studio where Dr. Meitner was waiting in Sweden. When I spoke to her I found a very famous but very frightened lady on the other end of the telephone. We could hear the NBC man in Sweden coaxing her to open her mouth and speak. She almost wept. Finally I tried to reassure her, saying: "Don't be afraid. Listen very carefully to what I say and then answer slowly, thinking exactly of what you want to say, and you will be very good. You really speak English very well." That was only one minute before we went on the air and I prayed that she would follow my advice. She did, and I believe the broadcast was very successful.

Of course, I do not spend all my time in New York City. I cannot even guess at the number of miles I travel a year, but during the winter I am on the road perhaps one week or sometimes two weeks in every month, including fairly regular trips abroad. Many of these trips to deliver lectures (I give about 150 a year) or to work for the A.A.U.N. are quick ones, because whenever I have to speak at a luncheon or a dinner I try to arrange it so I can go by plane, arriving just in time to keep my engagement, and return the same evening or at least early the next morning.

I do not grow weary of travel and I do not tire easily—not so easily as some younger people I know. Sometimes, it is true, my feet hurt. What I call my "White House feet," the doctors tell me, hurt largely because of a slight change in the bones in my instep that was caused by years of standing at receptions in the White House. I generally find pleasure in travel because it gives me an opportunity to catch up on my reading. In fact, I do most of my reading for pleasure on airplanes since at home there seldom seems to be time to pick up the many books that interest me. Incidentally, if I have a complaint about the kind of life I lead, that is it—I simply cannot find time to read as much as I wish.

Anyone who travels a lot knows what it means to encounter unexpectedly someone you have met years before and be unable to remember the name. But I doubt that anyone hears as often as I do the question: "Don't you remember me, Mrs. Roosevelt?" A typical incident occurred one evening after I had spoken in a Western city. A man came up to me with the inevitable question.

"Oh, dear," I exclaimed, "I know I've seen you somewhere but I really can't recall where."

Whereupon he pulled a tattered newspaper clipping from his pocket and flourished it before my eyes. It included a photograph of myself and this gentleman—when he was a Marine in a hospital in New Zealand in 1943! I was happy to tell him that I clearly remembered my visit to the hospital. Another time I heard the same question from another man who attended one of my lectures, except that he said:

"Don't you remember that time in New Guinea?"

"Why, I've never been in New Guinea," I replied.

"Yeah, that's right," he said. "It wasn't New Guinea. But I was in the Army in New Guinea and I came back to a rest camp in northern Australia and I sat at your table one night at dinner. I'm a miner from West Virginia and I remember what you said about the coal-mine strike going on then in West Virginia."

I did remember then. I had been warned by my sons when I toured the Pacific area during the war to get away from the brass and talk to the soldiers. So each morning I went alone to breakfast—and often to dinner—in the mess tent, standing in line and then sitting alone at a table. Always, after a short time, one or two soldiers would move over to my table to talk and then more and more would gather around. It was a wonderful experience, and I remembered the West Virginian because he had been the first to come to my table to discuss the coal strike and to talk about whether such strikes were justifiable in wartime.

I could tell of many more such incidents, including that of the taxicab driver I rode with in New York this past winter. When the cab stopped for a red light he turned around and wondered if I remembered him. I didn't because I must confess that a great many young men in uniform look very much alike or at least you remember them as looking alike.

"Well, I'm the guy who cooked lunch for you on Bora Bora," he said. No wonder he felt I should remember him! Bora Bora is a remote large island outpost in the Pacific and so isolated that anyone you see there you should remember forever. I certainly remembered going around the island in a jeep and eating with small groups of soldiers who were stationed there to watch for enemy submarines, which were seldom sighted. It was a dull and lonely assignment and a visit by anyone was an event to be remembered, especially if you cooked luncheon for your guest. It isn't always easy for me to remember these former soldiers, but I'm always happy when they speak to me.

III

SOME HYDE PARK GUESTS

When we lived in Washington the days were always crowded but after leaving the White House my life was so much changed that I feared I might find times when I wouldn't know what to do with myself. Fortunately, it has not worked out that way at all. I have a great interest in many things, a large family and a few very close friends. It has been nice to live in New York City and have the cottage at Hyde Park, too.

Perhaps I should explain that in the past my life at Hyde Park had been somewhat complicated and somewhat difficult. The big house was my mother-in-law's home. She lived there and ran it. She and her husband had lived somewhat after the fashion of an English county family, knowing their neighbors in the other big houses along the Hudson River, knowing also the people in the village and the people on the farms. It was a graceful way of life, even if in later years it became more and more difficult to get and train servants and otherwise maintain a large estate. Nevertheless, my mother-in-law had rigid ideas about how things should be done.

When Franklin and I stayed there we were her guests, although I can't say that my husband ever felt or behaved like a guest. Anyone who has ever run a large household may imagine the conflicts that sometimes arose between people accustomed to different conditions.

I was the mediator who somehow had to see that things ran smoothly. It was not always easy, particularly after Franklin became prominent in political affairs. His mother had not often rubbed shoulders with politicians and it was not easy for her to change her ways. Nor did she. In certain ways, she and Franklin were very much alike. Both of them could be completely obstinate, and I often found it advisable not to leave them too long alone if there was any controversial subject that might come up. Fifteen minutes was just about as long as it was safe for them to be uninterruptedly together. Yet nothing ever seemed to disturb the deep, underlying affection that they had for each other, and nothing disturbed the love of my husband and children for Hyde Park. So, of course, I wanted to keep the cottage there for my home after Franklin's death and as a place for the children to return to, but without the big house it was never the same to them.

My mother-in-law once remarked that I liked to "keep a hotel" and I probably still do when I am at Hyde Park. There usually seem to be plenty of guests there and they may include almost anyone from the Emperor of Ethiopia to my newest great-grandchild. Sometimes there are so many guests that they arrive by the busload—perhaps a group of college students from various foreign countries who come for a few hours to sit under the trees and talk with me on any subject they please, or perhaps a crowd of seventy-five or so employees of the United Nations who have been invited for a picnic. Each year I also have a picnic for about 150 youngsters from Wiltwyck School for delinquent boys. On that occasion I always try to enlist the help of my grandchildren, who wait on the guests and organize outdoor games. We feed the boys plenty and then they usually lie on the grass for a while and I read them a story such as Kipling's "Rikki-tikki-tavi" or "How the Elephant Got His Trunk." We also always have a package of candy for each boy before they go home.

My picnic ground is a large one and in summers it is used perhaps once or twice a week by some school or social group and, if I am there, I always try to stop by to speak to them for a few moments. Otherwise, they have to take care of themselves. For that matter, my own guests at Hyde Park usually have to fend for themselves much of the time because there are certain periods every day when I have to be busy at my work. There are a pool where they can swim, a tennis court, a stream full of water lilies and a boat and plenty of room for walking over the countryside—accompanied by my Scotty if he feels in the mood. When there are small children at the cottage, my son and I often pay my older grandchildren to organize and supervise activities around the pool and on the tennis court. There are always youngsters of some age around because John has a home next door and Franklin lives only about forty-five minutes away. Elliott, as I have mentioned, also lived for a while in the Top Cottage, which my husband had built on the hill about a mile from my cottage but he later moved to Colorado and the cottage has since been sold.

At Hyde Park, especially in the summertime, there are so many large groups of visitors that it is necessary for me to have more of a staff than when I am in New York City. In addition to a secretary, I have a couple who live at the cottage—Mr. and Mrs. Lester Entrup, a woman who comes in daily, a man who drives my car when necessary and two men on the place. We employ temporary helpers for special occasions. Most of the time, however, we make everything as simple as possible and life at the cottage is far different from what it used to be at the big house.

I drive my own car at Hyde Park, sometimes meet guests at the railroad station five miles from my cottage and do much of my own shopping at the roadside stands. I like to shop myself because at the roadside stands I pay cash and therefore I am able to check on prices and compare them, whereas in the city, where things are usually charged, I never seem to know what I am paying for food. During the summer months, I keep the deepfreeze well stocked and always try to be prepared to feed any number up to twenty—most of them unexpected—for luncheon.

One day, I recall, when there were eight of us staying at the cottage, a man with whom I had some business telephoned about mid-morning and said he would like to drop by. Then he added that he would like to bring his wife and daughter, too. A few minutes later a neighbor called to say he would like to bring over a friend—and the friend's two children. There were other calls and finally we had eighteen for luncheon. We eat outdoors a great deal, on the porch, or picnic ground, and the food is simple. I never cook if I can help it but any cook I have must be expert at whipping up a soufflé or scrambled eggs or other dishes that can be prepared quickly and eaten quickly. So, as is usually the case, we got by.

A number of my visitors are friends or acquaintances connected with my work for the American Association for the United Nations or with my earlier life in the White House, while others are official visitors to the grave of my husband. One of the most interesting was Emperor Haile Selassie of Ethiopia, who came to Hyde Park while on an official visit to the United States. He was a slight, bearded man with dignity and strength of character and, I felt, a desire to foster freedom, peace and progress in his country. It seemed to me that the Western clothes he wore on his journey were less impressive on him than the robes and sandals of his own land, but he was a person I liked and admired.

The Department of State had, of course, made all arrangements for his visit. A representative of the department advised me that there would be nineteen persons in his entourage. He would arrive at noon and I was to meet him at my husband's grave in the rose garden. He was to visit the library where the records of my husband's administration are kept. He positively must get to the house by one o'clock because he wanted to see a television broadcast of a film that he had made. Then the State Department representative added sternly that it was imperative that the Emperor have a half hour alone in his room before luncheon for rest and contemplation.

I thought this a rather crowded schedule but I didn't try to argue with the State Department protocol officer. I met the Emperor and accompanied him to the library. He was much interested in moderniz ing his own country, and when he saw the excellent system for keeping records in the library he became excited and summarily ordered his entire staff to be assembled.

"Look!" he exclaimed, waving his hand toward the library stacks. "Study this system. Here is how you do it—here is how you keep history!"

He was so busy examining the library that I barely managed to get him to the house on the stroke of one o'clock. He found a low stool in the living room and seated himself in front of the television set and seemed to forget everything else as the film of himself came on the screen. I am not sure that he had ever seen television of any kind before. In any event, he was fascinated and the minutes passed with no sign that he was ready to retire to his room for the scheduled half hour before luncheon. This rest period had been so strongly emphasized to me, however, that at last I approached and spoke to him in French.

"Your Majesty," I said, "I believe you want to rest for half an hour alone."

He did not turn his gaze from the television screen, but his reply was prompt:

"Oh, no. It is not necessary for me to be alone. I only wanted to take off my shoes for a little while."

Still watching the screen, he pointed downward.

"And," he added, "my shoes are off."

I looked down. The Emperor's shoes were certainly off and he was wiggling his toes comfortably.

At luncheon, I scattered members of the Ethiopian party among my American guests at a number of tables. I served from a side table and people either carried their plates to their places or some of the children carried plates to them. Members of the Emperor's staff were all eager—doubtless owing to his prodding—to learn all they could about American ways. But they were accustomed to many servants at home and I don't believe they ever understood our explanations of why the woman whose husband had been the head of a great state no longer was attended by a large number of butlers, maids and footmen.

After the Emperor returned to his own country, he thoughtfully sent me four hundred pounds of Ethiopian coffee beans.

Another distinguished visitor to Hyde Park was Prime Minister Nehru of India, who came to luncheon one day when a number of my grandchildren and their friends were there. A striking figure in his long, dark coat and white trousers bound tightly at the ankles, the Prime Minister seemed delighted to see the young people and after luncheon sat cross-legged in the middle of the living-room floor to talk to them for a long time. He appeared to be just as interested in asking them questions as they were in hearing his views, and it was an afternoon I will long remember.

Mr. Nehru was troubled during his visit to this country by the fact that he was unable to address large groups of Americans. In India, he was accustomed to speaking to many thousands of persons at great outdoor meetings and apparently he had assumed he would have the same opportunity in the United States. Our government, however, was responsible for his safety while he was here and our security officers limited his largest audience to about two thousand persons—

and they were at dinner at the Waldorf-Astoria Hotel in New York City. He was greatly disappointed, but otherwise considered his visit a success.

As I got to know the Prime Minister better when I later visited India, I felt he was a man with great physical and moral courage. But I discovered that his remarkable intellectual abilities did not free him entirely from prejudice. In the dispute between India and Pakistan over Kashmir, Mr. Nehru was completely emotional because of his personal ties to Kashmir. I felt that he suffered a stoppage of all reason on that particular subject and contradicted the high ideals that he normally expressed in regard to the right of peoples to decide their own destiny.

To an extent I had never before witnessed, Mr. Nehru has the power to concentrate. Once at a dinner, I noticed that he seemed to have completely detached himself from his surroundings. He ate but he obviously was "not present." He was far away and thinking about something entirely unrelated to the dinner-table conversation. On another occasion, I observed that he was really not listening to what I was saying to him and, for the moment, was even unaware that I was trying to carry on a conversation. This power of self-detachment and concentration is less unusual in India, but it was something I had previously observed only in persons who had been a long time in solitary confinement. Mr. Nehru has the point of view of a man educated in the West, but at heart he is very much an Indian as well as very much a human being.

It seems to me that Secretary of State John Foster Dulles's method of dealing with Prime Minister Nehru has been unfortunate and unwise. You have to remember that in the 1950's India was newly independent and the Indians were highly sensitive in regard to their independence. You have to remember, too, that after the Communists came into power in China, India was the only large non-Communist nation in Asia. Mr. Nehru firmly expects India will remain non-Communist, and this is of great importance to the West. Yet Secretary Dulles, in my opinion, has made several grave errors in dealing with India. When negotiating the Japanese treaties, for example, he visited various Far Eastern countries but did not go personally to India. Mr. Nehru felt this was an obvious slight, and I cannot see how it was wise to create resentment toward us in such an important country. Then when India and Pakistan were in conflict, we sent arms to

Pakistan, theoretically at least for defense on her northern (Russian) borders. It created against us in India a bitterness that might well have been avoided by limiting our aid to Pakistan to the economic field. I cannot help but think that Mr. Dulles fails to understand the feelings of many of the peoples with whom we deal—that he lacks antennae with which to reach out and sense the attitudes of others at times when such attitudes are of utmost importance in our struggle against Communism.

IV

THE ROYAL FAMILY

When I was a little girl I spent many hours alone with books. I lived so much in one place or in two places at most—my grandmother's home in New York City or her home in Tivoli, in Columbia County, New York—that I read avidly anything I could lay my hands on that told me about the world.

My father had talked to me often of a trip he made around the world when he was twenty years old, and his stories kept vividly alive in my mind some of the things that had happened on a trip to Europe with my parents when I was five. But after that I did very little traveling until I went to school in Europe and could travel there on my holidays. After our marriage my husband and I spent a summer in Europe but then, although we frequently talked about another trip, I seemed to take very few, either abroad or in the United States, because of the children. Even Franklin took comparatively few trips, although he felt he knew whole areas of the world, particularly China, because of his mother's family ties with trade in the Far East. In fact, he did have a remarkable detailed knowledge of distant lands, even if he had never seen them, because of his reading about naval affairs and his interest in collecting stamps. He could describe remote sea-coasts in amazing detail and once, during a critical time in World War II, he confounded the Prime Minister of New Zealand by his familiarity with an area he had never visited.

They were discussing the possibility of establishing an outlying Allied base on an island off the New Zealand coast. A particular small island was suggested by the Prime Minister but the President promptly suggested another tiny island in the same area.

"It has a good natural harbor," he added.

The Prime Minister looked at him in amazement. "Why, I never even heard of such an island," he exclaimed. "You must be confused."

Franklin insisted that he was not mistaken and a search of large-scale coastal maps showed that the island was there—and that it had a good natural harbor.

For my own part, however, such remote parts of the world were only glamorous dreams. After Franklin's death, I never really planned to travel alone or purely for pleasure, but as it turned out various circumstances have taken me on many trips that covered a large part of the world in recent years. I do not want to tell about them in chronological order—in fact, I fear there will be a minimum of chronology in this book—because that would doubtless be like a second-hand Cook's Tour. But I do want to say something here about the invitation I received in the spring of 1948 to visit England for the unveiling of the statue of my husband in Grosvenor Square, when I was also invited to spend a weekend at Windsor Castle.

I had met King George VI and Queen Elizabeth on two previous occasions. The first was when they visited America before the war and stayed with us both at the White House and at Hyde Park, where I served them a picnic meal of hot dogs and hamburgers that attracted quite a lot of attention in our newspapers. I admired both of them and found the Queen a warm and positive personality. I shall never forget the day they left Hyde Park to go back to London at a time when the threat of tragic events in Europe already weighed heavily on all of us. Franklin and I went with them to the Hyde Park railroad station, where their special train was waiting. Nobody had arranged any ceremony but, of course, the public knew the time of their departure and crowds had gathered. The steep little banks rising on the side of the river were covered with spectators who waited, rather silently, until our good-bys were said. But, as the train pulled out, somebody began singing "Auld Lang Syne" and then everybody was singing and it seemed to me that there was something of our friendship and our sadness and something of the uncertainty of our futures in that song that could not have been said as well in any other words. I think the King and Queen, standing on the rear platform of the train as it pulled slowly away, were deeply moved. I know I was.

Later, in 1942 I saw the King and Queen in London when they refused to leave Buckingham Palace to escape the wartime bombardment of their capital. At that time I stayed briefly at the Palace with them and also drove with them in the city to inspect the damaged areas where bombs had fallen. The people would gather almost everywhere they went, standing outside the ruins of their houses and waiting until Their Majesties had tramped through the rubble. Often the King or Queen spoke to them quietly and on other occasions the people would address their monarch, but these exchanges of words were always in a tone of sympathetic understanding. The people suffered stoically and I never heard them complain or speak bitterly.

When I accepted the invitation to return to London for the unveiling of the statue I arranged for Miss Thompson to accompany me. President Truman had appointed my husband's old friend and partner, Major Henry Hooker, as special ambassador to represent him and I knew I would be well cared for. But I was worried and I suppose that I was most worried about what I would wear. This had never been a problem that caused me a great deal of concern, and I sometimes remarked that I preferred to travel with only one evening dress because then I didn't have to worry about what to wear since there was no choice. But going to Windsor Castle was different: Queen Elizabeth always had such a wonderful wardrobe and always looked as if she had just a moment before been in the hands of a skillful maid and hairdresser as, indeed, she usually had been. When she visited the White House she was accompanied by three maids and there were hardly enough closets to accommodate all her dresses properly.

I could not travel in such style but as I worried over the problem I realized that I did not have much experience to draw on in deciding what I would need. Clothes had been of very little importance when I visited England during the war. I was flying then and was permitted to take very little luggage. Furthermore, there was no elaborate entertaining during the war and I did not need many changes. Even so, I had been a bit taken aback when I arrived at Buckingham Palace on that trip and was shown my dressing room with huge closets all around the walls. The maid who unpacked my luggage was well trained but I could see that she was surprised when all she could find to hang up in the enormous expanse of wardrobes was one evening dress, one afternoon dress, a few blouses and an extra skirt!

Remembering that occasion, I came to the conclusion that no matter what I decided to take on this trip my wardrobe might be rather skimpy for peacetime at Windsor Castle. One thing helped me greatly, however. I was in mourning and a black dress is a black dress. No one sees much difference in what you wear in such circumstances. So I took only one dressy evening dress in black, one less dressy evening dress in black, one afternoon dress, a kind of rough country suit and coat and a simple black dress and long coat. I had two black hats, one designed to withstand the ever-rainy English weather and one a little more dressy for special occasions. As I looked back on it later, I am quite sure that I was right and that clothes made no difference, for all black dresses look alike. I did not succeed, however, in looking as beautifully perfect on all occasions as did the Queen when she visited the United States.

If I was nervous about my visit before I left the United States I was still more nervous after arriving in England and being driven out through the countryside to Windsor. In some ways I rather dreaded the formality of a visit to a castle inhabited by a reigning monarch, but I knew some of my friends, including the Churchills, would be there and, in fact, once I had arrived everything was so interesting that I did not have time to think of my shyness.

The King and Queen were kindness itself. They showed me to my room and sitting room and told me that the King's mother, Queen Mary, was staying over at the Castle in order to greet me. During my visit, breakfast was brought to my room but luncheon and dinner were served in the big dining room, and at dinner a Highland piper, dressed in kilts, came in to march once around the table, playing his bagpipes. There was, of course, much formality but I was impressed by the easy manner of the King, dressed during the day in tweed jacket and slacks like a country squire relaxing on the weekend, and by the skill of the Queen in keeping their family life on a warm, friendly level even in such a historic setting as Windsor Castle. There were many occasions when I felt that I might have been in almost any well-to-do British or American home. Princess Margaret, for example, had some young friends in and they promptly turned on the phonograph to listen to popular records. I was amused to notice that, like most fathers, the first thing the King said when we came into the room was: "Meg, the music is too loud. Will you please turn it down?"

On our first evening at the palace we were taken on a tour of the galleries after dinner. Like my mother-in-law at her Hyde Park home, Queen Mary knew where every painting and *objet d'art* was placed— or at least where she thought each one should be placed. As a matter of fact, not everything was in the same place that it had been when she was the mistress of Windsor Castle. She promptly observed with no particular pleasure that the King had changed the hanging of several paintings. Then she must have noticed that some art object was missing, because she asked her son what had happened to it. Perhaps with some hesitation, he replied that the object in question was behind a curtain. It made me realize that the King, like any other son, must watch whatever he does in the light of his mother's interest.

During our tour, we came to a long gallery with a striking portrait in one corner. The King called Princess Margaret to join us and got a stool which he placed for her to stand on under the portrait. It was a painting of one of the Princess' distant ancestors—I simply cannot recall who—and there was a quite remarkable resemblance between the picture and the handsome young girl standing on a stool beneath it. The King seemed pleased to demonstrate the resemblance and I guessed that Princess Margaret was accustomed to being asked to climb up on the stool.

The next day we went through the library at Windsor, which I had seen once before. To me it is one of the most interesting I have ever visited because of its historic documents and prints. I was especially interested in one of the newer manuscripts, which will one day be a historic document too. Princess Margaret took it out of the case to show it to us. It was an account of the coronation of her father and mother written by Princess Elizabeth, who was a small girl at the time. It was charmingly done, and later when Elizabeth herself was crowned I thought how often her account of that other coronation must have come to her mind.

I was particularly struck by the then Princess Elizabeth, still a young girl at the time of my visit but very serious-minded. She came to me after a dinner given by the "Pilgrims" and said: "I understand you have been to see some of the homes where we are trying to rehabilitate young women offenders against the law. I have not yet been to see them but could you give me your opinion?"

I told her I was very favorably impressed by the experiment. The government had taken over some of the country's historic homes that the owners could no longer afford to maintain, and had put them under the care of young women prisoners who, with expert guidance and advice, had done the work of rehabilitating the houses and gardens to preserve them as national monuments. Thus it was hoped not only to maintain these monuments to the past but, in doing so, to assist the young women to rebuild their own lives. What struck me at the time was that this young Princess was so interested in social problems and how they were being handled. My friend Lady Reading headed an extraordinary organization of women doing volunteer work in England, and she, I am sure, influenced the young Princesses and helped them to understand the social needs of the country.

One evening during my visit at Windsor Castle, when Mr. Churchill was there, we played The Game—a form of charades which is also popular in America. Queen Elizabeth acted as a kind of master of ceremonies and chose the words that the rest of us were called upon to act out in such a way that they could be guessed. She puzzled for some time over various words and occasionally turned to Mr. Churchill for assistance, but without success. The former Prime Minister, with a decoration on the bosom of his stiff white shirt and a cigar in his hand, sat glumly aside and would have nothing to do with The Game, which he obviously regarded as inane and a waste of time for adults. Not even the Queen's pleas for advice could move him to take a small part in the activities. He just kept on being glum.

Mr. Churchill—now Sir Winston—is, of course, one of the very unusual figures of our time. He was frequently at the White House during the tense years of the war and he and Franklin had many interests in common—not counting winning the war—so that they enjoyed each other's company. They could talk for hours after dinner on any number of subjects. My husband, however, was so burdened with work that it was a terrible strain on him to sit up late at night with Mr. Churchill after working until 1 or 2 A.M. and then have to be at his desk early the next day while his guest stayed in his room until 11 A.M. I suppose I showed my concern about this at the time and the Prime Minister probably remembered it when on a later occasion in London he said:

"You don't really approve of me, do you, Mrs. Roosevelt?"

Looking back on it, I don't suppose I really did—though the cigars and the various favorite drinks I had to remember had something to do with it, too, which he doubtless guessed.

I said good-by to everyone at Windsor Castle on Sunday evening since I was leaving early Monday morning and did not expect to see them again before my departure. But Queen Mary did not say good-by. Instead, she raised her eyebrows in a question.

"Are not my son and daughter-in-law seeing you in the morning?" she asked in a surprised voice. "I shall see you in any case!"

I protested but, to my horror, the next morning she was up and dressed to perfection, her white hair perfectly waved in a kind of pompadour, and waiting in the big corridor to say good-by to me.

And she had made her son, the poor King, get up also to see me off!

I think I might interrupt my story here to say that I have seen Princess Elizabeth on several occasions since she became Queen. Her loveliness does not change but she seems to me still more serious, as one might expect her to be under the burden of her duties. It is my custom when on a visit to London to call at Buckingham Palace and "sign the book"—a large volume on a big table near the door. I did so during one quick trip to England and then continued on to Glasgow and Nottingham, where I had various engagements. After I left London, the Queen got in touch with Lady Reading and invited me to the Palace for a chat. I returned to London on my last afternoon in England, was met at the station by Lady Reading and we drove directly to the Palace. A lady-in-waiting and a secretary met me on the ground floor and, after a few moments' conversation, said that the Queen was ready to see me. We went up in the old-style cage-type lift and to the Queen's sitting room overlooking a garden. She was at her desk with a fire crackling in the fireplace, and she greeted me graciously.

Much of our conversation was about her son, Prince Charles, who had had his tonsils out only that morning. As soon as he recovered from the anesthetic, she said, he asked for ice cream as a reward and since then he had twice again wanted ice cream.

We talked for a while about the troubles facing our two countries and the difficulties in the relations of the United States and Britain. After half an hour—since it is protocol to wait for the Queen to end a conversation—she smiled and remarked that she knew I had to have time to get dressed for a dinner engagement, and I departed. I had noticed that the Queen's entourage seemed much younger than when I had previously visited the Palace, and a young secretary escorted me to my automobile.

"It must be terribly hard," I said to him, "for anyone as young as the Queen to have so many official responsibilities and also carry on as a wife and mother."

He looked at me with what I thought was a surprised expression and said briskly: "Oh, no. Not at all. The Queen is very well departmentalized." How *does* one departmentalize one's heart, I thought!

I saw the Queen again for a moment when she and Prince Philip were on their official visit to the United States in 1957. Our meeting was immediately before a big luncheon for her at the Waldorf-Astoria Hotel and there was no time in the crush to exchange more than a few words. What she did say, however, was to the point—she was very much frustrated because she was having only one day in New York and would not get an opportunity to visit the shops on Fifth Avenue.

But to return to the story of my visit at Windsor Castle, and the unveiling of Franklin's statue. I had been given detailed directions through our Embassy about what to do practically every minute during the ceremony at Grosvenor Square. I was to arrive, of course, before the Royal Family and to be seated. Our Embassy faces the square and the windows were crowded with spectators. Special tickets were required for admission to the enclosure around the statue and they were precious few, so the fortunate guests arrived clutching their invitations tightly and were admitted to a small seating area. But, in addition, large crowds without tickets stood around the square, which had been beautifully landscaped in the way the English know so well how to do.

The unveiling was even more interesting to me because there had been a warm behind-the-scenes controversy over the statue. Sir Campbell Stuart, head of the Pilgrims Association which raised the money for the memorial, and the sculptor, Sir William Reid Dick, strongly felt that Franklin should be depicted standing, facing into the wind. But Winston Churchill, who had not only been the Prime Minister most closely associated with my husband but who is an artist himself, took issue. He argued that because Franklin could not walk the statue should show him in a sitting position.

The controversy was very much in my mind after King George had spoken at the ceremony and then walked with me to the statue for the unveiling. I pulled a cord and, as the covering dropped away, I found myself looking at a statue showing Franklin as he was some years before his death. The figure was standing, with one hand gripping a cane and with the familiar cape flowing back from his shoulders. It gave the impression of a young, vigorous man and I think that is the impression my husband would have liked to leave with the British people. I have never regretted that it was done as a standing figure.

The sculptured figure has two shallow pools on either side of it and around the pools are low marble seats where, as the landscape architect explained to me, people could come and sit or eat their lunches. Carved on the back of the four seats are the four Freedom declarations. The architect said he felt Franklin had always liked to have the people close to him. "And here I have made this possible," he added. Judging by what I observed when I visited Grosvenor Square in later years, the people agree with him. There are always people there and I have rarely seen the statue without at least one small home-made bouquet resting on the marble base.

I could not help thinking during the unveiling ceremony how sad it was that Franklin could not have lived to visit England himself, as he had planned to do, and feel the gratitude of these people for his support before the United States' entry into the war. There is something in the acclaim of a people that gives a man a tremendous sense of satisfaction. Perhaps all of us need to feel now and then that our efforts have had some really beneficial results and are appreciated. My husband had looked forward to the joy of sharing with Mr. Churchill the gratitude of the people of England. But just as Moses was shown the promised land and could not enter, I imagine there are many men who see their hopes and plans developing but who are never actually allowed to have on this earth the recognition they might well have enjoyed. One can only hope that, if they have labored with the love of God in their hearts, they will have a more perfect satisfaction than we can ever experience here.

After the ceremonies in London we returned to Claridge's and soon afterward I left England.

V

WITH THE UN IN LONDON:
LEARNING THE ROPES

Now I want to turn back to late in 1945 when there began one of the wonderful and, I hope, worth-while experiences of my life. At that time I still had my apartment on Washington Square at the lower end of Fifth Avenue. It was, for the most part, a pleasant and interesting neighborhood with some familiar old hotels nearby, a few very expensive apartments, a good many old brownstone homes converted into apartments, the buildings of New York University, a congestion of tenements sprinkled with Italian stores and restaurants and much of Greenwich Village not a stone's throw away. The square itself was usually swarming on pleasant days with loafers, young stickball players, amateur artists and chess experts hunched over their boards. There were also plenty of boys and girls strolling, hand in hand, in the evening and I recall one night when, returning home late, I was followed by a young sailor who probably had consumed too many beers and who obviously had mistaken me in the gloom for a much younger woman. He quickly discovered his mistake. My own apartment was on the west side of the square. It was in a fairly modern building from which I could look out at the trees and, on the north, at half a dozen graceful old buildings whose high windows and ancient brick walls made an attractive picture that frequently appealed to Greenwich Village artists.

While I was living there in December of 1945 I received a message from President Truman. He reminded me that the first or organizing meeting of the United Nations General Assembly would be held in London, starting in January, 1946, and he asked me if I would serve as a member of the United States delegation.

"Oh, no! It would be impossible," was my first reaction. "How could I be a delegate to help organize the United Nations when I have no background or experience in international meetings?"

Miss Thompson, however, urged me not to decline without giving the idea careful thought. I knew in a general way what had been done about organizing the United Nations. After the San Francisco meeting in 1945 when the Charter was written it had been accepted by the various nations, including our own, through their constitutional processes. I knew, too, that we had a group of people headed by Adlai Stevenson working with representatives of other member nations in London to prepare for the formal organizing meeting. Then, as I thought about the President's offer, I knew that I believed the United Nations to be the one hope for a peaceful world. I knew that my husband had placed great importance on the establishment of this world organization. So I felt a great sense of responsibility.

I talked it over with Tommy and with my son Elliott, and with various other friends, all of whom urged me to accept. At last, I did so in fear and trembling. But I might not have done it if I had known at that time that President Truman could only nominate me as a delegate and that the nomination would have to be approved by the United States Senate, where certain Senators would disapprove of me because of my attitude toward social problems and more especially youth problems. As it turned out, some Senators did protest to the President against my nomination but only one, Senator Theodore G. Bilbo of Mississippi, actually voted against me. He had been critical of statements I had made previously in regard to discrimination against Negroes, but when some of the newspapermen in Washington asked him why he opposed my nomination he replied only that he had so many reasons he would have to write a book in order to cover them all. Anyway, my nomination was confirmed by the Senate, and I still marvel at it.

There was not much time left before the delegates were to leave for

London and I had to get ready in a hurry after receiving all kinds of
instructions from the Department of State. I might point out here that
as a delegate to the United Nations, and later, as a member of the
Commission on Human Rights I received a salary that would have
amounted to about $14,300 a year, except that one is paid only for the
days one actually works. My transportation and hotel room bills were
paid by the government and I received around $12 a day for expenses
when required to travel abroad. My actual expenses always exceeded
these figures, but I never knew just how much I was out-of-pocket
because I didn't keep a complete account of them. Therefore, the only
sums I could deduct from my income tax were those that I recorded
for official entertainment. I suppose my service as a delegate for seven
years actually cost me a considerable sum.

I did not know that I was permitted to take a secretary with me to
the meeting in London—one had to be assigned to me later—and
when I said good-by to Tommy I was rather heavyhearted at the
thought of crossing the Atlantic Ocean alone in January. I had always
been a bad sailor, although somehow in the years that my husband
had been Assistant Secretary of the Navy I had learned not to be seasick. Members of the delegation sailed on the *Queen Elizabeth* and
the dock was swarming with reporters and news photographers who
surrounded the Senators and Congressmen on the delegation to get
last-minute statements and pictures. Everything had quieted down,
however, when I drove in my own car to the dock and got aboard rather
late and managed to find my way to my stateroom.

I was feeling rather lost and quite uncertain about what lay ahead.
But as it turned out there was plenty to do even for a confused be-
ginner in such affairs. The first thing I noticed in my stateroom was a
pile of blue sheets of paper on the table. These blue sheets turned out
to be documents—most of them marked "secret"—that apparently
related to the work of delegates. I had no idea where they had come
from but assumed they were meant for me so I looked through them.
The language was complicated but they obviously contained background information on the work to be taken up by the General Assembly as well as statements of our government's position on various
problems.

So, I thought, somebody is putting me to work without delay. I
promptly sat down and began reading—or trying to read. It was dull
reading and very hard work, I had great difficulty in staying awake,

but I knew my duty when I saw it and read them all. By the time I finished I supposed that the Department of State had no more secrets from me, but I would have found it hard to reveal anything because I was seldom really sure of the exact meaning of what was on the blue sheets.

At the time, I feared this was because I couldn't understand plain English when it concerned State Department matters, but I changed my mind on this score because others seemed to have the same difficulty. I remember one occasion later when our Secretary of State, General George C. Marshall, summoned all members of the delegation to a special meeting to discuss our position on an important point, which is not pertinent to this story. Because of some question I asked, he evidently felt I was not clear on the matter and he went over it again.

"Is that clear?" he asked.

"I'm sorry, sir," I replied, "but that is not the way I read it in the newspapers."

Somewhat irritated, the General said that I was mistaken and that he would send me a State Department paper covering the subject.

He did and I read it carefully. Then I read it twice. Still I didn't know what our position was. I sent the paper around to one of the Department's best legal minds, and asked him to explain it to me. He sent me a note in reply: "If this is what they send to the President on the subject, God help the President!" Then I asked one of the delegation's most experienced advisers to come to my room and showed him the blue paper.

"You must be able to explain this," I said. "You must have had a part in writing this paper."

He studied it for a while and then said: "Yes, I had, but obviously it was not intended for you or anybody else to know what this paper meant."

But I am getting far ahead of my journey to London. People on the *Queen Elizabeth* were very kind to me, but nevertheless I felt much alone at first. One day, as I was walking down the passageway to my cabin, I encountered Senator Arthur H. Vandenberg, a Republican and before the war a great champion of isolationism. He stopped me.

"Mrs. Roosevelt," he said in his rather deep voice, "we would like to know if you would serve on Committee 3."

I had two immediate and rather contradictory reactions to the question. First, I wondered who "we" might be. Was a Republican Senator deciding who would serve where? And why, since I was a delegate, had I not been consulted about committee assignments? But my next reaction crowded these thoughts out of mind. I suddenly realized that I had no more idea than the man in the moon what Committee 3 might be. So I kept my thoughts to myself and humbly agreed to serve where I was asked to serve.

"But," I added quickly, "will you or someone kindly see that I get as much information as possible on Committee 3?"

The Senator promised and I went on to my cabin. The truth was that at that time I did not know whom to ask for information or guidance. I had no idea where all those blue documents marked "secret" that kept appearing in my cabin came from; for all I knew, they might have originated in outer space instead of in the Department of State.

Later, I discovered that there was at first some concern among the Democrats on the delegation over whether Senator Vandenberg would "go along" on the United States plans in London or whether he might stir up a fuss. But their suspicions proved groundless. The Senator had a little cubbyhole of a room across from my cabin as his office and I would hear him typing there for long periods every day. One day he invited me in to read what he had written. It was a speech he planned to make and he asked my opinion about it. I was interested in reading it, but didn't feel I could make any useful suggestions.

"When the Charter meeting of the United Nations was held in San Francisco," the Senator told me, "I didn't want to be a delegate. I didn't much believe in international organization on this line, but your husband urged me to go and insisted that I could vote exactly as I felt was right. On that basis, I went."

Needless to say, Senator Vandenberg became one of the strongest supporters of the United Nations; it was he who worked so hard to keep the budget moderate so that there would be no danger of driving out the smaller, weaker countries. His influence meant much in the early years when support was badly needed for this bold new concept of an organization that might be our only hope of avoiding future wars.

After our ship docked at Southampton and we were all officially greeted, I drove to London with Senator and Mrs. Tom Connally. I had once spent three years at school in England at Allenswood so I knew what the English villages and country estates looked like before the war. But now there were signs everywhere of what the war years had done. Broken fences might have been expected at home, perhaps, but until now I had never seen any on an English estate. Trees were down and the woods uncared for. Driving through villages, we saw gaps between houses with new, low brick walls in front of what had been a house. To American eyes this kind of thing looked natural enough even after we were in the suburbs of London. Senator Connally remarked that the war damage did not seem great. So I pointed out where the still-standing front of a house often hid complete destruction behind or where there was a neat fence around a hole where a building had stood. In America we are always tearing down and building up. In England everything remains the same for hundreds of years and I realized that somehow we Americans would have to try to see with British eyes if we were to understand what these scenes meant to them.

We stayed at Claridge's in London. Lady Reading came to see me and I was soon to find I had friends and acquaintances in England besides my two cousins, Mrs. Cyril Martineau and Mrs. Charles Fellowes-Gordon, and the Wolryche-Whittmores who had been so kind to me as a child. I unpacked and settled myself and began at once my custom of laboriously typing every evening an account of all that had happened during the day. I sent these reports to Tommy who copied them and sent them to the children and friends who were interested. Tommy wrote to me every day and gave me all the news of family and friends at home, for which I was grateful.

Our offices were on Grosvenor Square about two blocks from the Embassy. When I arrived there my adviser, Durward Sandifer, said that there were one or two members of the delegation's staff who would be available to discuss with me the problems of Committee 3. I had previously asked my friend Ambassador John Winant to find someone to help me with work on my daily column and mail. He found Louise Morley, whom I was delighted to see because I had known her for a long time in connection with some of the youth work in which I was interested in America.

As I learned more about my work I realized why I had been put on Committee 3, which dealt with humanitarian, educational and cultural questions. There were many committees dealing with the budgetary, legal, political and other questions, and I could just see the gentlemen of our delegation puzzling over the list and saying:

"Oh, no! We can't put Mrs. Roosevelt on the political committee.

What could she do on the budget committee? Does she know anything about legal questions? Ah, here's the safe spot for her—Committee 3. She can't do much harm there!"

Oddly enough, I felt very much the same way about it. On the ship coming over, however, State Department officials had held "briefings" for the delegates. We listened to experts on various subjects explain the problems that would be brought up, give the background on them and then state the general position of the United States on various controversial points. I attended all these sessions and, discovering there also were briefings for newspaper people aboard the ship, I went to all their meetings, too. As a result of these briefings and of my talks with Mr. Sandifer and others, I began to realize that Committee 3 might be much more important than had been expected. And, in time, this proved to be true.

One early incident in London gave me cold chills. Papers kept coming to my desk—a flood of papers, and most of them marked "secret" or something of the sort. One morning when I walked into my office I found a notice to report at once to the security officer. I did not know where to find the security officer but, after numerous inquiries, I was directed to his office in the building. He confronted me with the fact that his staff, making their rounds at night, had found on my desk a paper that was marked "top secret." I recalled then that I had left my office at a time when my secretary was out and I had presumed that she would put all papers away and lock up the office when she returned. Apparently, she had not and I was guilty of a serious offense, which I never repeated. Thereafter I made certain that the papers were locked away in the file and that the office was locked. I also always carried personally the brief case in which I took documents home for study, keeping it within reach or putting it in a safe place. I frequently noticed in later years, however, that information in papers marked "top secret" appeared in the newspapers even before it reached us. But that is one of the curious inconsistencies that you have to accept in government work.

In this connection, a bit of advice given me many years before by Louis Howe proved useful in London. He said it was much wiser to appear to know nothing about certain matters, even if it meant that people thought you were dumb. That way you would not be guilty of babbling about things meant to be secret. I have noticed that people sometimes try to seem important by indicating that they have secret information. But once that becomes known, anyone interested is likely to discover ways to ferret it out. You may find yourself giving away information quite as much by what you do not say as by what you do say. So it is well to resist the temptation to appear important and appear less well informed than you are.

Secretary of State James F. Byrnes had not accompanied the delegation, but he arrived by air soon after we reached London. He disliked delegation meetings and briefings and I never knew him to call one except on one occasion, when the meeting was a kind of cocktail party at which we talked about our work in desultory fashion. However, Mr. Byrnes stayed only a short time. Thereafter we had regular briefing sessions in which State Department experts—or perhaps Edward R. Stettinius, who later succeeded Mr. Byrnes as head of the delegation—discussed each morning the important items on that day's program. These meetings were often held in a large room where around nine o'clock in the morning all the U. S. delegates and their advisers would gather, perhaps forty or fifty persons in all. Normally the head of the delegation would preside and outline the high points of the work to be done while the rest of us followed his remarks by reference to the printed or mimeographed documents that had been prepared for us by the experts before the meeting. Then, when certain complicated problems were to be discussed in detail, a State Department official with special knowledge of the subject would take over. If any points were not clear, the five delegates or their alternates would ask questions.

In this way, all the delegates were able to keep up with what was going on in general—if they listened carefully and had time to read the prepared papers—and in addition each delegate and each alternate got detailed information about the particular committee or the special project on which he or she was working at the moment. These briefings, with everybody sitting around a big table on most occasions, became a regular part of my routine throughout the six years I was connected with the American delegation to the United Nations, regardless of whether we were in London, Paris, Geneva or New York. It meant that we usually had to get up early so that there would be time to study the prepared papers before the briefing session, which preceded the opening of the General Assembly or committee sessions at eleven. But getting up early and doing your preparatory work were exceedingly important if you expected to achieve anything in negotiations with representatives of other nations on the various committees or in debate in the General Assembly.

I drove to the first session of the General Assembly in London with Mr. Stettinius, who was then Assistant Secretary of State, accompanied by Mr. Sandifer and two other young advisers. We drove slowly through the streets, past the Parliament buildings and the impressive statue of Abraham Lincoln that stands nearby, to the doors of the big auditorium where large crowds of spectators had gathered to see the delegates of many nations arrive. The people were very hospitable and there was quite a lot of cheering, probably because people who had just survived a terrible war were desperately eager for the world's statesmen to find some better way to solve international problems.

We had some difficulty finding the way to our places inside the auditorium. Each delegate had a desk and there were several seats behind him for his advisers. The gathering of so many representatives of the large and small nations was impressive. There were a few whose costumes appeared unusual to American eyes and lent a touch of color to the scene—but the most colorful notes, I am sure, then and later, were the astonishingly large and fashionable flower-decked hats worn by the very able delegate from the Dominican Republic, Miss Minerva Bernardino.

The first business of the Assembly was concerned with organization and the election of the first president, Paul-Henri Spaak of Belgium, a wonderful diplomat, an eloquent (in French) orator and a statesman of stature who did much to help the United Nations get off to a good start. As president of the Assembly, Mr. Spaak sat at the top of the rostrum with the recording secretary on one side of him. On the other side, once he was elected, was the first Secretary General of the United Nations, Trygve Lie. He was a stranger to most of us, but, as a Norwegian, a choice on whom all the nations finally were able to agree. Mr. Lie was an able man who strongly believed in the ideas behind the United Nations, which he served well. He was a very positive personality, which possibly was a handicap in his position, for he eventually made enemies. I suppose it is important that the Secretary General not only should be a good negotiator but should be able to make practically everyone feel he is their friend—if such a thing is possible.

At the early sessions in London, which were largely concerned with technicalities of organization, I got the strong impression that many of the old-timers in the field of diplomacy were very skeptical of the new world organization. They had seen so many failures, they had been through the collapse of the League of Nations, and they seemed to doubt that we would achieve much. The newcomers, the younger people in most cases, were the ones who showed the most enthusiasm and determination; they were, in fact, often almost too anxious to make progress. It was fortunate that such men as Mr. Spaak and Mr. Lie were on hand and skillful enough both to give the veterans new inspiration and to hold the newcomers in check when necessary.

I might point out here that during the entire London session of the Assembly I walked on eggs. I knew that as the only woman on the delegation I was not very welcome. Moreover, if I failed to be a useful member, it would not be considered merely that I as an individual had failed, but that all women had failed, and there would be little chance for others to serve in the near future.

I tried to think of small ways in which I might be more helpful. There were not too many women on the other delegations, and as soon as I got to know some of them I invited them all to tea in my sitting room at the hotel. About sixteen, most of them alternate delegates or advisers, accepted my invitation. Even the Russian woman came, bringing an interpreter with her. The talk was partly just social but as we became better acquainted we also talked about the problems on which we were working in the various committees. The party was so successful that I asked them again on other occasions, either as a group or a few at a time. I discovered that in such informal sessions we sometimes made more progress in reaching an understanding on some question before the United Nations than we had been able to achieve in the formal work of our committees.

As a result, I established a custom, which I continued throughout the years I was connected with the United Nations, of trying to get together with other nations' representatives at luncheon or dinner or for a few hours in the evening. I found that often a few people of different nationalities, meeting on a semisocial basis, could talk together about a common problem with better results than when they were meeting officially as a committee.

The first small meetings with the women in London gratified me and I hope some of the others look back on our social gatherings with pleasure. As time went on, there were more and more women serving on various delegations, and ours later usually had a woman alternate even while I was still a delegate. Helen Gahagan Douglas, Mrs. Ruth

Bryan Rohde and Edith Sampson all were extremely valuable on the United States delegation.

As a normal thing, the important—and, I might say, the hard—work of any organization such as the United Nations is not done in the big, public meetings of the General Assembly, but in the small and almost continuous meetings of the various committees. In the committee meetings each nation is represented by one delegate or an alternate delegate and two or three advisers. Committees meet in smaller rooms and sit at desks arranged in a large circle. They elect officers and, if the chairman of the committee is a capable taskmaster, a great deal of work can be done. A proposal or a plan or a project must be thoroughly talked over and, if possible, agreed upon by a committee before it is presented to the General Assembly for final debate and a vote.

So, the discussions and the compromises and the disagreements that occur in committee meetings are of utmost importance. Personally, I always found such sessions more interesting than the plenary sessions of the Assembly. At first, of course, I was not familiar with committee work and not at all sure of myself, but Mr. Sandifer was always seated just behind me to give me guidance. As time went on I got so I could tell merely by his reactions whether the discussion was going well or badly. If I could feel him breathing down my neck I knew that there was trouble coming, usually from the Russians. But at other times when I felt that our opponents in some debate were getting out of hand, he would remain quiet and calm. "Just sit tight," he would whisper. "It will be all right. With these fellows you have to be patient."

There is a question many persons have asked me about the responsibilities of a delegate to the United Nations: "You are representing your government," they say, "but do you do exactly what you are told to do or say? Do you have any latitude for self-expression or for personal judgment in voting?"

The answer is perhaps a little complicated. In the first committee meetings I attended, in London, I was in complete agreement with the position of the State Department on the question at issue: the right of war refugees to decide for themselves whether they would return to their countries of origin. I was a little uncertain about procedure, however, and often I lagged behind when the chairman called for a vote. Finally, Mr. Sandifer said sternly:

"The United States is an important country. It should vote quickly because certain other countries may be waiting to follow its leadership. So you must vote promptly."

After that, you may be sure that I always tried to decide just how I would vote before a show of hands was asked for and, as soon as it was, my hand went up with alacrity. In deciding how to vote, it is true that a delegate, as a representative of his government, is briefed in advance on his country's position in any controversy. At London, fortunately, I agreed with the State Department position, because I do not think I would have dared to question it. But later I learned that a delegate does have certain rights as an individual, and on several occasions I exercised my right to take a position somewhat different from the official viewpoint.

Of course, a delegate cannot express his disagreement publicly unless he resigns, since obviously it would be impossible to have representatives of the same nation saying different things in the United Nations. But he may exercise his right to disagree during the private briefings. For example, before the start of a session of the Assembly we were told what subjects would be on the agenda, and we used to go to Washington for a meeting at which the State Department officials explained the government's attitude. If you disagreed, you had the right to say so and to try to get the official attitude changed or modified. You could, if necessary, appeal to the President to intervene, and you could, if there was no solution, resign in protest.

On one occasion I did object very vigorously to our official decision to rescind without explanation to our people, the position we had taken on recognizing the Franco government in Spain. I was joined by other delegates, and the State Department put off action until it could explain the situation fully.

However, it was while working on Committee 3 that I really began to understand the inner workings of the United Nations. It was ironical perhaps that one of the subjects that created the greatest political heat of the London sessions came up in this "unimportant" committee to which I had been assigned.

The issue, which I have already referred to, arose from the fact that there were many displaced war refugees in Germany when the armistice was signed—Ukrainians, Belorussians, Poles, Czechoslovaks, Latvians, Lithuanians, Estonians, and others—a great number of whom were still living there in temporary camps because they did not want to return to live under the Communist rule of their own countries. There also were the pitiful Jewish survivors of the German death camps.

I do not suppose that it had been generally foreseen that this situation would lead to a headline controversy in London, but it did and it flared up in Committee 3. It was raised originally by the Yugoslav representative, Leo Mates, a quick, bright young man whom I came to know well and who became Ambassador to Washington. Mr. Mates was engagingly innocent-looking and we often exchanged sympathetic smiles when we were both bored by some long-winded speaker. But he was highly skilled in his job, he knew how to take advantage of every parliamentary trick and, if he fooled you into letting down your guard for one instant, he would win his point every time. I learned to watch him with care. In later years I acquired a great respect for his ability and as he grew older and after his country had broken with the Soviet Cominform we began to see some things from more nearly the same point of view. But at that first meeting of Committee 3 he was my very dangerous adversary.

The Yugoslav—and, of course, the Soviet Union—position that Mates put forward was that any war refugee who did not wish to return to his country of origin was either a quisling or a traitor to his country. He argued that the refugees in Germany should be forced to return home and to accept whatever punishment might be meted out to them. This position was strongly supported by the Soviet representative, Professor Amazap A. Arutiunian, an Armenian who ably served for a long time in the Russian delegation.

The position of the Western countries, including the United States, was that large numbers of the refugees were neither quislings nor traitors and that they must be guaranteed the right to choose whether or not they would return to their homes. Since the London sessions were largely technical rather than political debates and since Committee 3 was the scene of one of the early clashes between the Soviet Union and the West, the newspapers found it convenient to make much of the refugee controversy. I felt very strongly on the subject, as did others, and we spent countless hours trying to frame some kind of resolution on which all could agree. We never did, and our chairman, Peter Fraser of New Zealand, had to present a majority report to the General Assembly which was immediately challenged by the USSR.

In the Assembly the minority position was handled, not by the

Soviet representative on Committee 3, but by the head of the Soviet Union's delegation, Andrei Vishinsky. It might be mentioned here that most nations would have had their committee representative discuss the question before the Assembly, since he presumably would be more familiar with the subject. But the Russians had a highly effective way of making the head of their delegation responsible for every subject that came up in the Assembly.

Vishinsky was one of the Russians' great legal minds, a skilled debater, a man with ability to use the weapons of wit and ridicule. And Moscow apparently considered the refugee question of such vital importance that he spoke twice before the Assembly in a determined effort to win over the delegates to the Communist point of view. The British representative on our committee spoke in favor of the majority report. By this time an odd situation had developed. It was apparent that in view of the importance of the issue someone would have to speak for the United States. The question of who this was to be threw our delegation into a veritable dither. There was a hurried and rather uncomfortable consultation among the male members and when the huddle broke up John Foster Dulles approached me rather uncertainly.

"Mrs. Roosevelt," he began, rather lamely, "the United States must speak in the debate. Since you are the one who has carried on for us in this controversy in the committee, do you think you could say a few words to the Assembly? I'm afraid nobody else is really familiar with the subject."

"Why, Mr. Dulles," I replied as meekly as I could manage, "in that case I will do my best."

Actually, I was badly frightened. I trembled at the thought of speaking against the famous Mr. Vishinsky. But when the time came I walked, tense and excited, to the rostrum and did my best. There was a little more than met the eye in this situation. The hour was late and we knew the Russians would delay a vote as long as possible on the theory that some of our allies would get tired and leave. I knew we must, if possible, hold our South American colleagues until the vote was taken because their votes might be decisive. So I talked about Simon Bolivar and his stand for the freedom of the people of Latin America. I talked and I watched the delegates and to my joy the South American representatives stayed with us to the end and, when the vote came, we won.

This vote meant that the Western nations would have to worry about the ultimate fate of the refugees for a long, long time, but the principle of the right of an individual to make his own decisions was a victory well worth while. The argument with Mr. Vishinsky was to be carried on in future meetings of the Assembly and on some occasions he even came to address Committee 3, but we always won out. And finally he gave up carrying the debate and left it to whoever might be the Soviet Union's delegate on Committee 3.

As the London sessions neared their end the austerity of life in Great Britain may have become more burdensome to us, although we suffered very few of the hardships that the British endured in their homes. Among other things, however, it was almost impossible to get eggs even at Claridge's hotel. For this reason, I was particularly touched one day when a lady who lived on a farm came to London and brought me half a dozen eggs.

That same morning Congressman Sol Bloom distressed me by saying that he was going home. Mr. Bloom was an expert on parliamentary procedure and served on the committee on rules. On one occasion I had complained to him that his committee seemed to talk endlessly; that they haggled for hours over whether to use this word or that word in a resolution. I asked if the rules must be so precisely worded. Mr. Bloom severely reprimanded me.

"These things," he said, "are more important than you know. When you are working in a parliamentary body you understand eventually the importance of using the right word in the right place. The phrasing of a sentence or the use of a word may later be of great importance in enabling you to win a particular point in debate. Or it may cause you to lose a point."

I never forgot the lesson he taught me and tried to overcome my impatience, and because I greatly enjoyed knowing him, his decision to go home before the session ended caused me to protest.

"No," he replied, "I am going home tomorrow. In my entire life I have never been without two eggs for breakfast each morning. Here I find it impossible to get anything but those horrible powdered eggs. I am going home."

At this point I had an inspiration. I promptly handed him the half-dozen eggs that had just been presented to me. "Now," I said, "will you please stay at least three more days?"

"Yes," he said. "I will stay."

By the end of the three days, Senator Francis Townsend of Maryland, who was an alternate on our delegation, had discovered that he could have eggs flown over from Canada. So we were able to keep the valuable services of Congressman Bloom through the rest of the session.

Toward the end of the sessions we worked until late at night. The final night the vote on Committee 3's report was taken so late that I did not get back to the hotel till about one o'clock. I was very tired, and as I walked wearily up the stairs at the hotel I heard two voices behind me. Turning around, I saw Senator Vandenberg and Mr. Dulles. They obviously had something to say to me, but for the life of me I can't recall which one of them said it. Whichever it was, he seemed to be speaking for both.

"Mrs. Roosevelt," he said, "we must tell you that we did all we could to keep you off the United States delegation. We begged the President not to nominate you. But now that you are leaving we feel we must acknowledge that we have worked with you gladly and found you good to work with. And we will be happy to do so again."

I don't think anything could have made the weariness drop from my shoulders as did those words. I shall always be grateful for the encouragement they gave me.

VI

TO GERMANY,
"TO SEE FOR MYSELF . . ."

The controversy with the Communist-dominated countries over the fate of refugees in Germany aroused in me a desire to see for myself what had happened to these many thousands of unfortunate people. So, as the Assembly sessions approached an end, I discussed my idea with Ambassador John Winant, who said he would arrange for me to visit Germany with the aid of the Army, which was then in control of everything in occupied areas. If I traveled by air, I could leave London as soon as my committee's work was finished and still get back to Shannon, in Ireland, in time to rejoin the United States delegation on its trip home.

The Air Force plane to which I was assigned left England at 6 A.M. in the gloom of a British winter morning, but the young officers in charge were pleasant and helpful and eager to show me the results of their wartime precision bombing on targets in Germany. They mentioned several cities with which I had been familiar before the war and said, rather proudly, that these would demonstrate the effectiveness of the blows that had been struck at the enemy. They did. I was stunned and appalled by what I saw as the pilot took our plane down to a low altitude and circled the ruins of Cologne and Frankfurt

54

and other places that I remembered as great and crowded cities. Later when we circled Munich and then looked down on the rubble of Berlin I felt that nobody could have imagined such utter, horrible destruction. I knew that the Air Force deserved great praise for its role in winning the war, but I thought that nothing could better illustrate the sickening waste and destructiveness and futility of war than what I was seeing.

I was, later, to see the effects of the first atomic bomb on Hiroshima. The bombing of Germany had continued over a period of months and months. The bombing of Hiroshima was over in a few seconds. But it made no difference. The results were the same.

We landed first at Frankfurt, where there were a number of refugee camps, including one for Jews in Zilcheim and others for refugees from Estonia, Poland, Latvia and other countries that were now under Soviet domination. In some of the camps the people lived in old houses but mostly they were in barrackslike buildings with a communal kitchen and dining room. Some families did not have even so much as one room for themselves but had to hang up blankets to divide off their quarters. In most instances each family tried to make a "home" for itself. Many would wade through the mud to the central kitchen and carry back food so that the family could eat together in its quarters, however small. If possible, each family had some kind of makeshift table and, although they had almost nothing to work with, the women often had embroidered sacking or other material to make decorations that would brighten up their quarters.

At Zilcheim I was greeted by leaders of the Jewish refugee group and they asked me to accompany them to the center of the camp. There they had built a small hill with steps leading to the top where they had erected a stone monument inscribed: "To the Memory of All Jews Who Died in Germany." In all the Jewish camps, there were constant signs of the terrible events through which these people had passed and of the hardships they continued to suffer, but I think they also showed with what courage and steadfast hope they could meet disaster.

Though every face I saw seemed to represent a story more tragic than the last, these people faced the future resolutely. One boy of twelve—he really looked no more than nine—wanted to sing for me. I was told that he had wandered into the camp holding firmly by the hand his smaller brother, who was about six years old. When he was asked for his name, he couldn't remember it. Nor did he know where he had lived nor who his parents were nor what had happened to them. He was just there, and he was taking care of his young brother. He sang for me "A Song of Freedom" so touchingly that no one listening could speak.

A young woman I talked to had a small baby. Both of them appeared to be so starved and ill that I thought they would soon die. When I had the opportunity, I spoke to the camp superintendent about them and he said he would try to do something. I left them despondently, but some years later I was to see them both in Israel. They had landed illegally on the beach at Haifa, they had survived and the baby had become a healthy young girl. The mother herself had remarried and had another child, a fine young son.

Most of all, perhaps, in the mud of Zilcheim, I remember an old woman whose family had been driven from home by the war madness and brutality. I had no idea who she was and we could not speak each other's language, but she knelt in the muddy road and simply threw her arms around my knees.

"Israel," she murmured, over and over. "Israel! Israel!"

As I looked at her weatherbeaten face and heard her old voice, I knew for the first time what that small land meant to so many, many people.

When we first landed at Frankfurt I had asked one of the military officers to make an inquiry for me.

"I went to school in England with a woman whose family lived near Frankfurt," I explained. "Her family and her husband are well known and it is just possible that she could be located if the family is still here."

The officer said he would try to find her and I gave him her name and such details as I knew. Later, when I returned to Army headquarters in Frankfurt, I was told that they had found my friend, who still lived at the family summer home at Zeigenberg.

I asked about the conditions in which she was living.

"They have a very good house and it wasn't bombed," the officer replied. "They seem to be getting along reasonably well but, like everybody else, they don't have enough. Her husband and one or two daughters are there but I think her sons were in the Army and at least one was killed."

"Was she a Nazi?" I asked. "Was her husband?"

He shook his head. "We didn't ask."

I remembered my friend, Carola von Schaeffer-Bernstein, born Passavant, as a very lovely blonde girl when we were at school together at Allenswood. She had a soft pink and white complexion, and she had been a very earnest kind of person. In the First World War, her husband was a general on the Eastern or Russian front and I remembered that following that war she had written me a rather sad letter in which she expressed sorrow about the war but said that "we are all to blame" because we have not lived by the teachings of Christ.

Now, in American headquarters at Frankfurt, I expected to find a greatly changed person but, in fact, she was no more changed by the passage of years and the long years of war than I, perhaps less. She was still lovely, and it was only when you looked the second time that you noticed that she was tired and worn by the strain of life in an occupied country. She was dressed plainly but well and her attitude toward me, while a bit reserved, was much as it had always been. I suppose, too, that our conversation was not much different than it had been when we met in earlier days. They were living in straitened circumstances but they were not destitute. If I had originally felt that she might be in difficulties and that I might in some way help her, it became obvious that she was not.

We said nothing—I suppose we avoided saying anything—in particular about the war until she was almost ready to leave, when I made some remark about the tragedy of Germany. She answered promptly.

"It was everybody's fault." Then, echoing what she had written me a quarter of a century earlier. "We are all to blame. None of us has lived up to the teachings of Christ."

I thought to myself that this was perhaps an easy way of not facing the problem, particularly for a German woman with education and social standing. But in my reply I pursued another thought.

"You have always been a very religious person," I said. "How is it possible that one can be so devoted to the principles of the church yet not protest the mistreatment of the Jews?"

"Sometimes," she replied, "it is wiser not to look over the hill."

Soon afterward she left to return home. I never did ask her whether she or her family had been Nazis, but then, after the war practically no one had ever been a Nazi!

I went on from Frankfurt to Berlin, where we landed at Tempelhof for a hurried twenty-four-hour visit. I managed with the help of American authorities to cover considerable ground, but in such a short time it is difficult to get more than strong over-all impressions. On a trip eleven years later I observed many specific differences between East Berlin and West Berlin—for instance the brilliant lights of the Western sector and the almost complete darkness of the Eastern sector as seen from the air—but in 1946 I was conscious only of mass destruction and human misery. If one had known Berlin before the war, one could only think that here was the real meaning of the word "devastation." Even worse were the faces—thin, cold and miserable.

We drove past the smashed Chancellery where Hitler had ruled and the bunker where he died and past the pock-marked Brandenburg Gate that had been a symbol of Germany's greatness. Now there were desolation and the sordid, degrading sight of men and women and children dealing in the black market. Watching the faces of these people, one got the impression that they would sell anything for food, and doubtless they had, although now they moved rather aimlessly back and forth across the vacant, beaten ground with only pitiful articles in their hands or in little piles on the dirt. Here, in the shadow of the Brandenburg memorial and close to the ornate temple of Nazi imperialism, all the degradation of war had come home to roost on the thin shoulders of the black marketeers.

Later I visited the quarters of refugees who had made their way from areas formerly occupied by the Germans—like the Sudetenland —into the Western sector of Berlin. The people were crowded into unsanitary and ramshackle underground shelters without proper heat or water or food.

"I say a prayer of gratitude every day that no epidemic has yet started," the woman doctor who accompanied me said as we parted.

Before I left Berlin I talked to several friends whom I had known before the war. They were Germans with children living in America and they themselves had lived in the United States for some time. They had endured Hitler but never admired him, and the war years had been an unbelievable ordeal for them. They had survived and they had hope now, but they were worn and saddened by the years.

It was good after boarding the plane at Shannon to be able to relax and sit still, but my mind was as busy as the aircraft's big motors as we roared along through the night. The faces of the women in the black market in Berlin kept crowding into my mind. I remembered with some emotion the old woman who could say only "Israel! Israel!" And, of course, I was filled with my impressions of the weeks in London, of seeing a new international organization take shape, come into being. I was less happy in my awareness of the skepticism of Europe's veteran diplomats about the United Nations and its future. But, I told myself again and again, there was also hope in the air. There had to be hope.

The whole journey, I thought, had been a good one for me. I believed I had grown and matured and gained confidence. After we landed in New York, I wrote my thanks to the President and to the Secretary of State for an unforgettable experience, and thought my work with the United Nations was over.

VII

I LEARN ABOUT SOVIET
TACTICS

I soon found I was mistaken in assuming that my career in the United
Nations had ended. Not long after I returned to New York I received
notice that the Economic and Social Council, which had been set up
by the United Nations in London, had created a committee* to make
recommendations on matters pertaining to the functioning of the UN
Human Rights Commission. It was to meet in New York in the spring
of 1946, and the members were named as individuals rather than as
representatives of their various governments. I was asked to serve on
this committee and accepted with more confidence than I had accepted
President Truman's invitation to be a delegate to the General Assembly.

We began work in temporary quarters at Hunter College in New
York and carried on at Geneva and the United Nations headquarters
at Lake Success, on Long Island, for the next two years. But during
the same period I was again nominated and confirmed as a member
of the United States delegation to the General Assembly, and con-

---

* The Nuclear Commission on Human Rights.

tinued as a delegate until 1953. At the same time I was also the United States representative on the Human Rights Commission.

Thus over the years, in one capacity or another, I saw a great deal of the Russian delegates and not infrequently felt I saw and heard too much of them, because of course they were usually the center of opposition to our ideas. I suppose a good many other delegates felt the same as I did at times—perhaps much more so. I remember one occasion during our first meeting in London when Senator Connally decided that he had reached the limit of his patience with the Russians. I do not remember the subject he had been negotiating and debating, but the discussion had gone on for days without getting anywhere at all. Then, one day when this deadlock was being discussed at a briefing session for the American delegates, the Senator arose with all the dignity he could summon.

"I would like to announce," he began with an angry toss of his handsome head, "that I have discussed this question with the representative of the Soviet Union for tho last time We made our position clear from the beginning, but he has brought the subject up three times as if nothing had been said. I will not discuss it again."

Red-faced, the Senator sat down in his chair with an air of finality, tugging his black string tie into place. I remarked as mildly as possible that the Russians were very tenacious in such matters because they seem to think they can wear down their opposition by never giving up a point, by just saying the same thing again and again. Their approach has nothing to do with reason, I added, and I was of the opinion that the Soviet delegate would keep right on bringing up the same point at every opportunity.

"I will not discuss it again," Senator Connally repeated. "In the United States Senate, when debate is finished it is finished!"

This was not, however, the United States Senate and, as I had feared, Senator Connally found himself discussing the same subject on several later occasions regardless of his own desires. He did it emphatically, too, raising his voice in dramatic fashion and sometimes bringing his fist down on the table with a bang. Whether he hoped to drive the Russians into some more reasonable position by these gestures I do not know, but I didn't feel it was likely. Once after the Senator's fist crashed on the table with unusual vigor, the head of the Soviet delegation, Andrei Gromyko, turned in dead-pan fashion to my friend, Frank Walker, who was on the American delegation, and asked:

"Does that mean that the Senator is sincere or does he do it just to be more emphatic? . . . In any event, it doesn't seem to help his logic."

Mr. Gromyko knew the ways of Westerners far better than he pretended, I always believed. I had a personal feeling about him because he had made a special trip to Hyde Park after my husband's death to pay his respects. But even there he gave me the impression of being always on guard, and he certainly maintained the Communist practice of never showing any kind of weakness in the presence of Westerners. We had invited him and his wife to luncheon, but after we were at table Miss Thompson observed that Madame Gromyko was not eating anything.

"Is there something wrong?" she asked. "Aren't you hungry?"

Madame Gromyko blushed but then explained that she was suffering from ulcers and that she had been told to confine herself to a soft diet.

"I will have some poached eggs and milk fixed for you," Tommy said.

While this exchange was in progress I had been talking to Mr. Gromyko, but he was the kind of man who missed nothing that went on. He turned to Tommy and, rather severely, said:

"My wife is quite capable of eating anything."

This, I suppose, was an order for Tommy to forget about the poached eggs or anything else special for Madame Gromyko—on the theory that Russians have no weaknesses. But for once I paid no attention to Russian stubbornness. I spoke up and told the cook to prepare the poached eggs. They were brought to Madame Gromyko and she ate them.

Perhaps Maxim Litvinov, whose wife was English, was the most skillful Russian diplomat in getting along with Western government officials. V. M. Molotov, who was so rigid as foreign minister and who helped make "Niet!" such a famous word at the United Nations, was always correct and polite. But, although I saw him frequently and sometimes sat next to him at dinners, I never felt that it was possible to know him well.

In fact, it was difficult to know any Russian well and I suppose the Kremlin planned it that way. After a good many attempts, I decided that it was really impossible to have a private and frank talk with Russian officials. As I have said, I followed for a number of years the custom of having small groups of United Nations delegates from various countries to my home for tea or dinner so that we could informally talk over problems that had arisen at official meetings. This often was an effective way to clear up misunderstandings or to explain the position of our government, and such off-the-record talks helped in reaching a formal agreement in numerous instances. But not too often with the Russians.

One of the Russian delegates over a period of years was a big, dramatic man with flowing white hair and a bristling black beard—Dr. Alexei P. Pavlov, a nephew of the physiologist Ivan Petrovich Pavlov, famous for his studies of conditioned reflexes. The nephew was an able delegate to the United Nations but, since he was obviously a man of education and social position, he seemed to feel the necessity of proving to everybody that he was a good and faithful Communist. He was a brilliant talker, good at repartee, and he often gave me a difficult time in committee meetings on controversial issues that provided the Communists with opportunities for ridicule or misrepresentation.

More than once Dr. Pavlov arose with a flourish, shook his white locks angrily and made a bitter attack on the United States on the basis of some report or even of some rumor that had to do with discrimination against Negroes, particularly in our southern states. Of course, I always replied vigorously, pointing out that, despite discrimination of one kind or another, the United States had done a great deal to improve the social and economic status of the Negro, but Dr. Pavlov never admitted any such improvement. On one occasion I took pains to explain that I had spent a good part of my own life fighting against discrimination and working for educational and other measures for the benefit of Negro citizens of the United States. But to everything I said, Dr. Pavlov replied by sticking out his black beard and barking:

"Yes, you worked. But where did it ever get you?"

Once, when I was irritated by his remarks to the point where I could no longer stand it, I interrupted him to say, as sternly as I could: "Sir! I believe you are hitting below the belt."

This may not have been very elegant language for a diplomatic exchange, but it expressed my feelings in American slang. It so amused some of my colleagues that they checked up on the phrase "hitting below the belt" to see whether it made any sense in Russian or any other language when translated by the United Nations interpreters, and they discovered that it was a familiar and accurate expression in any language you wanted to pick. So I presume he knew what I meant.

The Soviet delegates could be very thorough in seeking out American weaknesses or in distorting the picture of our country as a whole by citing some isolated fact to support their propaganda claims. In one meeting, the Russian delegate made much of what he said was a law in the state of Mississippi forbidding any man to strike a woman with an axe handle—or some such implement—more than two feet long. This was cited as an example of American brutality and it caused some lifted eyebrows among other delegates.

"In my country," a French delegate mused, "the law forbids a man to strike a woman even with a rose—long stem or short stem."

I had no idea what kind of law Mississippi might have about this but Louis Hyde, who was then a delegation adviser, quickly telephoned our legal adviser in Washington to check on the allegation. The uncomfortable answer he received was that an old law something like that actually was on the books in Mississippi, although I have no idea why. In any event, we had no very strong reply.

My practice of inviting delegates of various nations to tea or to dinner sometimes worked out well with the Russians and on other occasions didn't work at all. During one period of hard work, I had representatives on the Human Rights Commission to a series of luncheons in an effort to achieve a better understanding. At last, in checking over the list, I discovered that I had entertained all the group with the exception of one man representing one of the Soviet Republics. He was a rather quiet, unpretentious sort of man who seemed to have very little interest in other delegates and who never voted until he had a chance to observe how the leading Communist delegates voted. He was a kind of "ditto delegate."

It happened at this time that there was some rather important issue under debate in our committee on which the members were evenly divided, half taking the viewpoint of the Western delegates and half the viewpoint of the Russians. So I decided that I would invite only the ditto delegate to luncheon rather than have several at a time as I usually did. When I invited him, he seemed willing to accept but the next day he spoke to me.

"You kindly invited me to luncheon," he said, "but may I ask who else is invited?"

"Oh, I've invited only you and one of my advisers," I replied. "We will meet you outside the delegates' lounge at one o'clock."

He nodded, bowed and trotted away. At one o'clock, we looked for him outside the lounge but he did not appear. After ten or fifteen minutes we began looking in other likely places but we never did find him. Finally, we decided that he had become alarmed at the idea of being seen alone with American delegates. So we had luncheon without our expected guest.

But when we returned to the meeting room, I observed that our Russian friend was not there. Nor did he appear later when the issue under discussion was put to a vote. And, as a result of his absence, the Western point of view was approved by a single vote. It would have been a tie if he had been there to vote with the Communists, and I could not help feeling that my luncheon invitation had been responsible. In fact, the man did not reappear throughout that session of the United Nations, and I never did find out what had happened to him.

The fact is that the Russian delegates simply did not dare talk with a foreigner without taking the precaution of having a witness present, lest at some future time their superiors might accuse them of making traitorous statements. Not even brash, outspoken Dr. Pavlov, who so often berated me and attacked my stand at United Nations sessions, dared ignore this practice. One evening he and his colleague Alexander Borisov came to my apartment with several other guests. I usually tried to provide some kind of entertainment on such occasions and I had invited a friend who is an excellent pianist.

After dinner, my friend played the works of various classical composers, including Russians, and played very well indeed. Dr. Pavlov listened happily, his big shock of hair falling forward and his black beard touching his chest, but without ever saying a word. When he and Mr. Borisov were ready to depart, I walked to the door with them.

"Oh, I have left my hat in the other room," Mr. Borisov exclaimed. "I will get it."

He hurried away, leaving me alone with Dr. Pavlov. As soon as his companion was out of earshot, Dr. Pavlov leaned toward me and, in an almost conspiratorial whisper, said:

"Madame, you like the music of Tchaikovsky. So do I!"

Then he straightened up and smiled blandly as Mr. Borisov returned. And that was as close as I ever came to getting a frank and confidential expression of opinion from a Soviet official.

I certainly do not want to give the impression that the Russian officials or representatives are surly or even unfriendly at all times, because they are often quite the opposite. It is in official negotiations or in debate that they adopt such rigid attitudes and distort facts so irritatingly and display such stubborn unfriendliness toward Western ideas. Despite their difficult official attitude, I always felt that the American delegates should refuse to show unfriendliness toward representatives of the Communist bloc. Some of our delegates would not even be photographed shaking hands or talking with a Communist representative when the reporters and news photographers clustered around at the opening of each session of the Assembly or on some similar occasion. Presumably our reluctant delegates were taking the position that the Russians were mortal enemies, or perhaps they felt it would do them no good politically.

The Russians, on the contrary, were eager to be photographed shaking hands with and smiling broadly at the delegates of other nations, particularly Americans, realizing that this gave the impression all over the world that they were trying to be friendly and co-operative. I knew that after this shaking of hands for the photographers the Russians would stand up in the General Assembly and say untrue things about America, things that they were well aware were untrue. Nevertheless, I felt that our only course was to persist in what we knew was right in the belief that we would eventually get some kind of results. I wanted to be firm but I did not desire to be the one to show hostility and I never hesitated to shake hands with the Russians for the photographers.

I recall an amusing incident in Paris when the entire American delegation received a formal invitation to attend a reception at the Russian Embassy on the occasion of the Soviet national celebration of the October Revolution. This was the big affair of the year at the Soviet Embassy but it was also one year before the critical 1952 elections in the United States, and one of the most loudly exploited issues in the campaign was so-called "softness" toward Communism.

When the invitation was received, one member of our delegation who was coming up for re-election to Congress threw up his hands in horror.

"You won't see me within a mile of that place," he announced firmly. Another member, also facing a fight for re-election to Congress, expressed the same sentiment.

There were other delegates in our group who did not have to face re-election to anything at that time, but I suppose they had an eye to the future.

"You'll have to count me out," one of them said. "I have a prior engagement outside of Paris."

Then another explained that he would be unable to attend because of some complication that I cannot recall. By this time the situation began to look rather embarrassing, even to our two Congressmen.

"After all," somebody remarked, "we have diplomatic relations with our former allies and it would obviously be simply rude if none of us attended."

Nobody said anything to me but some of them glanced at me and I could tell they were waiting. I let them wait a bit before I said with a smile: "Well, I'm the only one left and, since I am not running for office and have no intention of running for office, I will attend the reception. You know, I don't really believe anyone will notice or care whether I pay a call at the Soviet Embassy."

So I went to the Embassy and, being a little early, I was one of the first guests to climb the long stairs and face the reception line. At that time, the Soviet Ambassador to France was none other than my old musical friend and deadly political enemy, Dr. Pavlov. But when I saw him I gasped. Instead of the quietly and correctly dressed professor I had been accustomed to seeing in the halls of the United Nations, the host now standing in the reception line was an erect and dignified diplomat wearing the full uniform of a soldier of the Soviet Union, liberally bestrewn with medals and ribbons. He was, indeed, an impressive figure. But when he saw me, some of the old Dr. Pavlov came through and he greeted me with more warmth and friendliness than one might have expected. I stayed only a short time and then explained that I had to get back to work.

"I will show you to your automobile," Dr. Pavlov exclaimed gallantly, stepping out of the reception line.

"Oh, no," I replied. "You simply can't do that. You must remain here to receive your other guests."

A number of new arrivals were approaching the reception line and, upon my insistence, the Ambassador remained at his post. But he gestured to another splendidly caparisoned figure.

"My aide will escort you," he said. So I was seen ceremoniously to the court where my automobile was waiting. I wondered what my

American colleagues would have thought if they had seen me but none of our delegation was within cannon shot of the Soviet Embassy that day—and I didn't even see any reporters. I drove away feeling that I must have been granted as warm a welcome as anyone could have received at the Soviet Embassy, but knowing that the next day I would doubtless be subjected to a violent Russian tirade at the United Nations to make up for it!

I made the point earlier that during the London sessions the head of the Soviet delegation, Mr. Vishinsky, took over debate on the refugee question when it came before the General Assembly, instead of leaving it in the hands of the delegate who had argued the issue all through the committee sessions, as most Western countries would do. This peculiar Russian practice is important to mention because it sheds light on the methods and training and abilities of diplomats from the Soviet Union. The head of their delegation is the only one who carries the responsibility for influencing decisions of the Assembly. I often marveled at the way in which Mr. Vishinsky must have been briefed for hours, right down to the last detail, in regard to what had gone on in the committee discussions. I marveled even more at his ability to absorb so many facts about a complicated subject that had been under discussion for weeks in the committee.

I once mentioned Mr. Vishinsky's remarkable memory to my son Elliott, and he replied that he wasn't surprised.

"The Russians are intensively trained and they have developed a remarkable ability to remember what they hear," he said. "In the Air Force during the war, they were the only foreigners who could arrive late in the afternoon, be given the book of detailed instructions on how to fly an American bomber, study it during the night and then fly the bomber away early the next morning, without an American flier aboard."

Mr. Vishinsky was like a highly trained technician. A white-haired, vigorous man with chill blue eyes, he gave me the impression of being a legal or business representative of a client rather than a man speaking his convictions. He was able but cold, and I rather thought he lacked any personal convictions. He just argued—bitingly and often eloquently—for his client.

Once at a formal dinner for United Nations delegates I was seated next to Mr. Vishinsky. He was polite and sometimes witty but I was never sure when his real thoughts were showing through his brittle surface. I had just read a book about the Hudson River valley and I told him something about it. He showed polite interest.

"Perhaps you would like to know more about it," I concluded. "If you can read English easily, I should be glad to send it to you."

"I read English very well," he replied, "but I read only diplomatic English."

It is possible that Westerners never fully understand the complexity of the Russian character, but I certainly kept trying throughout my service with the United Nations and later, because I know it is extremely important for us to learn all we can about our powerful international opposition. Sometimes I think I have learned what to expect from them and how to deal with them, but at other times I begin to wonder as I did at a large party given by Mr. and Mrs. Albert Lasker for all the delegates to the Human Rights Commission.

The peak of the party came when a huge cake was brought to the table. The icing, in bright colors, was made up of reproductions of the flags of all the nations represented on the Commission.

"Mrs. Roosevelt, will you please cut the cake?" Mrs. Lasker asked, handing me a long knife.

I looked at the cake with interest—and then with sudden concern. The flags made of icing covered the entire surface of the cake and I realized that I could not cut it without cutting through one of them. I stared. There was a Russian delegate standing next to me and he, too, stared at the cake, apparently realizing, as I did, that the knife was going to ruin at least one of those beautiful flags. I may have been wrong but I think he watched me carefully and a bit suspiciously as I raised the knife.

By that time, everybody else around the table was staring at me and the cake and the flags and I had to do something. I decided not to risk an international incident at such a gay party, and I cut through the American flag to produce the first slice. The Russian representative seemed to relax and nod pleasantly, the crisis safely past.

I am not certain that there is any moral to these observations about my dealings with representatives of the Soviet Union but they may help in understanding some of the happenings that come later in this book. On second thought, there is, of course, a moral and a warning for those who love freedom, and it was probably best expressed by a kindly but tragic man who loved freedom very much indeed. His name was Jan Masaryk, the son of Thomas G. Masaryk, the first president and founder of the Republic of Czechoslovakia.

At meetings of the United Nations General Assembly it happened that the Czechoslovakian delegation sat directly behind us. Jan Masaryk, as foreign minister of Czechoslovakia and head of the delegation, listened to the debates intently in the early days of the General Assembly, but when it came time for a vote he always followed the lead of the Russian delegation. In most instances, this meant that he voted against the position of the Western democracies. It was not difficult for us to understand because the Russian armed forces practically surrounded Czechoslovakia, but on one occasion Mr. Masaryk must have felt that he had to make some explanation. Leaning forward toward Frank Walker, he whispered:

"What can you do . . . what else can you do when you've got them right in your front yard?"

He found out that what he did made no difference to the Russians. In February of 1948 the Communists seized power in Czechoslovakia by a *coup d'état* and, a few days later, it was announced that Jan Masaryk had died by leaping from a window.

VIII

"MY MOST IMPORTANT TASK":
THE HUMAN RIGHTS COMMISSION

During my years at the UN, it was my work on the Human Rights Commission that I considered my most important task, though as I have explained I was also a delegate to the General Assembly, which at times when the two jobs more or less fused caused some confusion.

There is always, in any event, a certain amount of confusion and duplication and wasted effort in connection with any large group of delegations such as the United Nations, which represents so many different cultures and so many different political points of view. I remember when Senator Warren Austin, an able, dedicated and hard-working Republican from Vermont, became head of our delegation and our Ambassador to the United Nations. Senator Austin was a round-faced gentleman with a pince-nez and with hair brushed back smoothly from his forehead—a man who both looked and was orderly and efficient in almost everything. He always tried to plan a direct, well-organized approach to his work and to keep at it until it was accomplished.

When the second part of the first session of the first General Assembly was about to start in New York in 1946 Senator Austin called all of the delegates and advisers to a meeting, the first over which he pre-

71

sided. He was pleasant and helpful and, of course, he had had years of experience in the United States Senate.

"I think we should all organize our work carefully," he said, polishing his pince-nez with a big handkerchief. "I see no reason why we cannot be efficient enough to avoid working overtime or working at night. If we can arrange our work to avoid overtime, I feel sure everybody will be fresher and will have better ideas of how to achieve our goals."

At the time the Senator made this sensible little speech I was feeling that I was almost an old-timer in United Nations work, and I could not suppress a little smile. I looked over at my usually serious-faced advisers and I noticed that they, too, were thinking back and smiling faintly. I glanced at some of the others who had been through the mill and most of them were obviously but politely amused, and trying to suppress sardonic little smiles. A few months later, I'm sure Senator Austin also would have smiled because, while his words were certainly sensible, time proved that you can't always be well organized in United Nations work. Your work grows and branches out unexpectedly and sprouts new complications every so often. I know that some of my friends were amused by the fact that I started out at the first sessions in London carrying one thin brief case but ended up a few years later with one that bulged in every direction, while my patient advisers carried increasingly heavy brief cases wherever we went.

Now to get back to the commission that made recommendations on the definite composition of the Human Rights Commission at Hunter College in the spring of 1946. The facilities for our meetings were not perfect but we were comparatively comfortable. We usually met in a classroom, perhaps ten or twelve persons working on a particular phase of the program, and sat around a large U-shaped table. In the center of the U would be a table for the official interpreter because at that time we did not have the elaborate set-up for instantaneous translation that now exists at the United Nations. I remember one day at Hunter College when René Cassin, of France, was leading a rather involved discussion of the manner in which the Human Rights Commission would be set up. He spoke rather rapidly for fifteen or twenty minutes, it seemed to me, without any translation being made.

There was that day a new and quite handsome young blonde American girl at the interpreters' table and, for several minutes of Mr. Cassin's speech, she took notes furiously. Then she looked up, with a troubled frown, and laid down her pencil. When Mr. Cassin finished his remarks with an eloquent flourish, he turned and bowed in the direction of the young lady as a signal for her to start translating for the benefit of delegates who did not speak French. The girl started at the beginning of his remarks and translated a few hundred words. Then she blushed and stopped.

"I'm sorry!" she exclaimed, bursting into tears and running from the room, her notes clutched in her hands.

We waited for her to compose herself and return but she was gone for good! I was presiding at the meeting and I had to do something about it.

"Did everyone understand what Mr. Cassin said?" I asked.

Several delegates said they had understood nothing and that a translation was necessary. I looked around for help but there obviously was none.

"Well," I finally said, "I will try to remember it if Mr. Cassin will correct me in case I do not translate correctly."

So I repeated in English as much of his speech as I could remember and after complying with the rules in this way I announced that the meeting was adjourned forthwith. Such a thing could not happen now because of the modern system of simultaneous interpretation. Each delegate has earphones which he can put on, pressing a button for the language he understands. Then, while the speech is in progress, interpreters in sound-proof booths repeat in the various languages the words of the speaker, so that there is a lag of only a second or so before the translation is complete in each language. The same system is available at each seat for visitors to the United Nations so that the debate can be followed in French, Russian, English, Spanish or Chinese.

The work in this period was an intensive education for me in many things, including constitutional law, and I would not have been able to do much but for the able advisers who worked with me. I was more than grateful for the fact that Marjorie Whiteman, who has written a legal work on American treaties, sat behind me at almost every meeting and explained what we could or could not do for constitutional reasons. My first adviser at this time, James Pomeroy Hendrick, always remains in my mind with Mr. Sandifer as an ideal guide, philosopher and friend. Urbane and soft-spoken with a quiet sense of humor, he was tireless and devoted. He never spared himself and so he made me work hard. Once his wife accompanied us to Geneva and filled in, in an emergency, as my secretary, answering the telephone and replying to letters in several languages; in addition she was a delightful companion. There were quite a few others, too, including on various occasions James Green, James Simsarian, Herzel Plaine and Herbert Beaser.

As we began our work, the Russian representative designated for the task was Mr. Borisov, but he did not arrive. Instead there appeared a rather young gentleman sent by the Russian Embassy in Washington.

"Mr. Borisov will be here later," he explained. "Meanwhile, I will attend the sessions to listen but I do not have any authorization to cast a vote."

Having learned about Soviet tactics in London, I did not feel any great disappointment because of this development and, after I had been elected chairman of the Commission, I tried to push our work along as rapidly as possible. I might point out here that eventually we decided that our main task was to write an International Bill of Rights. This was to consist of three parts. First, there was to be a Declaration which would be adopted as a resolution of the General Assembly and would name and define all the human rights, not only the traditionally recognized political and civil rights, but also the more recently recognized social, economic and cultural rights. Since the General Assembly is not a world parliament, its resolutions are not legally binding on member states. We therefore decided that the Declaration would be followed by a Covenant (or Covenants) which would take the form of a treaty and would be legally binding on the countries that accepted them. Finally, there was to be a system for the implementation or enforcement of the rights.

We also finally recommended that the Human Rights Commission be composed of eighteen members, each of whom would represent one of the United Nations governments, and that they should be chosen on a rotating basis with due regard for geographical distribution, except for the representatives of the five great powers—the United States, Soviet Russia, the United Kingdom, France and China. As was customary, it was agreed that these five powers should be elected automatically to the new Commission as members, leaving thirteen seats to be rotated among other members of the United Nations. These recommendations, however, came later. At the Hunter College sessions we were just getting started.

Our early debates were lively, but I noted that the young Russian delegate sat quietly by and gave an impression of docility and even timidity. As the time neared to vote for approval of our preliminary actions Mr. Borisov arrived, and our quiet little man disappeared. Mr. Borisov approached me before the next meeting.

"Mrs. Roosevelt," he said, "I have not been able to attend and I would like to ask you, as chairman, to explain to me the actions on which the Commission has decided informally."

I said I would be delighted and carefully outlined the proposals which had been discussed. When I had finished, everything I had said was translated into Russian for Mr. Borisov. He looked thoughtful for a few moments and then shook his head.

"I am sorry," he said, "but I do not believe I clearly understand your plans. Would you mind explaining to me again?"

I said that of course I would not mind. So I went over the entire proceedings again, explaining as simply as possible what had gone on during Mr. Borisov's absence. Again it was all translated into Russian but again Mr. Borisov shook his head sadly.

"I really don't quite understand," he said. "Would you mind starting again at the beginning?"

After we had gone over it in the same way once more, Mr. Borisov was still frowning thoughtfully. "It is not entirely clear," he announced gravely. "Therefore I will not vote."

So, when we called for a formal vote on presenting our proposals to the Economic and Social Council, the Soviet Union merely recorded its "objections and dissent" to certain agreements and thus did not join in the recommendations of the preparatory Commission. The Council accepted our recommendations and President Truman then nominated me as the United States representative on the Commission, as I stated earlier. Being the first chairman of the Commission in addition to my duties as a delegate to the Assembly kept me on United Nations work during five or six months of the year. I always tried to be punctual for meetings—in fact, I frequently found myself waiting ten or fifteen minutes for others to arrive—and I had to keep my daily schedule on a crowded timetable basis, with no minutes to spare.

I remember once when the Assembly was in session at Lake Success, Richard Winslow, who was manager of the office of the United States mission, told me that he had been urgently asked to arrange a time when I could talk to Tyler Wood, who was then assistant to Will

Clayton, about a problem concerning the United Nations Relief and Rehabilitation Administration.

"Well," I replied, handing him my calendar, "here's my schedule. You figure out when I shall see him—if you can!"

He worked on the calendar for a while and then said that he and Mr. Wood would meet me at a certain hour when I would be leaving a New York hotel. They did. We got in the automobile that was waiting for me and Mr. Wood began talking. He talked until we had driven perhaps twenty blocks to the CBS studios, where I got out while they remained in the car. I did a broadcast with Mr. Dulles on some United Nations matter, then returned to the car and resumed talking with Mr. Wood while we drove from Madison Avenue to Broadway and Fifty-ninth Street. There I got out again and went into the United Nations Information Center, which was just being formally opened at ceremonies that I had promised to attend. I returned to the automobile and resumed my conversation with Mr. Wood as we drove downtown to the Hotel Pennsylvania, where Mr. Wood and Mr. Winslow left me. I continued on to my apartment at Washington Square, some twenty blocks away, but I had an appointment with Senator Austin at the Hotel Pennsylvania not long afterward, so I returned there within a short time. Arriving in the offices we had at the hotel, I discovered I had five minutes before meeting the Senator so I sat down in a big easy chair and closed my eyes.

A few minutes later I was awakened by a startled exclamation and looked up to see Mr. Winslow and Mr. Wood standing in the doorway, staring.

"How did you get here?" Mr. Winslow asked. "We left you on your way home. We walked across the street, had a quick hamburger and coffee and then came directly here—and you're already on the scene!"

"Oh, I went home and came back," I replied, "but I found there were a few minutes before our meeting with Senator Austin so I didn't see why I shouldn't take a catnap."

In those days my life went along at that pace for long periods at a time and I suppose I enjoyed it, because I like to keep busy, to have the hours and the days well filled with things to do. When the United Nations headquarters was at Lake Success my schedule was complicated by the fact that I always had duties to attend to in New York early in the day and then had to drive for forty minutes to reach Lake Success in time for the opening of the Assembly or some other meeting at eleven o'clock. This suited Mr. Sandifer or any adviser very well because he always knew that I would be starting out at twenty minutes after ten. He would climb into my automobile with the assurance that for the next forty minutes I would be his "captive audience" and that our discussion of the day's work would not be interrupted.

In the period that I presided as chairman of the Human Rights Commission we spent most of our time trying to write the Universal Declaration of Human Rights and the Covenants, and there were times, it seemed to me, when I was getting in over my head. The Officers of the Commission had been charged with the task of preparing the first draft of the Declaration, and I remember that on one occasion, thinking our work might be helped by an informal atmosphere, I asked this small group to meet at my apartment for tea. One of the members was the Chinese representative, Dr. P. C. Chang, who was a great joy to all of us because of his sense of humor, his philosophical observations and his ability to quote some apt Chinese proverb to fit almost any occasion. Dr. John P. Humphrey, a Canadian who was the permanent head of the Division of Human Rights in the UN Secretariat, and Dr. Charles Malik of Lebanon, one of the very able diplomats at the United Nations, were also at this meeting.

They arrived in the middle of a Sunday afternoon, so we would have plenty of time to work. It was decided that Dr. Humphrey would prepare the preliminary draft, and as we settled down over the teacups, one of them made a remark with philosophic implications, and a heated discussion ensued. Dr. Chang was a pluralist and held forth in charming fashion on the proposition that there is more than one kind of ultimate reality. The Declaration, he said, should reflect more than simply Western ideas and Dr. Humphrey would have to be eclectic in his approach. His remark, though addressed to Dr. Humphrey, was really directed at Dr. Malik, from whom it drew a prompt retort as he expounded at some length the philosophy of Thomas Aquinas. Dr. Humphrey joined enthusiastically in the discussion, and I remember that at one point Dr. Chang suggested that the Secretariat might well spend a few months studying the fundamentals of Confucianism! But by that time I could not follow them, so lofty had the conversation become, so I simply filled the teacups again and sat back to be entertained by the talk of these learned gentlemen.

Very early in the meetings of the Commission we discovered that while it would be possible to reach some kind of agreement on the

Declaration, we were going to be in for a great deal of controversy with the Russian representatives, particularly Dr. Pavlov, who attempted at every opportunity to write a bit of Communist philosophy into the document. For example, at the end of practically every article the Russians proposed to amend the Declaration to read: "This shall be enforced by the state."

When such an amendment was proposed I, or one of the other Western delegates, would argue against it on the ground that this was an international declaration by the United Nations and that we did not believe it should be imposed by the power of the individual governments. We would then ask for a vote and the amendment would be defeated.

But as soon as the next article was completed the Soviet delegate would again propose the same amendment and we would have to go through the whole business again with the same result—the defeat of the Soviet proposal. This naturally became monotonous but the Russians never gave up trying.

The drafting of the articles continued over many months. During our early work on the Covenants and measures of implementation it became apparent that it was going to be exceedingly difficult to agree on articles that would, if accepted, be legally binding on the various nations. This was difficult enough in regard to civil and political rights that have become fairly well accepted throughout the civilized world, but when it came to economic and social rights at times it seemed to me that agreement would be all but impossible.*

The reason for this, in part at least, was the vast social and economic differences between the various countries—the social and economic conditions in the United States, for example, as contrasted to existing conditions in a country like India. The gap was so great that it was well-nigh impossible to phrase concepts acceptable to both countries. Let me give one example to explain these difficulties.

With the aid of various specialized United Nations agencies, we set out to write the best possible article aimed at the encouragement of universal education. We achieved a preliminary draft that stated that everyone had a right to primary, secondary and higher education, the first two to be compulsory but all of them eventually to be provided

---

* The articles dealing with economic and social rights have now been adopted by a majority of the Committee.

free by the individual governments concerned. This might read well to a citizen of the United States but it was quite a different matter in India.

"Our economy is strained," Madame Hansa Mehta, the Indian representative, explained, "and we are only trying to give all children a primary education. What would happen if we suddenly attempted to provide secondary and higher education, too? The article should be amended to read that the goal is to be accomplished gradually with due consideration for the economy of each country."

"The trouble with that," I replied, "is that I do not believe the United States Senate would ever ratify a treaty so vaguely worded. The Senators would ask: 'What does gradually mean—five years or ten years or a hundred years?' I just don't believe they would accept it."

But if the economic problems of underdeveloped countries provided one stumbling block, the political systems of other countries, particularly the United States, provided another. Our delegation had to insist on including a states' rights clause because we could act only in regard to matters that were under jurisdiction of the federal government. We had to explain that in other matters which were under the control of the states we had power only to "recommend" that the states take appropriate action. Australia and Canada were the only other countries in a similar position.

Many of the other countries resented the fact that they were being asked to commit all of their people to the instruments we were drafting, whereas on certain matters the United States delegation could commit only a limited number of the people and hope that the various state governments would accept our recommendations. I could understand their resentment and their opposition to our "states' rights" system, but we always fought to get our amendment in. So far, however, the draft Covenants still lack a federal states' rights clause. We made very slow progress in drafting the legally binding Covenants and even slower progress in framing measures of implementation that would provide means to enforce the Covenants.

Late in 1947 it was decided that the next meeting of the Human Rights Commission would be in Geneva, so we left for that city early in December with the idea of completing our work in time to be home for Christmas. As chairman, I knew that it would require much hard work and long hours to be able to adjourn before Christmas but I was in a determined mood and I warned all the delegations of my plans. Mr. Hendrick had gone on ahead to prepare for our arrival in Geneva, but I was accompanied from New York by Mrs. Hendrick and several others, including my friend Dr. David Gurewitsch, who had been ill and was en route to a Swiss sanitarium. Unfortunately, when we arrived at Shannon airport in Ireland we were told that we could not continue because of heavy fog.

"We simply must go on," I exclaimed. "Here I have been telling everybody we would keep a tight schedule and now I—the chairman—won't even get there for the opening session!"

But you cannot, of course, argue with fog and we just sat there in agony for three days. Dr. Gurewitsch was put to bed in a little room at the nearby hostel. The weather was foul and there was very little hot water and I was worried about his condition. Mrs. Hendrick and I carried his meals to him each day, although the fog was so thick we could not see five feet in front of our noses. Mrs. Hendrick is a talented athlete and dancer but she and her husband also are expert pig raisers on their Virginia farm, and she was interested in buying a certain kind of pig that was available in Ireland. After numerous inquiries she was directed to a pig farm. She and a driver crept along through the incredible fog on a narrow road and eventually encountered a man who turned out to be a Lord Inchiquin and who, happily, was the owner of the pig farm. He guided her to the pig pen and she bought six animals for shipment to Virginia.

Finally the fog lifted and we continued to Geneva, where I discovered that all the other delegates also had been delayed because of heavy fog all over Europe. Although I was happy to make the opening meeting I resented the delay and I immediately laid out a schedule of work that, with night sessions, I believed would enable us to adjourn by eleven o'clock on the evening of December 17.

"I want to be home for Christmas and I assume everyone else does, too," I announced at our first session. "In fact, I have made reservations and I hope to keep them. If we work night sessions from the beginning instead of waiting until the last week as usual, we should get through in time."

Nobody objected to my plans, at least not until later, and I must say that everybody worked hard. My own day started at eight o'clock, when I met with my advisers at breakfast and went over the work schedule and any difficult problems. Then I would go to the Palais des Nations Unies, where the sessions were held, and get through my own correspondence, with the help of Mrs. Hendrick, in time for the morning session of the Commission. At luncheon, we usually got several delegates together to continue our discussions informally and then returned to the afternoon meeting. At night, we had an after-dinner session or a meeting of our delegation. Later Mr. Hendrick and I would talk for perhaps an hour about the next day's plans and, after he had gone to bed, Mrs. Hendrick would come in with a pile of personal letters on which we worked until after midnight. By the time I had dictated my daily newspaper column I was ready for bed.

This was a rather grueling schedule for everybody and within a few days I was being denounced—mostly in fun, I hope—as a merciless slave driver. But I must say we got through a great deal of work and kept to our schedule, for which I was very grateful to all the delegations. Only once did I encounter any real revolt and that was the fault of the Russians, but it was their fault only in a pleasant way.

As we neared the end of our sessions, the Russian delegation invited everybody to a cocktail party following the afternoon meeting. I could not attend nor could the Philippines representative, General Carlos P. Romulo, because both of us had previous engagements to speak at dinners. We expressed our regrets and everybody else trotted off to the Russian party where, I was later informed, there was available a considerable quantity of vodka.

I made my dinner speech and lost little time in finishing my meal so I could be sure to get back to the meeting room by eight o'clock. I had worked hard to train all the delegates to be on time and I did not want to set a bad example at this late stage. When I arrived a few minutes before eight there was no one there, but promptly on the hour General Romulo arrived and we sat at the big table in the big empty room and chatted. Ten minutes later, I realized that absolutely no other delegate, adviser, secretary or whatever had arrived. Another ten minutes passed and General Romulo and I were still alone at the big table. This was, I thought, no less than mutiny!

At eight-thirty there was a commotion at the door and the lost sheep began arriving. They were in a happy if unhurried mood, and, I observed, a little shaky on their feet. They took their accustomed places, leaned back in their chairs and gazed at me with pleased, rather foggy eyes. They were, as one of the younger members of our party put it later, loaded!

I had planned to dispose of a rather simple matter at the meeting—
I cannot remember exactly what—and I spent about five minutes out-
lining what I thought we should do about it. General Romulo then
discussed the question for a few minutes.

"Now," I said, when he had finished, "is that clear to everyone?"

There were several mumbled questions and Colonel William Roy
Hodgson, a wonderfully old-school gentleman from Australia, said that
it seemed a bit confused to him—Br-r-umph! So I then put into the
simplest possible words what had already been explained by General
Romulo. There was silence as I concluded.

"All clear?" I asked with some irritation after a few moments.

Colonel Hodgson rose, possibly with some slight difficulty, and made
me a courtly bow.

"Yes, Madame Chairlady," he said in a deep voice. "It is all just as
clear as mud!"

I knew when to acknowledge that the Russians had me licked.

"The meeting," I exclaimed, banging the gavel on the table, "is
adjourned until tomorrow morning!"

Despite the plenitude of vodka, we kept to our schedule thereafter
and we did end our work at eleven o'clock on the evening I had originally designated. I said Merry Christmas and good-by to everyone and
started down the long corridor of the Palais des Nations Unies for a
final stop at my office before hurrying to catch my plane to New York.
But in the corridor I was overtaken by Alexander E. Bogomoloff, the
Soviet delegate, who was then also their Ambassador to Paris. Madame
Bogomoloff had acted as his translator throughout the sessions and had
also translated for the delegate of one of the other Communist
countries.

"Madame," Mr. Bogomoloff said to me as we walked down the
corridor, "I have never worked so hard at any international conference,
and my wife is nearly dead!"

"I can quite understand that your wife is exhausted," I replied.
"She must have been under a strain, sitting first behind you and then
behind your colleague. But I am glad that you have discovered that
even in a bourgeois democracy, as you insist on calling the United
States, some of us know how to work."

The Soviet delegate laughed heartily and we parted. And all of us,
I hope, reached home in time for Christmas.

Eleanor Roosevelt

At the unveiling of the British memorial to Franklin D. Roosevelt in London in 1948. Left to right: Princess Elizabeth; Princess Margaret; Prince Michael with his mother, the Duchess of Kent; Mrs. Hooker; Queen Mary; Mr. Hooker, President Truman's personal envoy; Mrs. Roosevelt; Prime Minister Clement Attlee; Queen Elizabeth; partially hidden by Queen Elizabeth, Sir William Reid Dick; King George VI; Field Marshal Viscount Alexander.

Christmas dinner at Hyde Park.

Queen Elizabeth meeting one of the staff at Hyde Park.

Haile Selassie watching television with Mrs. Roosevelt at Hyde Park.

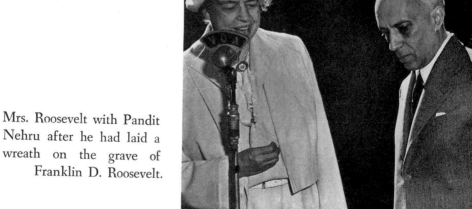

Mrs. Roosevelt with Pandit Nehru after he had laid a wreath on the grave of Franklin D. Roosevelt.

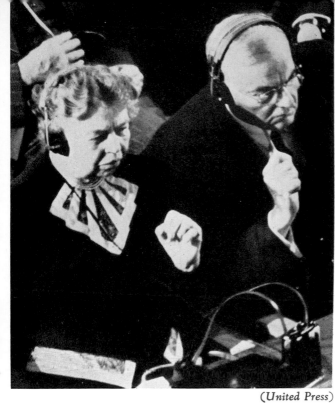

American delegates to the UN, Mrs. Eleanor Roosevelt and John Foster Dulles, hear Soviet chief delegate Andrei Vishinsky accuse the U.S. of planning atomic war against Russia.

(*United Press*)

Andrei Vishinsky congratulates Mrs. Roosevelt at a dinner in honor of her 70th birthday.

(*Wide World*)

Mrs. Roosevelt holds a press conference in Tokyo after her arrival there in May of 1953.

(*United Press*)

(*Gurewitsch*)

Mrs. Roosevelt at the border between Hong Kong and China.

(*United Press*)

Queen Frederica of Greece taking leave of Mrs. Roosevelt after a shopping trip in New York, December, 1953.

Mrs. Roosevelt talking with Adlai Stevenson at a dinner in Washington in 1955.

(*United Press*)

(*Gurewitsch*)
With Tito on his yacht. (Center, rear, Joze Vilfan, Director of Tito's private secretariat, formerly on the staff of the Yugoslavian Delegation to the UN.)

(*Gurewitsch*)
Mrs. Roosevelt in Bali.

A typical scene in Bali.
(*Gurewitsch*)

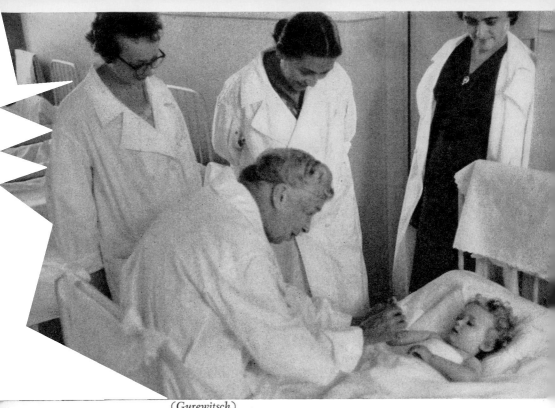

(*Gurewitsch*)
Visiting a day nursery in Tashkent, Uzbekistan, U.S.S.R.,
September, 1957.

(*Gurewitsch*)
Workers packing cotton on a collective farm in Tashkent.

Visit with a Mohammedan mufti in Tashkent.

(*Gurewitsch*)

(Gurewitsch)

(Gurewitsch)

In the Moscow subway.

ding in line to visit the mau-
m where Lenin and Stalin
n state in Moscow's Red
re.

Mrs. Roosevelt interview-
ing Khrushchev, interpre-
ter at her right.

Eleanor Roosevelt in Mos-
cow's Red Square.

Showing some schoolchildren Franklin D. Roosevelt's bedroom in the big house at Hyde Park.

Mrs. Roosevelt and Mrs. David Gurewitsch at Hyde Park in May, 1958.

IX

THE PARIS SESSIONS:
SUCCESSES AND SOME FAILURES

Our efforts to write a Charter or International Bill of Human Rights reached a kind of climax at the Paris sessions of the General Assembly in 1948. After our Geneva meeting we made steady progress on the Declaration, despite a good many controversies with the delegates from Communist countries.

Dr. Pavlov was a member of the Commission and he delivered many long propaganda harangues that appeared to be more for the purpose of publicizing the Communist point of view than in the hope of making changes in the Declaration. He was an orator of great power; the words rolled out of his black beard like a river, and stopping him was difficult, indeed. Usually, we had to sit and listen, but on one occasion it seemed to me that the rash accusations he brought up against the United States and Great Britain were proving a real detriment to our work. Dr. Pavlov knew that most of us were getting tired of listening, but toward the end of one week when we were preparing to recess he began speaking again. He seemed likely to go on forever, but I watched him closely until he had to pause for breath. Then I banged the gavel so hard that the other delegates jumped in surprise and, before he could continue, I got in a few words of my own.

"We are here," I said, "to devise ways of safeguarding human rights. We are not here to attack each other's governments and I hope when we return on Monday the delegate of the Soviet Union will remember that!" I banged the gavel again. "Meeting adjourned!"

I can still see Dr. Pavlov staring at me in surprise. But this maneuver may have had some effect, because his orations were brief and to the point for about a week after that.

Eventually we completed a draft of the Universal Declaration of Human Rights that we foolishly felt would be quickly accepted by the General Assembly, which was meeting in Paris in the autumn of 1948.

"I believe," General Marshall, who had become Secretary of State, said before we left for Paris, "that this session of the General Assembly will be remembered as the Human Rights session."

Immediately after those pleasing words, he asked me if I would be willing to deliver a speech on human rights at the Sorbonne in Paris prior to the opening of the Assembly.

"In French?" I asked.

"Yes, in French," he replied.

"Of course, I will try if you want me to," I said. "I learned French even before I learned English, but it always takes a little while when I get back to France to attune my ear to the language and to be able to speak easily. I'm afraid I will be very nervous."

I wrote my speech and had it checked over by some of the diplomatic officers and then I practiced it very seriously. I was still nervous the evening I was to speak at the Sorbonne, but as Mr. Sandifer and I drove from the hotel to the big auditorium I became really frightened for an entirely different reason. The French had sent several automobiles to pick up our party at the hotel and there also was a police escort. I'm sure that all the drivers and motorcycle police had once been racing drivers and were eager to get back to that profession. They drove at exceedingly high speed, with the motorcycles and automobiles almost bumper to bumper, and almost scared all of us to death as they whirled through the crowded streets of Paris.

When we reached the Sorbonne and stepped safely to the pavement again I was so relieved that I could have nonchalantly faced even a larger crowd than packed the big auditorium to its rafters. There was quite a lot of cheering both outside and inside the building. I delivered my speech and everyone was kind enough to say that I had done my job well.

As the session opened I was full of confidence that we could quickly get the Declaration through the formal hearings before Committee 3 and have it approved by the Assembly. My confidence was soon gone. We worked for two months, often until late at night, debating every single word of that draft Declaration over and over again before Committee 3 would approve its transmission to the General Assembly. While this repetitious work was in progress, a number of developments outside the United Nations kept me on the go.

For one thing, the Paris police suddenly informed me about a month after we arrived that the chauffeur they had assigned to me was being relieved of his duties. This young man had performed his duties well and had done many little services for me so I did not want to lose him; in fact, I had no intention of losing him, and I asserted myself rather vigorously. Upon inquiring of the police, we were told that the chauffeur had been removed because he had a criminal record.

"How could this happen?" I demanded. "All of the drivers assigned to the foreign delegations were investigated and cleared before we even arrived."

"Yes, madame," was the reply, "but in this case the young man's record had been removed from the Ministry of the Interior files or it had never been there. His record was later found in the files of the Prefect de Police in Paris."

"What did he do?"

"Well, during the German occupation of Paris he was charged with forgery of gasoline ration tickets. It is true that after the war such crimes were generally regarded as patriotic crimes and were wiped off the books, but in this case it was not removed from the local police station files."

By this time I was no longer irritated. I was outraged. I pointed out to the police that this was a technical trifle and I said that I had on various occasions left my pocketbook and other valuable things in the care of my chauffeur and he had carefully protected them.

"Doesn't the Ministry of the Interior record take precedence over the Prefect de Police records?" I asked.

"Yes, madame, in ordinary circumstances. But not in the case of such an important person as yourself. We cannot take any chances in the case of the widow of an illustrious President of the United States. The honor of the French police is at stake!"

Then it came out that the chauffeur's mother ran a restaurant which, the police suspected, was a center for Moroccan nationalists plotting against the French Government. The police were firm in their position and said they would return the man to his duties only if the government of the United States wrote to them officially saying that the chauffeur was acceptable and absolving the police of any responsibility for my safety. We finally decided against doing any such thing as that, but I was still outraged when the weeping chauffeur came to say good-by.

I made a couple of trips away from Paris during the Assembly sessions. One was a journey of United Nations delegates to Amiens to inspect the restoration of the cathedral and a new housing development, where Herbert Evatt of Australia, the President of the General Assembly, had been invited to speak. I asked Mr. Sandifer to go with me and I also took Miss Thompson and my grandson Curtis Roosevelt, who was with me during this session.

We left at seven o'clock of a cold, snowy morning, riding in little French automobiles with no heaters. Most of the United Nations party went directly to Amiens but our guides insisted on taking us about fifty miles out of the way to visit an old château. Then we had to stop at various towns along the way where the crowds were very friendly. So we arrived late at Amiens, and found, to my surprise, that the city officials had delayed the ceremonies until I got there. I am sure that this did not particularly please Mr. Evatt, who, after all, was the chief figure at the ceremonies whereas, as far as I knew, I was not to take any part.

The Mayor of Amiens and other officials were very hospitable and friendly toward me and there were so many people at the various places we stopped at during our tour of the city and the housing development that I made a couple of very brief talks upon the request of the Mayor. When we returned for the ceremonies at City Hall I also was asked to speak, so I tried to explain to the large crowd the importance of the work of the United Nations and to encourage their support. Mr. Evatt's annoyance with the way the program was being run was no doubt increased by this procedure and I can't say that I blamed him. When it came time for him to make the principal speech, I noticed that he did not even mention the United Nations but devoted his remarks to the exploits of Australian soldiers who had fought so gallantly in the Amiens area during the First World War.

The other trip I made was to Germany at the request of General Lucius Clay, who asked me to address a group of German women doctors in Stuttgart. This was not an easy assignment. There had been, during the conflict with Hitler, a considerable campaign of hatred in Germany directed against me personally because I had spoken out as strongly as I could against most of the things represented by Nazism, including the persecution of Jewish people. Furthermore, any occupation force whether good or bad, just or unjust, is detested if not hated by the people it rules, and I have never had reason to believe that an exception is made of American troops, other than in degree, regardless of the standard of their performance. General Clay, however, was attempting with considerable success to carry out a difficult assignment in Germany and he told me he believed it might be helpful if I spoke to the women in Stuttgart. So, of course, I agreed to do so.

I also decided that I would speak in German. I had not really practiced my German since I had been on my honeymoon in the Black Forest of Germany forty-odd years earlier, but I believed it would be worth a good deal of effort to deliver my speech in the language of my audience. I wrote the speech in English and sent it around to the United States Embassy in Paris to have it translated. When the translation was returned I began reading it over and over at every opportunity to get the feel of the German words. I asked a young man recently returned from Germany to listen to my delivery and tell me if I could be understood.

Hesitatingly, he said: "I understand you, but your pronunciation is pretty bad." That made me work!

I carried the German translation in my pocketbook and whenever I had a couple of spare minutes I read over parts of the speech. The rest of the time I went around repeating German phrases over and over, to the amusement and sometimes the annoyance of my friends. I asked Mr. Winslow, who had been with UNRRA in Germany until he was attached to the United States mission to the United Nations, to accompany me on the trip, and on the airplane en route to Germany I declaimed vigorously above the noise of the motors.

There was a large crowd at the Stuttgart meeting and, as I had feared, they were cool and reserved if not bitter toward me when I arrived at the dinner. I had no intention of letting their coldness prevent me from saying certain things I had on my mind, so I began with a denunciation of the Nazi philosophy and actions. I made it as strong as I could and I expressed the opinion that the German people must bear their share of the blame. I had not expected my audience to be pleased by such remarks and they were not. The atmosphere became cooler.

But then I talked to them more approvingly. At that time the Russians were blockading Berlin, cutting off all coal and other supplies that moved over the normal land routes and forcing the United States to organize a gigantic air lift to supply West Berlin. The purpose of the Soviets was to force the Western Powers to move out of Berlin. In this crisis, the German people had acted magnificently and I praised them for supporting the democracies and defying the Communist power. I talked about the future, the recovery of Germany under a democratic form of government and the hope that the United Nations would mean the end of international wars. Slowly, the audience warmed up and I could feel a change of attitude as I concluded: "And now I extend to you the hand of friendship and co-operation."

When I had finished I did not feel that my audience was enthusiastic by any means, but I believed that at least some of the bitterness was gone and that we understood each other better.

On this trip I lunched with the women doctors and they told me about their problems with their own German refugees, who had to live on the German economy because they were German citizens but who could not at that time of hardship find work. They were existing under miserable and dangerous conditions. I was also told of the difficulties of tracing children taken by Hitler from conquered Poland and other lands, under his plan of destroying their nationality. Now as the records were found an effort was being made to restore the children to their families. Many of them did not even know they were not of German birth. It was one of the tragic situations that followed the war.

I stayed only a little more than a day in Stuttgart, but the visit taught me much and I returned with zest to the work of the Third Committee of the General Assembly.

In the final vote in Committee 3 on presenting the Declaration to the Assembly, delegates from four Moslem countries abstained, explaining that they believed the article on religious freedom was contrary to the Koran.

This setback came at a critical time near the end of the Paris sessions but, fortunately, we consulted with Sir Zafrulla Khan, the foreign minister of Pakistan, whose delegate on the Commission had abstained, and he courageously rose in the General Assembly to defend the Declaration. Since Pakistan was the largest Moslem nation involved his position was important.

"It is my opinion," he declared, "that our Pakistan delegate has misinterpreted the Koran. I understand the Koran to say: 'He who can believe shall believe; he who cannot believe shall disbelieve; the only unforgivable sin is to be a hypocrite.' I shall vote for acceptance of the Universal Declaration of Human Rights."

In the end there was no vote cast against the Declaration in the General Assembly, but there were some disappointing abstentions. The Soviet Union and its satellite countries abstained, since the Russian delegate contended that the Declaration put emphasis mainly on "eighteenth-century rights" and not enough on economic, social and cultural rights. The delegate from Saudi Arabia, Jamil M. Baroody, abstained, saying that he was quite sure King Ibn Saud would not agree with Sir Zafrulla in interpreting the Koran. South Africa also abstained, I was sad to note; its delegate said that they hoped to give their people basic human rights, but that the Declaration went too far. Two small countries were absent. The Declaration was finally accepted by the General Assembly on December 10, 1948.

After the Declaration was accepted it seemed to me that the United States had held the chairmanship of the Commission on Human Rights long enough. So at the 1951 meeting of the Commission in Geneva I nominated Charles Malik of Lebanon, with the consent of my government. He was elected and from then on I was just a member but a most interested member, for I believed the Human Rights Commission was one of the very important parts of the foundation on which the United Nations might build a peaceful world.

The Commission continued to work on drafting the Covenants, but this was so difficult that the United States group finally decided that it would be possible to progress only if we moved forward a step at a time. We proposed that there be two Covenants, one covering legally binding agreements on social and economic rights and another covering political and civil rights. This plan was vigorously opposed by some delegations, including the Soviets, on the ground that the economic and social rights were the most important and that they probably would not be accepted for years if they were in a separate

Covenant. But it seemed to our delegation that it was better to try to get what we could at that time. The civil and political rights already were a part of the law in many countries and were not so difficult to phrase in legal language that would be generally acceptable, although we knew that even this first step would be exceedingly difficult.

We finally won our point by only four votes, but taking the first step turned out to be even harder than we had expected. Progress had been made but the Covenants are not well drafted, nor is the drafting yet complete, and I doubt whether they are likely to be accepted in their present form. Looking back over the work that has been done, I now believe it would be best to start anew by putting into the Covenant on civil and political rights only a few basic rights on which all could agree and to provide for adding other rights as it becomes possible to have them generally accepted.

In these pages I have, of course, touched only on a few phases of my six years of work with the United Nations. There were many other struggles and successes and failures in the various committees and in the General Assembly, and I was on the go much of the time between New York and Paris or Geneva in connection with my work.

I recall one time when I found myself opposing all the other members of Committee 3 on the very delicate issue of the Children's Emergency Fund, an occasion when the United States was defeated on all points, though in the long run almost everything we stood for was accepted. The United Nations International Children's Emergency Fund (UNICEF) had been set up to deal with the European emergency at the end of the war. When the plight of children in Europe began improving, the people working in UNICEF, seeing that the needs of children elsewhere in the world were often greater, began doing some work in other areas. But our Congress decided the money was being spent in a way not authorized and they stopped American funds, except for small sums, until certain changes were made in the UNICEF organization. These changes were to drop the word "emergency" from the title of UNICEF, and to make all plans for care of children in conjunction with the other organizations that would be needed to carry out the work, such as the World Health Organization and the International Labor Organization. Because of past differences of opinion among the various specialized agencies, the United States reasonably felt that all the children's work should be properly coordinated, and that emphasis should be placed on helping needy nations to develop their own supplies of food and, if possible, of medicine.

This proposal, which I advanced as representative of the United States, kicked up a very heated argument. One of the opposition leaders was Ahmed Bokhari of Pakistan, a very learned and eloquent man who later became head of the United Nations Public Information Department. In a most impassioned speech, he asserted that my position meant that the United States did not care what happened to the children of Asia. "After all," he said sarcastically and bitterly, "they are colored children and the United States cares only about helping the children of Europe, who are white."

Such a vicious and unjustified attack was, I suppose, an effective emotional way of opposing our proposals. In any event, the feelings aroused were so great that no other nation dared join the United States in making the changes, although I responded to Mr. Bokhari as best I could. This was one of the few times when I could find no way to "get through" the barrier of misunderstanding among the delegates of many nations, although I tried in various ways to talk calmly and informally with Mr. Bokhari.

I felt that our position was right, but I also felt very uncomfortable, especially when a motion was made to continue UNICEF in its old form and I cast the lone vote in opposition. Yet our position was reasonable, and a few months later we were justified when the name of the Fund was changed as we had suggested (although the initials UNICEF were retained simply because they had become a kind of world symbol) and the organization was re-formed to provide for closer co-operation with other specialized agencies. The only proposal we made that has not yet been accepted was that all nations share in the overhead expenses.

There are many other important and unimportant flashes of life at the United Nations that stick in my mind. There was, at one time, a Senator on the United States delegation who could never get to his office at the United Nations in time to read the documents that the State Department so carefully prepared each day to keep us abreast of what had happened in various committees and of what was scheduled to happen that day. The delegation documentary secretary always arrived early and put the documents in order on his desk but you could be sure that the Senator would come dashing in, out of breath, two minutes before the delegation met for its regular briefing. He would grab up the documents and puff into the briefing room—and usually he would not have the slightest idea what we were talking about.

Often, if I happened to sit next to him, I would have to find the proper document for him and point out the paragraph that pertained to our discussion. Then he would hurriedly and unsuccessfully try to catch up but by that time we had moved on to something else. I sometimes lectured him about doing his homework, but there was never any improvement.

There was the time, too, when we were in session in Paris during the United States Presidential elections of 1948. Most newspapers and many political observers forecast an easy victory for Governor Thomas E. Dewey, the Republican nominee. Mr. Dulles was close to Governor Dewey, and in many ways showed that he expected to become Secretary of State as soon as the voters elected a Republican President. I must say that I felt sorry for him when President Truman was re-elected to the surprise of practically everybody except President Truman. It was interesting to me that immediately after Mr. Truman's re-election the correspondents of many European newspapers came to me and asked how this could have happened.

"Why, everybody in all the newspapers in the United States told us that Governor Dewey was certain to be elected," they said. "How could they be so wrong? Do you have a 'controlled' press in the United States? Could they have purposely misled us?"

I gave them quite a little lecture on the fact that the press in the United States is completely independent, and I pointed out something else that many people fail to understand—the voters in the United States also are completely independent and cast their ballots as they wish.

There was also a memorable Thanksgiving Day in Paris. Whenever our delegation was abroad on Thanksgiving I tried to have a special dinner to which I asked all who worked with me and did not have a family with them. On this occasion my granddaughter Sistie, who is Mrs. Van Seagraves, and her husband were in Paris as Van was then working there with one of our government agencies. I asked Sistie and Miss Thompson to try to find some pumpkins to decorate the table for our Thanksgiving party. But when they went to the Paris markets and asked for pumpkins they were regarded as slightly crazy.

"A whole pumpkin!" the farm women exclaimed. "Who ever heard of buying a whole pumpkin. It's ridiculous! What would one do with a whole pumpkin?"

They persisted, however, and finally found a few. We ordered six turkeys and we carefully explained to the hotel chefs how we wanted them cooked and what kind of stuffing and gravy we wanted. The whole thing was difficult for the French cooks. When our guests arrived —thirty or so—the table had some faint resemblance to a real Thanksgiving table, thanks to Sistie and Miss Thompson, but the turkey trimmings were slightly European and the pumpkin pie was definitely a French instead of a New England version. I picked out among our gentlemen the ones I thought would best meet the responsibilities of carving and they tried. Later some of them told me they had never carved a turkey before, but somehow they managed. The fact that all of us were together made it a little less lonely on this very special American holiday.

The last session of the General Assembly that I attended in Paris was in the autumn of 1951, a session that continued after a brief Christmas holiday into February of 1952. Toward the end of this session, Ambassador Austin became ill and for a short time I presided over the United States delegation. The heads of other delegations frequently came to discuss with me various problems and all of them were quick to ask after Senator Austin and to express affection for him personally. I thought they paid him a great tribute both in his position as Ambassador to the United Nations and head of our delegation and as a man.

"We have not always agreed with the policies of the United States," most of them said in one way or another. "But if Ambassador Austin told us something was true, we knew it was true."

It was a great responsibility to preside over the delegation, especially when it included such able men as Senator Mike Mansfield of Montana and Representative John M. Vorys of Ohio. But if you have to do things, somehow you get through them. And of course I had Mr. Sandifer and other helpful State Department advisers, so I managed to keep the delegation working as a team without any real catastrophe.

There was one touchy incident toward the end of the Paris sessions. Throughout there had been an effort to get France to permit discussion in the United Nations of conditions in Morocco. But the French delegate insisted that trouble in those areas was purely a domestic issue to be dealt with by the French government, although some of us wondered whether human rights could ever be labeled a domestic issue.

Then, without warning, an American Negro who was backed by both Communist and non-Communist groups in the United States arrived in Paris and demanded that an item be placed on the agenda charging the United States with genocide because of lynchings that had occurred in our country.

What should our delegation do? We talked it over and finally decided that we would not object to having the subject discussed by the General Assembly. We did not realize it at the time, but as things turned out it was technically too late for any new item to be added to the agenda. So the charge did not come up in the Assembly. The Soviet delegate, Dr. Pavlov, tried to make up for this by raising the same charge in Committee 3. He made a vicious attack on our government in relation to discrimination against Negroes in the United States.

"The United States," he cried in a burst of uncontrolled oratory, "cares so little about its workers that at this very minute they are dying of hunger in the streets of Los Angeles by the hundreds of thousands."

I replied quietly: "The representative of the Soviet Union knows that what he is saying is not true. And to prove that his charge is false I will be happy to secure affidavits from the workers in Los Angeles."

The Communists, however, seemed to be off on a wild propaganda spree. A young Ukrainian representative followed Dr. Pavlov's lead.

"Mrs. Roosevelt tells us the workers are not dying of hunger in the streets of Los Angeles by the hundreds of thousands," he said. "What she does not know is that they are crawling back to their hovels and dying in their hovels." A slight murmur of amusement ran through the committee. "The workers of Los Angeles," I said, "will not like having their homes called hovels!"

Later, as I felt no white person could adequately answer this false charge, Dr. Channing Tobias, one of America's foremost Negro educators, delivered an honest and fine explanation of our situation and of our efforts to remedy inequalities among our citizens.

This was nearly the end of my work for the United Nations. I served during the autumn of 1952 but at the end of each session all delegates automatically resign to permit the President to have a free hand in choosing his representatives. In the 1952 elections, a Republican administration came into power and all of us who were Democrats knew that our services with the United Nations had come to an end. But my interest in the United Nations had grown steadily during six years and later I volunteered to work with the American Association for the United Nations so that I would not be out of touch with the work of the one organization that has the machinery to bring together eighty-odd nations in an effort to maintain world peace.

X

GOING HOME THE LONG
WAY ROUND

Although I had been bustling back and forth across the Atlantic Ocean rather like a harassed commuter for six years, my really extensive foreign travels did not begin until 1952 after the General Assembly in Paris. The end of my duties as a delegate later that year meant that I no longer had to adjust my life to a schedule of meetings of the Assembly or the Human Rights Commission in various cities at frequent intervals. Though it was necessary for me to spend a certain amount of time traveling in connection with my work for the American Association for the United Nations, I had much greater flexibility in my schedule and was able to take longer trips abroad, always as a newspaperwoman and sometimes also as a representative of the AAUN. There were many parts of the world in which I was interested and which I wanted to see at first hand. It had been a good many years since I was a little girl reading anything I could find that told me about the world, but the fascination of faraway lands had not waned.

I had received a number of invitations to visit various countries. One was extended by Prime Minister Nehru, on the afternoon that he sat on the floor of the living room in my Hyde Park cottage and chatted for several hours with the young people. In the midst of some discussion of conditions in India as compared with those in the United States, he turned to me.

"I would like to invite you to come to India," he said. "You would be the guest of the government and you would see these things for yourself."

"I am grateful for the invitation," I replied, "but I am not planning to make any journeys for a while. Later, I would like very much to see India."

The invitation stuck in my mind and, as the Assembly was ending its sessions in Paris early in 1952, I decided the time might be right. "Instead of going back to New York as usual," I remarked to my secretary, "why not go home the long way—around the world? We've already got a good start."

So Mr. Nehru renewed his invitation and our ambassador to India, Chester Bowles, seemed pleased with the idea, and I decided to go. Another thing that influenced me was that I had long wanted to visit Israel, particularly since I had seen the Jewish refugee camps in Germany and learned more of the eagerness of most of the refugees to migrate to Israel. As soon as I began making arrangements to stop in Israel on the way to India, I was approached by Charles Malik of Lebanon, whom I had come to know well on the Human Rights Commission.

"I hear that you're going to stop in Israel on the way to India," he said. "I really don't think you should stop there without visiting some of the Arab countries. You should see more than one country in the Middle East."

"That is perfectly true," I replied. "But since there has never been any formal peace established between Israel and the Arab states on her borders, it is impossible to get an Arab visa if you have your passport visaed for Israel. The Arab states refuse to recognize Israel as a nation. And in retaliation Israel refuses to give passports or visas to anyone from the Arab states. So far as I know, the only way to go from Israel to the Arab states or vice versa is to fly back to some neutral country like Greece and get a visa and then retrace your steps. I don't have time for that."

"I believe I can arrange it so you can visit Lebanon, Syria and Jordan and then go directly on to Israel," he replied. A little later he did make such arrangements for me and my secretary, Miss Corr, and we flew directly from Paris to Beirut, Lebanon, where we arrived late one evening. Beirut was a beautiful and peaceful-looking city even at night, with the Mediterranean breaking softly on its beaches, and I was in fine spirits when I arose early the next morning to start an automobile tour that had been arranged for me. I went out to get in the car, however, and discovered I was to be escorted by a lorry filled with soldiers.

I had wondered a bit about the attitude of the people toward me because I had always been outspoken in my support of the state of Israel, but everyone seemed friendly and I decided to ignore the presence of the soldiers for a time. When we halted to visit some historic site, the truck dashed up behind us and the soldiers leaped out to set up "lines of defense" around us. This was indeed an indication that the government was not at all certain about the kind of reception I would be given by the people. Or at least the officials were taking a rather alarmist view of it.

Actually, there was no sign of any hostility, and after a short time I became thoroughly irritated by what seemed to me to be intolerable nonsense.

"No one is bothering us," I protested to the official in charge. "No one even seems slightly interested in what I am doing. So please get rid of those soldiers and at once!"

"Very well, madame," he replied with some reluctance. He gave an order and the soldiers once more leaped into their truck and departed. I was certain, however, throughout my visit that there was always a guard of some kind nearby, although they did not admit as much to me.

I found my visit to the Arab countries extremely interesting. Lebanon was fascinating, with its hills so carefully cultivated in tiny plots, and there were many signs of important archaeological exploration in this ancient part of the civilized world. Some excavations had revealed six or seven different periods of ancient history, one above the other. We were interested in one mountain pass through which early conquering armies had come and where men had carved their names on the rocks from the earliest days of history.

Lebanon is perhaps the most westernized of the Arab countries. We had planned to drive to Syria, but there was so much snow in the mountain passes that we changed our plans and went by air to Damascus, an amazing city with narrow streets and bazaars. I asked our Ambassador if we could visit the home of an ordinary workman in

Damascus and he arranged it. We wound through the crowded streets, past many walls with doors opening from the curb into dim courtyards and came at last to our objective—another door opening through another wall into a center courtyard.

Inside I was greeted by the workman, who was employed in a crafts shop. He was cordial and invited us to a kind of living room off the courtyard where there were couches along the walls. I noticed in the courtyard a large pile of uncolored tiles.

"Are you building something with these tiles?" I asked.

"Oh, no," he replied. "I make enough at the shop to support myself but I need to earn more to support my wife and two children. So at odd times I color tiles, for which I am paid by the tile."

He brought us coffee, black and bitter in the fashion of the country. I knew that it would be a great discourtesy to refuse the coffee so I gritted my teeth and drank it. The room in which we sat was plain and almost bare except for the couches around the wall, which presumably served as beds at night.

"Could we see the rest of your home?" I asked.

Our host led us back into the courtyard and then to another room, which was almost exactly the same as the room in which we had been sitting. There was, however, a kind of grille in the wall and beyond it I glimpsed two dark, glowing eyes above a veil. Our host's wife was preparing more coffee—the idea of more coffee at that moment caused me considerable pain for I knew I could not refuse it—but she never did appear to meet us, though we met the children, who seemed very friendly. Nevertheless, I found my visit to the workman interesting and I learned something of conditions in the country by seeing his home.

The newspapermen to whom I talked in Syria were particularly difficult. They were bitterly nationalistic and bitterly opposed to Israel and they badgered me with questions about why I should support the Israeli cause.

"The Balfour resolution for establishment of a Jewish homeland was accepted by the United States and Great Britain after the first World War," I usually replied. "This action encouraged the buying of land by the Jews on the assurance that a homeland would be created for them in Palestine. I feel that it practically committed our government to assist in the creation of a government there eventually, because there cannot be a homeland without a government."

The Syrian reporters were never satisfied with this answer and the most I ever persuaded them to admit was that I was honestly expressing my point of view. That, however, obviously did not mean to them that I was entitled to a point of view on this controversial and explosive subject.

One evening in Damascus we had dinner with the head of the Syrian foreign office in a kind of night club and restaurant. There were a number of guests and I noticed that a handsome, uniformed man who sat opposite me at the table seemed to be someone of importance.

"Who is that gentleman?" I asked the man sitting next to me in a low voice.

He looked startled and raised his finger to his lips.

"That," he said in a whisper, "is the dictator of Syria, General Fawzi Selo."

The General seemed to have little to say and did not even speak to me during the meal, so I paid no more attention. But after dinner, with no preliminaries but with the air of a man accustomed to giving commands, he walked around to me and said.

"Madame, you have been very friendly to Israel."

"Yes," I replied, "I am friendly to all. I am equally friendly to your people."

"But," he persisted with some signs of irritation, "you have worked for Israel!"

"That is true," I said. "When I think a thing is good, I also think it should be given help."

He did not reply, but he stared at me with what I thought was anger. Then he turned on his heel and, without another word, walked away.

From Damascus, I drove to Amman, Jordan. The United States Embassy there took good care of us, but our time was short and I had a chance to meet only two or three government officials. They were greatly concerned with the problem of the Palestinian refugees who had moved out of Israeli territory during the warfare between Israel and the Arab states and had been put in camps in Jordan. I visited many of these camps during my trip and found them distressing beyond words.

I had seen various refugee camps in Europe, as I related earlier, and had been impressed by the way the inmates kept their hopes alive and tried to make their temporary quarters into "homes" even under the most difficult conditions. I had been particularly impressed by the burning desire of many Jewish refugees to get to Israel. Now, in the Arab countries, I learned something of the grave problem of refugees from Israel.

The Arab refugee camps were the least hopeful I had ever seen. One of the principal reasons for this, I believe, was that nothing had been done to preserve the skills of the people. They seemed to have little or nothing to look forward to and nothing to do. Under such conditions, of course, the adults are likely to lose their skills and the children grow up uninstructed.

"Why," I asked my official guide, "are these people not given something to do? They might be making things to go on the market or helping produce food. If they lose their skills, they will be worthless citizens in any country they may finally settle down in."

My guide gave a kind of helpless shrug. "You see, there is unemployment in most of the Arab countries," he replied, "and it is felt that we cannot permit these people in the camps to seek work that would put them in competition with the citizens of the country."

The standard of living in the camps we visited was low and the housing was inadequate. This was not a cold climate but there were times when rain and chill weather made it exceedingly uncomfortable even in a good house. Some of the refugees lived in solid houses in the towns but many of them were living under wretched conditions in tents out on the hillsides. I visited one tent where a woman showed me her small baby, who was ill.

"The baby was bitten by a snake yesterday," the woman explained, as she put it back on the floor of the tent. Looking around, I could see that there was nothing to prevent snakes from entering and that babies lying on the floor would be easy prey for them.

The refugees were fed on a budget of three cents per day per person. That would seem to be a pitifully small sum even for countries with a low standard of living but, in fact, it represented more food than was available to some of the nomads living in the desert. The officials told us that it was difficult to persuade the refugees to leave the camps and find some place to settle permanently because they hoped to see Israel defeated and to return to their old homes. But some of them were gradually giving up this hope and permitting the authorities to resettle them in new areas. The nomad tribes nearby kept a close watch on the camps and, if a refugee family was moved out to a new home, their places were taken overnight by nomads who infiltrated the camps in order to be assured of three meals a day—poor as those meals might be.

Going from the Arab countries through the Mandelbaum Gate into Israel was, to me, like breathing the air of the United States again. The Mandelbaum Gate itself is nothing much—a movable barrier, with soldiers on guard. But once I was through the barrier I somehow felt that I was among people with a purpose, people dedicated to fulfilling a purpose.

I spent seven days in Israel, the same number I had spent in the Arab countries. Michael Comay of the Foreign Office accompanied me on various visits to all types of institutions throughout the country and Dr. Chaim Sheba, who was the government health officer, showed me some of the efforts being made to improve conditions everywhere. The health program is a monumental work. Much had been done in the past by Hadassah, which built and ran hospitals made possible by generous private donations of persons in many countries. The government has worked hard to organize public health services and Dr. Sheba's task was to weld all these efforts into an expanding program.

I visited Degania, which is one of the oldest kibbutzim (or communal farm settlements) in Israel and was welcomed by a vigorous old-timer, Joseph Baratz, and some members of his family. I have great admiration for Mr. Baratz and for the work that has been achieved in this kibbutz under great difficulties, including warfare with the Syrian armies.

During the war the central government was so hard pressed for military supplies that it could not even provide arms and ammunition with which the men and women of the kibbutz might make a stand against the Syrian army, which was well organized and had armored groups poised for the invasion of Israel. The members of the kibbutz, however, had no intention of standing by while the Syrian soldiers overran the farms they had worked so hard to develop in what had been rough desert country. They had some arms of their own and they quickly improvised others by making bombs out of bottles filled with gasoline and with a fuse attached—the kind of bomb known during the Second World War as a Molotov cocktail. Then they dug an antitank ditch across the path of the attackers and waited. The first Syrian tank approached almost to the ditch without meeting any opposition, but then a strong-armed man hurled his Molotov cocktail so accurately that the tank caught fire and was stopped short of the ditch. The sight of the tank exploding in flames gave the Syrian commander the erroneous impression that Degania was strongly defended. He ordered his troops, which far outnumbered the defenders, to withdraw and the kibbutz was saved from destruction. By the time the Syrians learned of their mistake, the Israeli armies had struck at the main Arab forces so fiercely that the invasion was thwarted.

I believe I should mention here that I was greatly impressed by what the Israelis had done to reclaim the desert and make it productive, to develop the country industrially and to accept as permanent citizens hundreds of thousands of refugees from war and persecution in Europe and elsewhere. But I was even more impressed when I returned to Israel for another visit three years later and saw how much had been done in that short time. Of course, no one should imagine that everything is perfect in Israel. The country has many large and small problems of all kinds to overcome, including the necessity of establishing a sound basis for its economic existence. A great deal has been done. The desert has been made to blossom but there remain grave obstacles —such as the efficient use of water—to a peaceful and prosperous future. With reason and patience, I believe solutions can be found and they will greatly benefit not Israel alone but the entire area.

Not all of Israel's problems are economic. One issue that must be faced by the government is that of separation of church and state. At present, the influence of the church is so great that it is often difficult to distinguish between it and the state. I was surprised, for example, to be told about a young man who had been refused the right to marry the girl with whom he was in love because she was an Orthodox Catholic. The authorities, because of the power of the religious leaders, simply refused to grant them a license to marry. This is merely one example of the injustices that can grow out of such a situation and the incidents will greatly increase in time. Apparently leaders of the state do not now feel that their country is strong enough to undertake a solution of this problem because it would arouse bitter controversy, but someday it must be faced. When it is, I am confident there will be a separation of powers as there is in the United States.

There is one more experience I want to mention in connection with Israel. On the occasion of my first visit I called on Sheik Suleiman near Beersheba. Not a great many Arabs chose to remain in Israel after the war with the Arab countries, but Sheik Suleiman is a large landowner and he continued to live in rather feudal fashion under the Israeli government. However, only his style of life was feudal. His ideas of farming were modern and he used machinery to work the land where possible.

A big, bearded and strong-looking man, the Sheik received us in a large but sparsely furnished room at his home. I imagine he was in late middle age. He wore the robes of Arabia but spoke excellent English and made us feel welcome at once. As we entered, I had noticed a number of women near a door in the big courtyard and many children running about. Knowing that the Sheik practiced polygamy, I asked him how many children he had.

"I think about seventy-five," he replied thoughtfully, stroking his beard, "but I am not sure . . . I am not sure."

We had a pleasant visit and enjoyed seeing him. As usual in these countries, we were served bitter black coffee. On this occasion I had consumed several cups and would doubtless have taken more out of politeness if someone had not been kind enough to tell me that I should shake my hand hard on replacing the cup on the tray if I did not want the servants to keep on refilling my cup.

Several years later, in 1957 some friends of mine, Mr. and Mrs. Joseph Lash, were going to Israel for a visit and I wrote them a letter of introduction to Sheik Suleiman. They called on him and he received them warmly, inviting them to an Arab dinner of roast kid. In the custom of the country this is eaten with the fingers of one hand and without the benefit of any kind of cutlery except perhaps a sharp-pointed knife. When I heard about how well the Lashes had been received I wrote a note of thanks to the Sheik, and he later sent me a beautiful silver dagger, with a letter saying that the dagger had been his own for thirty years and had never been touched by anyone but himself. I couldn't think of any need I had for a dagger so I gave it to my son Franklin, who was very much pleased.

In the autumn of 1957 my son James made a trip to Israel and upon my suggestion he, too, called on Sheik Suleiman. In the course of their conversation my name was mentioned and the Sheik called James's attention to a photograph that he had of me. He tugged thoughtfully at his beard and my son insists that he said:

"I have thirty-nine wives, Mr. Roosevelt." He paused and pointed at my picture. "She should have been the fortieth. I will never understand why she did not accept my offer."

That, at least, is the way James told the story when he came home. I would like to make it very clear that, so far as I know, the Sheik had never made me an offer, I believe he must have been joking, but when James told me about it, possibly with some elaboration to make a good story, we enjoyed a chuckle over the idea that I might have had a chance to be the fortieth wife of a sheik!

The most notable personality in Israel, I thought, was Prime Minister Ben-Gurion, and I still think so. Before leaving Israel, Miss Corr and I were joined by Dr. David Gurewitsch, who continued with us to Pakistan and India, a trip I described in my book, *India and the Awakening East*. When Miss Corr and I eventually arrived back in New York, I thought my around-the-world journeying was ended, but as things turned out I was soon to have an opportunity to visit another exciting distant land—Japan.

XI

JAPAN: EXPERIMENT IN
DEMOCRACY

In the spring of 1953 I came home from a short trip in the United
States to find bad news waiting for me. Miss Thompson was in the
hospital.

I went immediately to see her, but she did not recognize me. Dr.
Eugenia Ingerman told me that Tommy had had a heart attack a
day before I reached New York and that she had been taken to the
hospital that morning. She had not been feeling well for several
days before the attack, and had had a slight stroke. The doctors were
doubtful whether she would ever be able to move about again. I had
arrived home on April 7, and for the next few days I spent most of
my time at the hospital, making several trips a day to be near her.

The anniversary of my husband's death falls on April 12 and there
is always a ceremony on that day at his grave in the rose garden at
Hyde Park.

"I always try to be at Hyde Park on the 12th," I told Dr. Ingerman.
"I don't want to go away while Tommy is in such serious condition
but she isn't conscious and doesn't recognize me. If you think she's
not likely to change, I will drive up to Hyde Park in the morning and
return in the afternoon."

The doctor said she thought I should go and I did. I returned late in the afternoon and walked into the hospital just as dear Tommy died. There had been no sudden change. She just died.

I could only believe that it was a blessing that she did not live as an invalid, which was the most the doctors could hope for. She was a most active person and invalidism would have been sheer agony for her. Tommy had been with me for over thirty years and some of that time she had lived with me. She had an apartment in my cottage at Hyde Park and my children and grandchildren were devoted to her as a member of the family. She was really a remarkably selfless person and a wonderful judge of people. She had a keen sense of humor and her values were clear, so nothing ever changed her. She wanted to be useful and in many, many ways she not only made my life easier but gave me a reason for living. In almost anything I did, she was a help but she was also a stern critic.

"You didn't do that very well," she frequently told me after I had made some speech or written some article. "You didn't take enough time to prepare for it."

No one can ever take the place of such a person nor does one cease missing them, but I am sure she would not have wanted to live to suffer the torture of being an invalid.

Though my work for the American Association for the United Nations began in the spring of 1953, it did not become intensive until autumn. Consequently I accepted an invitation that spring to be one of a group of exchange people going from the United States to Japan. The trip was under the auspices of Columbia University, which acted as host in this country for the Japanese who came here. Our hosts in Japan were Shigeharu Matsumoto and Dr. Yasaka Takagi, who represented the International House of Japan and the Committee for Cultural Exchange. There had been two Americans ahead of me, Dr. Charles W. Cole, the head of Amherst University, and Father George Ford of Corpus Christi Church, who studied Japanese prisons and other institutions.

The reason the Japanese invited me was that their women were just coming into the responsibilities of functioning in a democracy after centuries in which feudalistic concepts had dominated their lives and customs. The attempt to change over to more or less democratic concepts in a short time naturally created many problems both of a political nature and in regard to family life. Some of the Japanese leaders hoped that an American woman, talking to groups of Japanese women and men, would be able to explain to them the meaning of democracy and the manner in which a democratic government functioned. The fact was that after World War II the United States had rather arbitrarily insisted on giving the Japanese a democratic constitution, telling them that now they were going to be a democratic country. But this, of course, did not automatically change the old customs or turn feudalism into democracy. There were various articles in the new Japanese constitution that had been taken almost verbatim from Western documents, as I will explain later, and some of these meant nothing to the Japanese or merely confused them because of the great differences between their social and economic background and the social and economic concepts of, say, the United States or France. So, a period of education obviously was necessary, and I was happy to have a chance to do whatever I could to help spread the idea of democracy.

I left New York on May 21, accompanied by Miss Corr and my daughter-in-law Mrs. Elliott Roosevelt. Minnewa and Elliott had not been married very long and I think she felt the need of understanding the motivations of her new family, since the environment into which she had married was very different from anything she had known in the past. So she as well as Miss Corr went with me to Japan. Minnewa proved to be a good traveling companion and we enjoyed many delightful experiences together.

Our first glimpse of Japan after we got off the plane was on the long drive into the city, most of it through drab streets and past dreary houses and shops—the kind of uninteresting approach you find to so many of our cities in the United States. Seldom in traveling around the world have I seen an attractive drive from an airport into a city, and a visitor often gets a completely erroneous first impression of the community he is visiting. But when we reached the Imperial Hotel in downtown Tokyo we found that we had a charming sitting room, a pleasant place for breakfast in the early morning.

In fact our hotel accommodations were very much like those in a hotel at home, except for the sunken bathtub, which I like because it is easy to step down into. There were flowers everywhere in our rooms and later members of the United Nations Association of Japan who came from the northern prefecture of Aomori to see me brought a beautiful basket of firm and juicy apples, as good as those grown in New York State. Coming from me, that is a compliment because I particularly like the fruit of my own home state.

I went over my schedule for the next few days with Dr. Takagi and Mr. Matsumoto. One of the first persons I encountered in the lobby of the hotel was Marian Anderson, who had been singing with great success all over Japan. Later, I held a press conference. I had always heard that the Japanese were avid photography fans, but I never expected to see as many news photographers as greeted us in Tokyo. They were all over the landscape all the time. I was told that Adlai Stevenson gazed in wonder at them during his trip to Japan and exclaimed: "This is a photographic dictatorship!"

I will not attempt to describe our experiences in Japan in any chronological order because we covered so much ground in the five weeks we were there, but there were some highlights that stand out in my mind. A few days after our arrival, we visited Princess Chichibu, the widow of the Emperor's brother. The Princess had gone to the Friends School in Washington when her parents, Ambassador and Mrs. Tsuneo Matsudaira, were stationed there. After her marriage she was apparently able to keep in much closer touch with the people of Japan than were other members of the royal family. For years while her husband was ill, they lived on a farm at the foot of Mount Fuji and knew many of the farm families in the district. Now she was living in a small house with a very small garden nearer to Tokyo, but she still raised delicious strawberries that ripen all year around. Her farmer friends still came to see her regularly to talk over problems of farming. She also kept busy working with the Girl Guides, which is similar to our Girl Scout organization, and with Four-H Clubs, which have been active in Japan since the war in an effort to help young farmers learn modern methods of production.

We were served black tea, English fashion, with dainty sandwiches and cakes and a dish of strawberries with whipped cream. But later everyone was given a bowl of green Japanese tea and it was explained that such tea is always given to guests when they are making a ceremonial call. One of the guests was Madame Takagi, lady-in-waiting to the Empress, and she said that it used to be a custom to call on all your friends and relatives to say good-by before starting a trip.

"You had to drink a cup of this green tea without sugar or lemon at

each place," she added. "By the time you had finished making all of
your calls you really had consumed a lot more tea than you needed in
one afternoon."

The photographers continued to swarm around us. The previous day
two of them had even followed us up into the mountains in a rain
storm when we went to spend the night at the home of Mr. and Mrs.
E. J. Griffith, Americans with business interests in Japan. One of
them remained somewhere in the neighborhood all night, although we
were not aware of it until breakfast time, when he sent in a little
drawing of himself with a camera and one of me with an umbrella—
an invitation for me to come outside for a photograph! Mr. Matsumoto
went out and told him that on Sunday one should not be disturbed
by newspaper photographers and he retired, but when we reached
Princess Chichibu's house there were numerous photographers there.
The Princess said that she did not appear in public, but she did
consent to have a photograph taken with our party in the garden.

The next day I had an interesting meeting at the Ministry of Labor
with the people who run bureaus for women in industry, for improvement of rural life, child welfare and the like. These government
bureaus bear the stamp of American organization but that does not
mean they operate the way they do in the United States. The organization was imposed in Japan by the occupation authorities and, as usual,
American methods were not entirely suited to the facts of life in
Japan—the place of women in the industrial system, the necessity
for children to contribute to the family income, the ability of the
economy to support such public services. In order to make these organizations practical they had to be adjusted to fit conditions in Japan, and
that has been a very complicated task.

There is also the very important question whether such services are
welcomed by the public. As I was leaving the Ministry a group of
Communist party women, led by an American who is married to a
Japanese, were waiting outside. The American woman stared at me
and seemed to be highly strung to the point of fanaticism. As I stepped
out the door the group began shouting anti-American slogans.

"Go home to America. We women who went through the war do
not want any more war!"

The obvious answer was, of course, that neither did I want war, but
it is groups such as this one that keep the fear of war constantly alive
in the peoples of the free world. I made numerous inquiries about

Communist activities and strength in Japan. On one occasion I met with a number of college presidents at Nara and made a point of asking them about the attitude of students and professors.

"Do you think a majority of students in your colleges are convinced Marxists?" I asked. "How many of your professors advocate the Marxist ideology?"

It was a little difficult to get these men to warm up to a frank discussion—perhaps we were somewhat awed by each other—but they generally agreed that both students and professors like to study Marxism.

"But," one of them added, with the agreement of the others, "I doubt that more than a few are really convinced Communists. A few, however, can make a good deal of noise and gain a prominent position because they know what they really believe in, while the others are divided and groping to find their way."

This seemed to me to be a familiar situation. I was inclined, however, to believe there was more real acceptance of Marxism as a theory among the students in Japan than these college presidents were willing to acknowledge to me. They did say frankly that democracy was not making headway among the students and that it was not being well taught.

Not long afterward in Tokyo I dined with three eminent professors and we discussed the relative responsibility of the Soviet Union and the United States for the tensions existing in the world and the fear of another war. The Japanese attitude was to put more blame on the United States than I would admit was deserved, but I suppose this was only natural since they constantly were seeing and sometimes suffering from the fact that we have military installations in their country. They are thus far more conscious of our military power than they are of the threat of Soviet military expansion.

The Japanese, of course, resent the presence of foreign soldiers as much as any other people would, but the space taken up by our military installations is an important factor in their grievance. It is difficult to realize that every acre, almost every yard of land is needed if it can be used to raise some kind of crop in Japan. The dinner I shared with the three professors, for example, was in an excellent restaurant on the French style. The big range was part of the dining room so you could see the orders being cooked, and the food—mostly fish—was as good as any in Paris, to my taste. But even here very little meat was served and for the mass of the people there is rarely any meat and often not enough food of any kind.

It seems to me that the Japanese have tended throughout their history to deal in theory and to shun reality. In their difficult economic situation, the Marxist theory as an ideal has a certain definite appeal. But I doubt very much whether the Communist reality as developed by Lenin and Stalin in Russia would have any real appeal to the Japanese. One can only hope that the arguments one puts forth in behalf of democracy will bear fruit later. The men with whom I was talking on these occasions were scholars and I believe their integrity will oblige them to examine what has been said in spite of their dislike of facing realities.

I talked to countless groups of women in many cities of Japan and there were certain broad themes that ran through all of our discussions. One was the attitude of young people toward their elders and the attitude of the elders toward the young. Since the Japanese had been urged to accept the democratic idea of free discussion, there had developed a great deal of criticism between the two groups and this antagonism was increased by the fact that the young people blamed their elders for telling them that Japan could not lose the war. Much of the authority of the elders was undermined when the Japanese armies were defeated and the Emperor was declared to be a man rather than a god. The young people became cynical and disillusioned.

Another theme in our discussions was the age-old question of prostitution, and of babies of mixed blood. These matters were very serious in Japan because of the American soldiers, who had plenty of money and food while the Japanese standard of living for the masses was so low that the main consideration of many was how to get enough to eat.

There also were many questions, particularly from the students, that I answered as best I could. Sometimes I was asked why the United States used the atom bomb and how I felt about it. I tried to explain the urgent reasons that prompted our leaders to make the decision in an effort to end the war quickly, but at the same time I expressed my feeling of horror about any kind of warfare. Another question was "Do the people of the United States understand that the young people of Japan dislike rearmament and that, in order to rearm as urged by Washington, we have to change our constitution, which was adopted at the request of the United States in the first place?"

Of course, world conditions had changed since they adopted the constitution that renounced war forever, but it was not so easy to see the threat of Soviet expansion through Japanese eyes as it was through American eyes. And I don't suppose my explanations of the danger to the democracies were entirely satisfactory to people who had never really experienced democratic life.

These sessions were often exhausting, particularly if there were a large number of students in the audience, but what was most tiring to me was the fact that everything had to be translated. I had fine interpreters, including Yoko Matsuoka, who had spent seven years in America and is the author of a book called *Daughter of the Pacific*. But whenever I made a speech I would talk for only two or three minutes and then stop while the translator told the audience what I had said. Then I would resume for a few minutes and halt again for the translation. This makes it difficult sometimes to keep to a train of thought and in any event it is far more wearying than making an ordinary speech. And the same system, of course, had to be followed in asking and answering questions, which made the meetings much longer than they would have been otherwise.

My daughter-in-law Minnewa was one of the most patient persons I have ever known. She went with me to every meeting and listened to many speeches over and over again, yet she never seemed to be bored or weary. Once when I spoke to a group of women and men in a village there were many questions from the audience, one of which sounded quite unusual to American ears.

"In the United States," a young woman asked me, "what do you do with your mothers-in-law?"

I replied that I didn't think there was any set formula for that problem in America. But then I glanced at Minnewa and thought how tired she must be of listening to my speeches and I added with a smile:

"Perhaps my daughter-in-law can answer your question better than I can."

My joke was taken seriously by our audience and poor Minnewa found herself confronted by a battery of Japanese eyes, curious and earnestly anxious to know the answer to a very serious question. But my daughter-in-law only blushed, shook her head and refused to answer.

The question was an important one for the Japanese. In their country the mother-in-law is in authority over the women of the household and, in fact, over all members of the household except her husband and her eldest son. She also often is the keeper of the purse and all earnings of members of the family are turned over to her. She doles out money as she thinks it is needed, even to married sons and their wives.

I remember one charming and rather sophisticated Japanese newspaperwoman who was beautiful in her native costume yet seemed to be familiar with Western customs. She told me that her greatest difficulty at home was with the "system of the pouch."

"What is that?" I asked.

"My mother-in-law," she said, "is old-fashioned. She has a large leather pouch and each week she puts into that pouch all of the family earnings. Then all of us become dependent on her ideas of how much we should spend or whether we should spend anything—in fact, she can practically tell us how to run our lives."

I found that this custom was practiced in many places. A woman who worked in a factory told me she went home on weekends to the farm where her family lived and that she always placed her earnings on the household shrine the night she arrived. The next morning they were gone—into the mother-in-law's pouch. I found that most of the Japanese mothers in the working class look forward to the day when they will be mothers-in-law and can tyrannize over their daughters-in-law. Slowly, these outdated customs are changing under the present government but it will be a long time before they are entirely gone.

In some of the rural areas we visited it was usual for the mother-in-law to take care of the children while other members of her household worked in the field. But in general the daughter-in-law is almost a slave indoors. She must arise early and prepare the food and serve everyone before she kneels a step below her husband and his mother to eat her own meal. She works in the fields and then returns to prepare the Japanese bath. In many farm homes, this is a huge copper caldron which has to be filled by hand from a water supply quite a distance away. Once the tub is filled, she builds a fire under it and keeps it going so the water will be at the right temperature. Members of the family bathe according to their importance but the daughter-in-law is always last.

I mentioned earlier that principles in various Western documents had been incorporated into the new Japanese constitution and that this had caused confusion. As I read the Japanese constitution, it seemed obvious that there was much in it that required interpretation and that it might well be interpreted in different ways by the Japanese and by the experts in Washington. I was told that the document written in English is regarded as the original but that the Japanese translation is not identical with the original. Some Japanese have insisted that the original document is the document they accepted and that they did not accept the Japanese translation. The United States had a great deal to do with the writing of the constitution and with its acceptance by the Japanese, but I wonder if we really know exactly what we and they accepted? The exact meaning of the constitution was a burning question whenever I spoke to students or to members of the labor organizations.

Basically, this controversy arises from the differences between the cultural and political backgrounds of the Japanese and American people. Let me give one example, a rather amusing one which would never have been noticed by anyone who had not participated in drawing up the Universal Declaration of Human Rights. I discovered that the Japanese constitution included some of the articles, verbatim, from the Declaration but without any background material. That is, there was no reference to the record of the hearings that preceded the drafting of the Human Rights Declaration.

Now this makes a great difference in determining what the words of the Declaration mean. Quite often, the record shows, the United States would say that they accepted this article because it meant thus and so. But at the same time, the Soviet Union would say that they accepted the same article because they interpreted it to mean something quite different.

The article on economic rights says: "Everyone has the right to work." The United States interpretation of this, which went into the record, was: "We take this to mean that a government has an obligation to strive to create an economic climate which makes it possible for everyone in the country to find work if they want it." Also it means to us that if people cannot find work through no fault of their own a government must create work, since it cannot let its people starve. But the Soviet Union statement said only the Soviet Union could implement this article because in Russia the government controlled all jobs and the government would see to it that every individual not only had a job but worked at it. The Communists always looked down on what they called "eighteenth-century rights," which were the rights of freedom of religion, of assembly and of equality before the law. So, in reading the Japanese constitution, which we had given them, I could not help wondering which of the two explanations of the right to work had been presented to the Japanese people, feeling they had a right to be clear about which interpretation they were accepting. Later, I was told that no explanation at all had been given them.

There are minorities in Japan and although some of them have been there for hundreds of years they are still considered backward people. The Koreans are still looked down on and so is a group called the Ettus. They are generally engaged in the slaughter of animals, which is repugnant to a Buddhist. Their standard of living is still lower than that of the average Japanese, as I discovered in one minority village we visited—a village where I was to learn from the head man how important it is to recognize that there is a bond among all peoples.

The rain was pouring down when we left Osaka to visit this village in the middle of June. About two thousand people belonging to the minority group live there and, by law, they are equal citizens, but in practice it proves difficult to break with the old customs and the old relationship. This minority descended from the aborigines who originally inhabited the island and were conquered by the Japanese. To them, quite naturally, was given the lowest and most degrading work. They were butchers. They tanned hides and made shoes. They were day laborers. When Buddhism became powerful in Japan, they were more than ever looked down upon. The average income of a worker in this village was perhaps 13,000 yen a year as compared to some 300,000 yen a year earned by a well-to-do farmer. The village had no sewage system but there were public baths. The oldest one was small and dirty, but the cost of a bath was only three yen and everybody took advantage of them. Most of the houses had two rooms, a kitchen with a mud floor and another room with the floor raised off the ground. The average family had five members but as many as seven lived in one house we visited. Attached to that house was a shed where bicycles and materials for making shoes were kept. On the floor of the entrance, where there was very little light, sat an old woman of sixty-eight, who looked as if she were eighty. She was weaving the straw sandals that are worn by so many Japanese.

The head man of the village escorted us in considerable discomfort through streets that were rivers of mud. The rain beat on our umbrellas and dripped down our necks. It was, indeed, a miserable village and you might have said a pitiful people, but the head man attempted to show us what was best. There was not much.

"I suppose," he said as we were preparing to depart, "that you have never seen such misery as you saw here today."

Listening to his voice, I suddenly realized that this was an important moment; that his words were both an appeal and a kind of defense of his village.

"Sir," I said quickly, "misery is the same in any country. There was a time in my country when certain areas were poverty-stricken. I have seen misery in those areas and nothing I saw today is any worse than what I saw in some mining areas in West Virginia, Kentucky and Pennsylvania some years ago. I hope you will be able to raise the standards of your people in just the way we have been able to do it. One must never give in to discouragement."

His eyes lit up, and I was glad that I had said the right thing.

"The government," he told me eagerly, "has just granted me some money for better public baths, and that will make a difference in my community!"

The friendliness of the Japanese people seemed to me to be surprisingly warm considering that they had been defeated by our armed forces and that many of our peacetime actions had been most irritating to them. I was pleased to have old Admiral Kichisaburo Nomura, who was in Washington during the period just before the war and was a friend of my husband, tell me that he hoped I did not believe he had been in favor of the attack on Pearl Harbor or had acted in any way unbecoming to his ambassadorial position. He said he had always wanted peace with us and had done his best to bring it about and that he knew nothing of the plans of the military for the attack on Pearl Harbor at the very time he was trying to negotiate some kind of settlement in Washington.

I believe I may have learned more from the Japanese than they learned from me. Even my visit to the Emperor and Empress of Japan, despite its rigid formality, taught me that human beings have great adaptability.

XII

I CALL ON THE EMPEROR
AND EMPRESS

I have had a good many experiences in my life but I could not help feeling a twinge of anxiety as I prepared for my interview with Emperor Hirohito, the 124th of his line, and Empress Nagako. I had originally asked to call on the Empress because there was a question I had long wanted to ask her. Knowing that old habits and customs were changing, especially for the women of Japan, I felt it would be interesting to know whether she was able or desired to give some leadership in these changes. I mentioned this to many Japanese and all of them said that, of course, I must ask the Empress about it, but they added that I really did not understand the position of the Japanese Imperial family.

During my five weeks in Japan I had begun to learn. I came to see that in the past the advisers around the Emperor had on many occasions used his power—almost that of a god—to influence the people. But in the past there had been no possibility for the Imperial family actually to make contact with the people and take part in their activities. Since Japan's defeat in World War II, however, the Emperor had declared that he was not a god and had gone about the country in an effort to see things with his own eyes in a way that was unthinkable in the past. But, I wondered, had the Empress made a similar change?

The more I talked with groups of women in Japan the more I was convinced that, while the women were a force in their homes behind the scenes, they had not gained direct equality with men as provided in their new constitution, despite the fact that there were thirty women members of the Diet or parliament. The constitution of which, of course, General MacArthur was the chief architect, not only gives labor organizations full recognition for the first time and establishes a social security system, but it specifies that women shall have full rights as citizens. But how, I kept wondering, were the women going to develop their power under this constitution, and I did not find any very satisfactory answers.

I met many charming and beautiful ladies of high station, including several princesses, but observed that these women did not attend the meetings of women's organizations that were actively trying to change the pattern of Japanese society. There were certainly some intellectuals among the prominent women in the field of labor, in farm organizations and in social work, but they could not be called the most influential in Japan from the standpoint of social prestige. The society leaders were still merely gracing a charity here and there by their honorary presidencies or by appearing at some fund-raising affair. They were not—if I except Princess Chichibu—finding out how the girls in the factories lived or how the farm women worked in their fields and their homes. So, I wanted more than ever to ask the Empress for her views on the problem of leadership among women.

When I finally received word that my request for an interview had been granted I was told that both the Emperor and Empress would see me on the day of my departure from Japan. I discovered that they often did this, presumably because they wanted to get the visitor's last impressions of the country. I was also informed that I must wear a long-sleeved dress or, if I did not have one, I could wear a dress with three-quarter-length sleeves providing I donned long gloves which would meet the sleeves. As it happened, I had only one dress and one pair of gloves that met these specifications—a little flowered print dress—so I planned to wear that. Two members of the staff of the Exchange Committee met me the morning of the interview and remarked that they liked my other dress better.

"But there is a rule that one must wear long sleeves or gloves that reach the sleeves," I replied. "And my other dress doesn't meet that requirement."

"In that case," they said with a laugh, "you must abide by the regulations."

So I wore the little flowered print.

Our ambassador, John M. Allison, in frock coat and striped pants, called for me at the Imperial Hotel at exactly fifteen minutes after ten on the morning of June 24 and we drove to the Imperial Palace. It is surrounded by a moat and a high stone wall and we could only wonder how these walls had been built so solidly without cement in the distant past. We crossed a bridge spanning the moat and in a moment came to the steps of the Palace. To my amazement, there was one of the omnipresent Japanese photographers waiting to snap our picture as we stepped out of the car. One just couldn't get away from them.

A gentleman in frock coat met us and conducted us to the elevator, and when we stepped out on the upper floor another frock-coated gentleman bowed low and led us into a room with gilt furniture in the French style and with pink damask hangings. The paintings on the walls were Japanese, however, and there were priceless carved objects in a cabinet. Here we waited a few moments and then a young man entered and introduced himself, saying he would translate for the Emperor. He led us through two other rooms furnished in much the same fashion and into a third room where we were seated according to rigid protocol. We were told that we should stand when the Emperor and Empress arrived, sit when they sat, speak only when spoken to. I was seated on a sofa. Mr. Allison was seated in a chair. There was room on the sofa for the Empress to sit beside me and there was a chair nearby for her lady-in-waiting, Mrs. Takagi, who acted as interpreter for her.

We had waited only a few minutes when their Imperial Majesties entered, accompanied by Mrs. Takagi, another lady-in-waiting and two gentlemen. The Emperor and the gentlemen wore frock coats and striped trousers. We all bowed to each other and then the Emperor shook hands with me, followed by the Empress and Mrs. Takagi, whom I had already met. The Empress sat with me on the sofa and the Emperor sat in an armchair almost facing me but looking more directly at Mr. Allison. His interpreter sat on my left.

The Empress, as well as the other ladies, wore a kimono. The one worn by the Empress was light in color and flowered. The others wore dark kimonos. (Perhaps I should explain that the color of Japanese kimonos is significant. I had been told that only a bride wears red and she wears white with it to indicate that she has died to her own family but is reborn in the family of her husband. White kimonos are never worn except in death, and women attending funerals wear all-black kimonos. Gray is the usual color for older women.) On her feet the Empress wore the usual white cotton slippers with a slit at the big toe for the sandal thong and, of course, she wore sandals. Her hair was done almost in Western fashion and her make-up was hardly noticeable, which is customary with Japanese women of high social status.

I was particularly interested in her obi because I had been in Kyoto where the finest obis are woven by hand. The work is so intricate that women who do it for long periods invariably develop eye trouble as they grow older. I remembered one old woman who worked with her nose practically touching the cloth she was weaving, but strangely enough she had spectacles which she put on when she stopped work on the obi.

An expensive obi usually has much gold thread in it and the designs are lovely. Japanese women often wear a woolen band under the obi or perhaps a stiff piece of cardboard to keep it straight as it is wound around the waist and formed into a large bow at the back. A cord goes from the bow and ties in front to keep the obi in place. This cord can be simply tied or fastened with a pin and, in the case of the Empress, a very beautiful pin clasped her obi cord in front. As I looked at her sitting calmly with her hands in her lap, with her face unlined and impassive, I could not help wondering what lay behind that placid surface. She must be, I thought, a woman of extensive education. Her husband is a student of the sciences and has written several books. The Empress had always taken an interest, I had been told, in child education. An Oriental woman in the position of royalty, I thought, must have a kind of severe discipline and must suppress many of the natural emotions. For instance, I was told that the children of the Imperial family each had a separate palace and visited their parents only a few times each week. What a strange family life! Perhaps it leads to the look of calm that was on the face of the Empress, but I wondered, too, if that calm could be attained without missing something of life.

Once we were seated, the Emperor began a conversation, saying he feared I was very tired since I had gone to so many places and seen so much in a comparatively short time. "But," he said, "I am very grateful for your visit." The Empress added that I must be worn out.

"Oh, I am not a bit tired," I assured them. "I have found my visit most interesting. The Exchange Committee had everything very well planned and I am grateful for the opportunity to get to know something of Japan."

We talked about conditions generally and at one point the Emperor said he had always regretted that we had gone to war in spite of his vigorous efforts to prevent it. Now, he said, he hoped we were embarked on an era of friendship and peace.

I had been studying the Emperor and had thought at first that he did not have a strong or impressive personality; yet, as he spoke about the war and the future, he showed both strength and courage. He has the appearance of a student and it occurred to me that perhaps this was inevitable for a man in his position. As a godlike Emperor before the war, he was permitted very little outside activity in which he might express himself. But he could study the sciences. The sciences strive to prove the truth and the Emperor must always speak the truth. His word was law. If he were to say anything about his work, if he were to express himself at all it would be necessary for his words to be provable as truth. So it was perhaps natural that he became a student of the sciences.

Under the new constitution, of course, his position is somewhat changed but the Emperor can be an important figure. I think he was sincere in saying that he had tried to prevent the war and I decided that, if we behaved with tact and caution, we could count on him to help us build friendly relations with the Asian world. Even at that time he was hoping that Japan would become a member of the United Nations, as it later did, and that we could all work together for harmonious international relations.

It was not possible in the years after the war for the Japanese really to like us. Under all of their politeness there must have been many resentments. Most thoughtful foreigners in Japan told me that the Japanese people suffered from an inferiority complex. They had felt sure they could win whatever military adventure they undertook, and when they were defeated they not only lost the war but they lost much of the psychological attitude that gave them strength, or seemed to. So, if we desire to make friends with them, we must understand that we are facing a difficult psychological problem along with everything else. No one can visit the Far East and not realize that fundamentally the Asians want to feel their own importance and to be independent of the West. They are ready to work with us when it is to their advantage and when it adds to their importance, but it is natural—after all of the humiliations of the past—that they intend to act as the equals of the white people who once exploited their countries. They want white people to know it and to treat them with the proper respect. I thought that perhaps the Asian peoples would find a way to work together in order to achieve this overriding desire for equality among the nations and races of the world. I wondered whether the Emperor had something of the same feeling, but he did not indicate any definite opinions other than that the Japanese want peace and will work for it.

I am afraid that during this interview I did not observe the rule that one should speak only when spoken to. I asked a few questions myself, or rather I made some remarks intended to draw out the ideas of the Empress.

"When I visited Pakistan and India," I said, "many changes were taking place, particularly in the status and activities of women. It seemed to me that women of all classes were drawing closer together and gaining in strength because of their greater knowledge of each other."

I paused and looked at the calm face of the Empress, waiting for her to comment. She said nothing for a few moments and then replied: "We need more education." The Emperor broke in with some comment and I thought perhaps that would be all the response I would get from the Empress, but she seemed to be thinking over my remarks for a few minutes and then said to me:

"There are great changes coming about in the life of our women. We have always been trained in the past to a life of service and I am afraid that as these new changes come about there may be a loss of real values. What is your impression, Mrs. Roosevelt?"

"In all eras of change," I said, "there is a real danger that the old values will be lost. But it seems to me much less dangerous when the intelligent and broad-minded women who have had an opportunity to become educated take the lead to bring about the necessary changes."

I mentioned Begum Liaquat Ali Khan of Pakistan, and the important social work she had done with her husband's support and which she continued after his death. For a moment, the Empress did not seem to know of her work but when I explained she at once remembered. But she shook her head doubtfully.

"Our customs are different, Mrs. Roosevelt," the Emperor broke in. "We have government bureaus to lead in our reforms. We serve as an example to our people in the way we live and it is our lives that have influence over them."

And that seemed to be the final word on how far the Imperial family, or at least the distaff side of it, might go in assuming leadership in the new era in Japan. But I cannot help believing that, since the elder women have been such an important influence in the home in the past, the future may see greater leadership exerted by the women of high social status, including members of the entourage of the Imperial family.

The Emperor talked of other matters and I inquired about the Crown Prince, whom I had entertained at Hyde Park when he was touring the United States. I said I feared the young man had found his visit to America tiresome because there was so much formality and he was expected to pay so many official calls, but that I felt he had done his duty well. The Emperor replied that he was pleased with his son's conduct and that it had been an important trip for him.

After about an hour, their Imperial Majesties arose, wished me a very happy and safe journey and, after saying good-by to Mr. Allison, left us, bowing again as they went out. We, of course, returned their bows. I never hope to be able to bow as gracefully as do Japanese women but by this time I had learned much about the art and the shades of feeling that the Japanese can express merely by the way they bow.

After the Emperor and Empress had departed, I talked briefly with Mrs. Takagi and thanked the gentleman who had interpreted for the Emperor. We bowed to each other and then the two gentlemen who had met us when we arrived accompanied us to the door, bowing as we departed. As usual, the news photographers were waiting outside the door and I had to stand there long enough to be photographed. Then I bowed again to the last of the protocol officers and got into the automobile with Mr. Allison.

We drove to my hotel, where the Ambassador said in characteristic

American fashion: "I will meet you for luncheon in about an hour—after I go home and get out of these formal clothes!" We did not bow as he departed.

As I looked back on my visit to Japan, many incidents stood out as illustrative of the problems of establishing a democratic form of government in the Far East, and especially of educating women to take an active part in public affairs. One day in Tokyo I attended a round-table conference at the national Young Women's Christian Association with perhaps the most representative women leaders in the country. They were gravely concerned about progress in the new era of freedom, although they had long fought for woman's suffrage and should have been particularly pleased by the changes taking place. They made me see more clearly the difficulties created by an army of occupation or even by the presence of many American boys stationed at military bases in Japan. Unfortunately, we do not train our youngsters carefully enough before sending them throughout the world. They do not always remember that they are not merely soldiers but ambassadors, representing all that their own country stands for and all that democracy means to the rest of the world. The women were particularly concerned about the growth of prostitution and believed that it could be controlled only by the closest co-operation between Japan and the United States.

The Japanese have an active organization working in co-operation with the Children's Fund of the UN in an effort to provide more food and better conditions for young people. They expressed gratitude for the work that had been done by the Children's Fund but pointed out that after the war the health of the children generally was greatly impaired. In one Tokyo school, I was told, the children were found to be a whole year behind normal in weight and general development.

The education of Japanese in democratic ways also was made more difficult at times by news from the United States telling of racial discrimination, of instances in Los Angeles and Texas where the work of UNESCO was attacked as communistic, and of the methods employed by the late Senator Joseph McCarthy in his congressional investigations. Again and again, Japanese told me they were confused and bewildered by these news dispatches, which were displayed prominently in the newspapers. "Will you please explain these attitudes?" one leading Japanese businessman asked me. "Japan hopes one day to be a member of the United Nations and to work loyally with that organization. But we are unable to understand why these things happen in a great democratic nation like the United States."

On another occasion a young man showed me a news dispatch from the United States saying that the Japanese Government's victory in a recent election was due to the fact that the majority of Japanese were accepting the policy of gradual rearmament which had been urged on the Tokyo government by our State Department.

"Do people in the United States really believe that?" he demanded. "Everybody knows that the government in Japan has been very careful to say practically nothing on the subject of rearmament. Don't you realize that there is deep resentment here because many Japanese feel the United States used economic pressure at the time of the election in order to put into office people who favor the U.S. State Department's policies? For that reason, many feel that the United States is trying to make Japan economically a slave."

These are some of the suspicions and some of the grave problems that must be overcome—and, I feel sure, will be overcome—if our relations with the Far East are to be secure. Progress has been made toward this goal, but there are constantly arising new causes of misunderstanding, so that the road is a long and rough one. Perhaps our best hope is that the Japanese as well as ourselves want peace above all. This was impressed upon me strongly at the tragic city of Hiroshima.

To arrive in Hiroshima is an emotional experience. Here is where the first atom bomb ever to be dropped on human beings was actually used. The people of the United States believe that our leaders thought long and carefully before they used this dreaded weapon. We know that they thought first of the welfare of our own people, that they believed the bomb might end the war quickly with less loss of life everywhere than if it had not been dropped.

In spite of this conviction, one still cannot see a city and be shown the area that was destroyed by blast and fire and be told of the people who died or were injured, one cannot see the photographs of some of the victims, without a deep sadness. To see the home where orphans were being cared for was to wish with one's whole heart that men could learn from this that we know too well how to destroy and that we must learn instead how to prevent such destruction. It is useless to say that Germany started the war and even started the research that led to the atomic bomb. It is useless to remember, as I did, the feelings of my husband and of the people of the United States when we heard the shocking news of the Japanese attack on Pearl Harbor. Pearl Harbor was only the climax of years of mounting misunderstandings and antipathies throughout the world. And out of all this came Hiroshima.

But it was not just here in this sad Japanese city that men and women and children suffered. All the world suffered. So, it seems to me the only helpful thing we can do as we contemplate man's adventure into the realm of outer space is to pledge ourselves to work to eliminate the causes of war through action that is possible only by using the machinery of the United Nations. If we do, then the peoples may understand each other a little better; they may have a better chance to be heard.

Contemplating the fate of Hiroshima, one can only say: "God grant to men greater wisdom in the future."

XIII

HONG KONG, ISTANBUL
AND ATHENS

My daughter-in-law flew from Japan back to the United States but Miss Corr and I continued on a westward route around the world, stopping first at Hong Kong, which has become a fascinating cross-roads of the free world in Asia. I was very kindly received at Government House by Governor General Grantham and by American diplomatic officials who are stationed at this sensitive spot adjoining Communist China. At dinner the Governor General had several Chinese dignitaries who had escaped to Hong Kong and we discussed the plight of refugees from the mainland.

"Would you like to see the border of Communist China?" the Governor General asked me.

"Indeed, I would," I replied, "if that is possible."

As it turned out, it was no problem at all. The British general in charge of the border patrol called for me at my hotel the next morning and we drove over the hills to a little stream that separates Hong Kong from China. To my surprise, the "line" between the free world and the Communist world at this point is only a single strand of barbed wire and there is a bridge, guarded by police, over which a considerable number of Chinese go back and forth every day. These Chinese live on the Communist side but they own land on the Hong Kong side of the border stream and are permitted to cross each morning—often driving cows or pigs and carrying their farm tools—to work the land. Then in the evening they return across the bridge to the Communist side.

There were rice paddies and vegetable gardens all along the frontier. "Some food comes across the border," the General explained, "because Hong Kong does not begin to grow enough for its present population."

There did not seem to be many guards on either side of the border but it was patrolled regularly. Nevertheless, a number of Chinese continued to flee across the frontier to Hong Kong every day or so.

"Nine Chinese escaped to Hong Kong only yesterday," the head of the border police told me. "They had walked about twenty miles along the railroad until they spotted a place where there was no fence. As they crossed the border there, the Communist soldiers saw them and opened fire. It was quite a scramble for them to get away but they made it, although they arrived here in a bit of a mess."

"What kind of people were they?" I asked.

"Ordinary people, storekeepers, people with small means. They would have remained at their homes but they said the Communist officials kept calling them up for questioning and bedeviling them until they finally decided they could stand it no longer."

Talking with other officials and with refugees, I got the impression that many of those who had fled to Hong Kong were neither Communists nor anti-Communists. They just wanted to be let alone and to be given a chance to earn a living. If the government did not try to tax them too heavily, they did not really care who ran it or whether it was corrupt—they just wanted to be left in peace.

We visited the area where many refugees lived. At first they had lived literally in holes dug in the hillsides but now the government had moved them to barracks where each family had a small space perhaps ten by ten feet square. This was usually divided into two parts, the space at the front being used as a kind of shop where the man of the household carried on his business. Then there was a space in the rear for a raised platform where the family, which might number half a dozen, lived and ate and slept on mats. There was no sewage system and the children were constantly carrying pails of water from a distant supply; it was amazing to me that there had not been any epidemic.

Later, a Chinese gentleman, Dr. Wan, took me to a friend's home where I had dinner with a group of refugees. It was my first real Chinese dinner at which I enjoyed Charles Lamb's famous roast pig. "You must eat the crackling skin," I was told, "because that is the real delicacy." We also had bird's nest soup and duck's feet and I had quite a struggle eating them in the proper manner with chopsticks.

The next day I met two gentlemen who had come from Taipei (Formosa). They represented the United States Committee to Help Chinese Refugees and were also busy trying to counteract the flood of Communist propaganda literature which comes into the Hong Kong area. This propaganda was largely cheap little books with pictures that misrepresent everything done by the United States or the United Nations as bringing death and destruction. Such propaganda was circulated widely among even the poorest Chinese and, so far as I could discover, very little was being done by the democracies to offset these false stories.

I was glad to have an opportunity to talk to the gentlemen from Taipei, but I did not desire to go there. I have always had admiration and affection for Madame Chiang Kai-shek, who had stayed with us at the White House when she was in America some years before and who had visited me at Hyde Park after my husband's death. She seemed to me to be a woman of great ability with an intellectual understanding of democracy, but I had never ceased to be perplexed by her ideas about the establishment of democratic government in China.

I remember when General George C. Marshall was the President's Ambassador to Chungking after the end of World War II with the mission of bringing about a settlement of the conflict between Chiang Kai-shek's government and the Communists and other groups in order to further the establishment of a unified China. General Marshall later told me that he would get the Generalissimo to agree to various reforms that might further a peaceful settlement, but the next day Chiang Kai-shek would talk to some standpatter war lord who would persuade him to forget the whole thing. As a result, the idea of democracy was projected but never put into practice. Madame Chiang once told me that she and her husband felt it was their duty to carry on to the bitter end from Taipei or anywhere else their struggle to establish democratic government in China. But I could not feel that she really understood what it is to live democracy, or that her husband had really made the effort to establish representative government.

I could not go to Taipei and not see Madame Chiang. But I knew that if I saw her I would have to tell her I did not think her dream of regaining China was possible. I felt that Chiang Kai-shek had had his chance and had not used the right methods to unify the country. And I did not believe that he any longer had any chance to do so. So I did not visit Taipei.

Many things have been written about Madame Chiang's visits to the White House which were not completely accurate. She was ill much of the time and had to have trained nurses and special care. She had with her as secretaries her niece and nephew, who were not always as understanding and careful as they should have been about the comfort and convenience of other people. On the whole, I found Madame Chiang a warm and able woman who, however, could be, when dealing with matters of state, completely cold and completely determined to achieve what she felt was necessary for her government's good.

While I was at Government House in Hong Kong, I met Mr. Keswick, a British merchant whose family has been in China for a very long time. I remarked that my husband's family had been in the China trade and it turned out that he knew much about Russell & Company, in which the partners were Franklin's grandfather, Warren Delano, and his son-in-law Will Forbes and another son-in-law, Frederick Delano Hitch.

"There is one thing that you may be able to clear up for me," I told Mr. Keswick. "At home during the New Deal era, certain newspaper writers who were opposed to the administration often liked to assert that Franklin's family had made money in the opium trade in the days when the clipper ships sailed to China. I never knew whether such statements were true, so I never made any attempt to refute them. But perhaps you know."

"I have an excellent history of that period," Mr. Keswick replied. "I will lend it to you and you can find out for yourself. But it is true that all foreign merchants trading in tea in China in those day were required to obtain special permits. And one of the requirements for getting a permit was that they agree to take a small amount of opium when they were purchasing tea and other goods. Everybody who wanted tea to take to foreign lands had to do the same."

I later read the history Mr. Keswick lent me and found that his version was supported by the book. So I suppose it is true that the Delanos and the Forbeses, like everybody else, had to include a limited amount of opium in their cargoes to do any trading at all.

I might mention here that in 1955 I made a second visit to Hong Kong and found that there was more traffic across the little bridge leading to Communist China than when I had been there the first time. There were Chinese soldiers with rifles on the other side of the border and one of them had a camera with which he took a picture of our party. Dr. Gurewitsch, who was with me on the second trip, quickly adjusted his camera and took a picture of the Chinese guards, but before he could snap the shutter all the Communist soldiers lowered their rifles and more or less concealed them behind their backs. I suppose this was according to their instructions to avoid giving an appearance of stern military rule on the Communist side of the barrier. No one spoke, however, and we were told that there was no fraternization between the soldiers on either side of the line.

Miss Corr and I flew on our first trip from Hong Kong direct to India, with stops for a few minutes in Bangkok and Rangoon. Approaching Calcutta we ran into the monsoon and landed there in a pouring rain. Aboard our plane was U Nu, the Prime Minister of Burma, who was enroute to visit the Prime Minister of India, and he and his party sat silent and immovable throughout the storm, although I did not believe they enjoyed it any more than I did. The air continued turbulent as we flew on toward New Delhi, where a severe dust storm was just dying out. After some delay we were able to land. It was late at night but Mrs. Pandit had come to the airport to see someone off and remained to greet me. For other reasons she had already been to the airport twice that day, and after we had chatted for a few minutes I persuaded her to go home and get some rest. Later, I was glad I had done so, because just as we were getting on the plane again they discovered some mechanical trouble and, after another hour's delay, they told us we would not leave until the next morning. So we went to a hotel and I was happy to be there, because I would always rather be overcareful if there is any possibility of something going wrong.

We did not get off until after luncheon the next day, and it was five o'clock in the morning on a beautiful day in late June when we skimmed over the brown fields of Turkey and caught a first glimpse of the wonderful greens and blues of the Mediterranean just before landing at Istanbul. I had not expected anyone to meet us at that hour of the morning but, to my horror, there stood our Consul General, Mr. Macatee.

"You should not have come!" I exclaimed.

"Oh, yes," he replied, always the perfect diplomat, "it is so rare for me to get up at this time of morning that I am grateful to you for the opportunity to see the world when it is so beautiful."

He told us there was a hotel nearby and asked if we wanted to go there.

"I believe not," I replied. "We missed yesterday afternoon in Istanbul by being delayed and I think we would like to make up for it by driving through the city now and seeing some of the mosques. We have only five hours now."

Mr. Macatee was a game diplomat and he said that would be a splendid idea, although goodness knows what he really felt. I could well imagine that he would have much preferred to go back to bed instead of escorting us to the Blue Mosque, Hagia Sophia, the Byzantine Wall and the Bosporus. Of course nothing was open at that time of day and we could not go inside the buildings. We walked around outside some of the most impressive mosques and the early-morning light made the minarets and the domes beautiful. At the Blue Mosque we got a glimpse of the wonderful color above one door.

"Well," I said, "that at least gives us an idea what it is like inside."

"Ah!" said Mr. Macatee, gazing up at the glow of morning light on the dome. "I feel certain that very few other visitors have seen these sights at six thirty o'clock in the morning."

It was a pleasant thought and I didn't even feel that he was being sarcastic, and the empty streets and the coolness of the morning made our lonely tour so enjoyable that we no longer felt disappointed at not having arrived the previous afternoon. About eight o'clock, Mr. Macatee took us to the Consulate, where his bewildered wife and daughter, who had only recently arrived themselves, were wondering what on earth he had been doing. They were probably even more bewildered when he walked in with two strange ladies and announced we were going to have breakfast on the rooftop where we could get a good view of the Golden Horn. We did, too, with Mrs. Macatee making us very welcome, although I doubt that she ever quite understood why anyone would go sightseeing in Istanbul at dawn.

We had a leisurely breakfast and recalled the old tales of the city and the love story of Hero and Leander, who swam the Hellespont, and spent a great deal of time just looking at the beautiful view. Much too quickly it was time to return to the airport and catch the plane to Athens. It was an odd feeling to fly over a part of the world that I had read and heard so much about, to see the thick old Byzantine Wall that had once been a defense against invaders, to see the domes of the mosques built so many years ago, to soar high in a British Comet jet airplane over the ancient land of the Greeks. Here were all the things I had long been familiar with in pictures and books and now they were before me. It was an almost awesome feeling, not overshadowed even by the impression the age and beauty of many of the treasures of India and the Far East gave me.

We found upon arrival at Athens that it was a holiday, the name day of King George of Greece. But we got through customs quickly and zigzagged our way through narrow, twisting streets—getting a first glimpse of the Acropolis—to our hotel. I was pleased to learn that Governor Adlai Stevenson was in Athens and that he would come to tea that afternoon. We also were joined in Athens by Dr. Gurewitsch, who had come from Paris, and with him and Miss Alison Franz, an archaeologist, we arranged to visit the Acropolis and to see some of the excavations being made in Athens by our American group under Mr. Thompson. With such expert guidance we got much more out of our visits to the ancient ruins than would otherwise have been possible.

One should see the Parthenon not only in the morning, as we did, when everything stands out clear and rather hard but also in the soft light of the setting sun when the marble takes on a rosy hue and, somehow, the entire effect is different. When we arrived there in the morning my mind was racing back over history, recalling the numerous wars and the many armies of destruction that had rolled against this hill that was primarily a fortress against the Persians and the barbarians. One could not help wondering if humans every really understood the meaning of history, ever really looked at the remnants of past glory and beauty and pondered how often the hand of man had destroyed beauty in destroying other human beings. Still we go on; we destroy through war in this century just as men did twenty centuries ago.

I was impressed and perhaps a little disturbed by the evidence uncovered by archaeologists which demonstrates how little we change in some ways. Miss Franz showed us in a museum case the bits of clay which had been found in the rebuilding of the market square of ancient Athens. The Athenians used these clay bits in an unusual kind of balloting, in which each private citizen put down the name of any other citizen who he felt might someday become a dictator. If as many as six thousand voters put down the name of the same man as being dangerous, that man was exiled from Athens for ten years. After that time he could return, presumably on the theory that by then he would have lost interest in stirring up trouble or seizing power. I wonder whether the archaeologist is discouraged to see how history has repeated itself down through the centuries and whether he must conclude that it is the destiny of human beings always to be destroying something and then spending ages in rebuilding it.

But when we went back to the Acropolis as the sun was setting I did not even think about what had happened there in the past. I just stood in the soft evening light and enjoyed the beauty and was grateful that so much of it was still there to give us pleasure.

We made various trips through the countryside which I greatly enjoyed; and it was strange in Delphi to sit on one of the old stone seats of the amphitheater where Greek games took place two thousand years ago and watch some children of the neighborhood playing a modern game of football. There was, too, back of the little church of Daphne a hillside where there were lovely green trees but where the earth was completely barren. I never have been able to understand how the people living in those hills that produce so little food could exist, but I discovered that they did get along, and with dignity.

On some of our trips we saw many signs of American influence in Greece. Near Delphi there was a huge threshing machine near the road and I noticed that it was well labeled to show that it had come from the United States as part of the Marshall Plan. We stopped to talk with the people running the machine and they told us that it quickly did work that would have taken days with slow-moving animals and men using old-fashioned implements. It was obvious in many places that America was having an influence on the Greeks as well as on other parts of the world. But whether this was bringing us friends I did not know.

It was very evident that the people of Greece were poor but I did not get an impression of real squalor. The children looked healthy and on the whole were well dressed. Many of the older women wore black shawls and black dresses, but I noticed the custom was not prevalent among the younger women and I hoped it would die out, for it seemed to me a gloomy habit.

One picture of Greece I will not forget is the blue sea of the Gulf of Corinth and the little red-tiled roofs of whitewashed houses shining in the sun. Because of the flies, all the houses had their doors and windows shut, seeming almost to be unoccupied. As soon as the light came each morning, the flies buzzed in in huge numbers but at night they disappeared with the evening light and the windows could be opened. You can't help feeling that a few American screens would be useful. However, another purpose is served by shutting up the houses, people keep cool within their thick walls during the hottest days.

In Corinth we were fortunate enough to have as guides Professor and Mrs. Dinsmore, who were living at the American excavations nearby. Mr. Dinsmore told us many of the old legends as we walked around the excavations and the ruins. For instance, the story of Medea and Glauke and how Glauke threw herself into the well after wearing the poisoned cloak presented to her by Medea, who did not like having her husband take a second wife. The old drinking well which we saw in the city dates back to 400 B.C. and today is much the same as it was originally. We also saw in one corner of the excavations the spot where St. Paul is said to have spoken to the Corinthians.

Early one morning I stepped out on the balcony of the Bourdzi Hotel and the sea was beautifully calm. I dressed and then took the path around our picturesque little hotel and sat on the wall over the water, with the mountains rising out of the sea opposite me. The origin of this little castle that has been turned into a hotel was not a happy one. It was once a prison and the executioners of the early times were so unpopular that they had to live in the castle for protection. The cells are now all made into pleasant little rooms with circular balconies and we had our breakfast table in what must have been the prison yard which the unfortunate prisoners first saw when brought to the prison. It had been planted with flowers and was quite gay and cheerful.

In talking to Professor Dinsmore in Corinth I discovered that archaeologists often have a great deal of amusement guessing how some of the buildings now in ruins were really used when they were new. One theory that he mentioned concerned a building that apparently had been used for treatment of the sick by a kind of hypnotism. One suggestion was that the treatment had gone something like this:

patients were arranged in a chamber at night, like spokes in a wheel. Beneath the chambers there was a great open space and it was surmised that priests walked around and around in this space, muttering incantations which they wished to have enter the minds of the patients up above. Hocus-pocus, we might call it today, but it was claimed the treatment cured many patients, and I am not sure that it was any stranger than some of the treatments we employ today.

While in Athens, I had the good fortune to go out to luncheon in the country with King George and Queen Frederica. Our Embassy had handled the arrangements and, as usual, they sent a very dignified-looking but slow-moving limousine to take me from my hotel to the palace. I started out about half past eleven, rolling sedately out of the city and up into the hills where the summer palace is located. It was cooler there and we were rolling happily along when there was a roar of a high-powered motor behind us and a racy sports car zipped around us and went bowling along the road at a very high speed.

I got a quick look at the occupants and suddenly realized that the King was driving and the Queen was beside him. They were dashing along the road as if they were racing drivers out for a morning's test spin, and making the most of it. They went so fast, in fact, that before we reached the palace we caught up with two automobiles which had passed us in pursuit of the King's car, but had broken down later.

"Those are the men who guard the King," my driver said with a chuckle. They were evidently secret service men whose cars could not keep up with the pace set by His Majesty and who had had to stop to make repairs.

I arrived at the palace exactly on time, as the Embassy had planned, and we had a very pleasant luncheon. I found the Queen to be charming, warm and intelligent. Perhaps the King's personality is not so warm, but he is an able man and greatly interested in the young people of his country, where there are so many orphans from war and disaster, and where so many are hungry. I believe that I receive more letters asking for help from Greece than from any other country and I know that need much. At luncheon, the Queen told me of her efforts to alleviate this situation, and gave me an account of what had happened to a group of Communist guerrilla youths who had been taken prisoner the year before.

The prisoners numbered about one thousand boys between the ages of fourteen and twenty-one. The King had them sent to an island that had been returned to Greece after the last war, and asked the islanders to start a school which would train the boys and enable them to find jobs. The islanders were poor but they got together and helped renovate buildings where the boys could be housed. The boys were told that their past records were wiped off the books and that they would be making new records from the day they started to school to learn a trade or to get academic instruction. They were permitted to choose the trade they would learn and craftsmen on the island acted as instructors.

"The boys were told they did not have to go to school," she continued, "but every one of them decided to attend. They had lived almost as savages during the fighting, existing in the mountains in any possible way, and they really had to be taught how to live in a civilized community."

Most of the boys learned crafts in the school and have since done well, and the school has been continued to help poor boys who would not otherwise have a chance to learn a trade.

The Queen told me that she hoped to visit the United States before long and to study our rehabilitation hospitals, where great progress has been made in helping handicapped or crippled children. She and the King did make the trip later—if I may jump ahead of my story—and were escorted many places by representatives of the Department of State. I noticed, however, that they reserved five days at the end of their official trip for an unofficial visit in New York on their own. So, when they arrived in New York, I wrote the Queen a note, recalling our conversation in Athens and asking whether she had been able to see the things she wanted to see.

I have little idea what the State Department had shown them at great expense and effort, but she replied that she had not seen any of the things she really wanted to see. Then I wrote her again, saying I would be glad to arrange a short tour for her, and she accepted the invitation. As a result General Willis D. Crittenberger, Mrs. Joseph P. Lash and I (together with city officials) guided her one morning to several institutions in New York City that I thought she would want to visit. We went to the new hospital on the East Side where Dr. Howard Rusk has done so much to help the recovery of crippled children. The Queen was wonderful with the patients. One little boy who had had polio attempted to show her how he had learned to walk again. But in his eagerness to demonstrate he slipped and fell. It was the Queen who got to him before anyone else and picked him up.

"Don't worry," she said. "Many of us fall when we try to show what we can do. But I'll help you and you show me again."

We also visited the Alfred E. Smith housing project, which includes a settlement house, and stopped at the apartment of a second-generation Greek couple. They had made special preparations for our visit and their relatives, who had been born in Greece, were there to greet the Queen. She seemed to be impressed by the quality of the housing.

"I wouldn't mind living here myself," she remarked as we departed.

Later, visiting the Henry Street Settlement House, as we were walking along in a sedate little procession, accompanied by members of the staff, on our way from one building to another, we passed a city fire house. Looking through the big open door, the Queen saw the brass fire pole and paused.

"Do you think they would mind if I went in?" she asked.

"I'm sure they would be delighted," I said. I went in and found a fireman on duty and introduced him to the Queen. She was much interested in the equipment and asked many questions.

"Perhaps it would be possible for you to demonstrate how the men answer an alarm," I remarked to the fireman.

He said that would be simple, and rang the bell. An instant later the men began sliding down the brass pole from the second floor and quickly jumped on their trucks. Then, last of all, their big cat came sliding down the pole. The Queen laughed and clapped her hands in delight. Then she thanked the firemen, said good-by and we rejoined our little procession.

XIV

YUGOSLAVIA IS NOT RUSSIA

We left Athens by airplane on July 6, 1953, for Yugoslavia. Our Greek pilots did a wonderful job of flying around and under some very black storm clouds which dropped so much rain on Salonica, where we stopped briefly, that everything was afloat. Flying over Macedonia, in Yugoslavia, I was impressed by the fact that it looked like good farming country in contrast to the arid appearance of the land in so many parts of Greece, particularly in the mountains.

"One reason for the difference is that the Yugoslav Government has made a determined effort to reduce the number of herds of goats," a Yugoslav told me. "Goats have been almost completely forbidden in some places. I can't say this program has been entirely successful in the forbidden areas, but at least the number of goats is more or less controlled and they no longer eat every blade of grass down to the roots as they often do in Greece. Why, they even eat the trees and I have actually seen them climbing up into the branches of trees to feed."

We landed at Belgrade, where I was greeted by a number of old friends from the United Nations meetings—Mr. and Mrs. Joze Vilfan, Dr. Vladislav Ribnikar, Mr. and Mrs. Branko Jevremovic and Mr. and Mrs. Vladimir Dedijer. We went to the Hotel Majestic, where Dr. Ribnikar and Mr. Vilfan sat down and helped me plan my program for the next three weeks. I also was assigned as interpreter a very charming young woman, Mrs. Yovanka Luki, who usually interprets for the wife of the President. She accompanied me to a dinner that evening at the United States Embassy but later I learned that she had to make a quick night train trip after she left me in order to be on hand to interpret for the President's wife. I felt a little guilty because she was being overworked but it was considerate of the government to make the effort to give me an excellent interpreter.

My main purpose in visiting Yugoslavia was to interview President Tito (or Josip Broz, to give him his real name) but I was greatly interested in learning all I could about the country and its governmental system. I wanted to meet Marshal Tito and make my own observations of this man who had successfully fought the German army of occupation in Yugoslavia, who had established a government closely harmonized with Communist Russia after the war and had finally broken with the Comintern, declaring his independence of the dictates of Moscow.

I had been informed correctly that Yugoslavia was very different from Russia, where for generations peasants had been accustomed to living under the strict Czarist regime, to being attached to large family estates and to doing what they were told to do. It had always been difficult to tell the Yugoslavs anything. They fought foreign invaders and they fought each other for racial and religious reasons and sometimes perhaps for no reason at all. The Montenegrins, for instance, were never really conquered through the centuries of Balkan warfare. If an invader fought his way into the country, they retired to the mountains and defied anybody to come after them. The men were such traditional warriors that the women did—and continue to do—practically all of the hard, everyday work.

"They are unusual people," a German doctor told me in relating his experiences at a Montenegrin hospital. "It is not at all uncommon to see a little procession come up to the hospital—a man riding on a donkey and a woman walking six paces behind him carrying a baby or perhaps some bundles on her back. The man dismounts at the hospital door and tells the doctor that he has brought his sick wife in for treatment. It never strikes him as odd that he had ridden and she had walked!"

The background of many of the Yugoslav republics is somewhat similar and they have always valued individual freedom. Why, then,

I had wondered, did Communism develop in Yugoslavia and how could it be maintained by Tito's dictatorial methods? Why didn't these people throw out the commissars and resume their ways of individual freedom? These were some of the questions I wanted to ask President Tito, but he had suggested that I see as much of the country as possible before visiting him. It was a good suggestion and I learned at least some of the answers in my talks with members of his cabinet and my trips to all but one of the republics. The Tito regime, I discovered, was, without any question, communistic, but it was in many important ways different from the Russian dictatorship.

At a luncheon with several government officials on my first full day in Yugoslavia, one of the undersecretaries of state told of changes that were being made in industrial management. "The state," he said, "will not run the industries. They will be operated by councils of workers, and this system, where it is being tried out, already has improved production. Workers quickly find out that good management is necessary, that all must do their best and the deadwood must be eliminated if an industry is to pay."

This seemed to me to be a kind of compromise between Communist and capitalist ideas, and it was obvious that the Yugoslavs were experimenting in an effort to find governmental theories that would permit limited individual freedom within a socialist framework. Such experimentation might be a valuable contribution, I thought, to the development of countries where resources do not make it possible for even a limited type of capitalism to develop naturally.

In the next few days the people I talked with, including American officials and newspapermen, seemed to agree that there had been great changes in the government in the past year. Decentralization of governmental power had been encouraged, which I thought was quite remarkable in a dictatorship, where the leader or leaders usually want more instead of less absolute power. Certain supervision and a measure of ultimate control by the central government would be continued, but it was evident that many more decisions were being left to the people's committees even in the smaller village groups.

A day or so later I went alone to Banja to see a wine co-operative, which was started fifty years ago and is one of the oldest in the country. There are 120 members who own their own land but bring their grapes to the co-operative where the wine is made. About ten of the members, including some members of the people's council, drove me through the beautiful countryside and then showed me the cellars where wine is stored. Later, we sat around a big table and tasted wine, ate excellent homemade bread, two kinds of goats' cheese and hard-boiled eggs.

"Is it true, Mrs. Roosevelt," one of the farmers asked me, "that the people of the United States are losing their freedom?"

I was amazed that in this little village, quite a distance even from Belgrade, a peasant farmer would ask me about domestic politics in the United States. I could only express my confidence that the people of my country intended to hang on to their freedom very firmly.

"But what about Senator McCarthy?" another demanded.

I could only express my disapproval of the Senator's activities.

Their questions showed that they knew a great deal about various phases of politics in the United States, even if some of their conclusions were distorted by Communist propaganda. Finally, one of them asked me with a sly smile: "Have you found the people of Yugoslavia as barbarous and uncivilized as you expected, Mrs. Roosevelt?" I insisted that I had not expected to find the people barbarous, but I acknowledged that I had been surprised by some things, including their questions showing a real awareness of what was going on in the world.

Later we visited the home of one of the members of the co-operative, where I became interested in the family's homemade blankets. The wool is spun and dyed in the home and the final result is a blanket with colors and designs very similar to those woven by our Navajo Indians. I had previously noticed the same kind of blankets at Delphi, and I could not help wondering how this similarity in design had come about.

One thing that I observed almost immediately in Yugoslavia was that the people were neither worried nor afraid. I did not hear a single Yugoslav say anything about the danger of war, although their old enemy Germany was rapidly gaining strength on one side of them and they had broken with the Soviet Union and its satellites, which lie on the other side. Perhaps if you have always lived with danger you can't afford to think with fear, or perhaps the people were too busy.

Later I made a trip to Sarajevo and on the way drove to Zemica, a good coal and iron ore center which was busily trying to become the Pittsburgh of Yugoslavia. The plants had been rebuilt and enlarged after the war and were already producing three times as much as they had before.

"We bought that plant from the Krupps in Germany before the war," the manager told me, pointing to a large building. "During the war the Germans needed steel so badly that after they invaded our country they picked up the whole building and moved it back to Germany, set it up again and started it producing. Then, when Germany was defeated, part of the reparations awarded to Yugoslavia was this same plant. It was moved back here and erected for the third time and is again producing."

I asked many questions about how the plants were run and cleared up some of the theories that had been explained to me in Belgrade. For example, the theory is that the plants will be run by workers' councils. But, while that is technically true, the fact is that the councils sensibly employed technical experts actually to operate the plants and the experts report to and are responsible to the councils. I also met two American engineers employed by one plant to direct operations.

Once when I was driving along a road near Sarajevo I stopped at a small and poor-looking farmhouse. An old woman, probably about sixty, welcomed us and showed us around.

"Who works the farm?" I asked her.

"I do," she replied, looking out over her three acres. "My husband and son are dead and my married daughter lives quite a distance away. She comes to help in the busy season. But I have six grandchildren living with me."

"What do you have to eat?"

"Oh, I have two cows and a little vegetable garden and I make butter and cheese and bread."

The state paid her a modest sum for each child, but I didn't feel they were getting much variety in their diet. The old woman cooked on an open hearth in summer and baked bread by putting it on the coals and spreading ashes and coals over the top. It was a good solid loaf.

I saw children living in quite a different environment a day or so later when we visited an island near Dubrovnik where an old monastery had been turned into a home for war orphans. This was the monastery that the Emperor Maximilian and Carlota often visited and where, after his death, Carlota frequently came to sit at a stone table to look out over the peaceful shore and the water. The children were bathing when we arrived and were having a wonderful time.

They attend school on the island and once a week they go into Dubrovnik, which is about their only contact with urban life.

"They look upon city life as nothing but visiting museums and historical monuments," said Mr. Jaksic, who was showing us around. "The trouble is that the authorities now feel we are making a mistake in bringing the children up on this island. They are fine, but the atmosphere in which they are growing up will not fit them for the hard facts of the life they must live." He gave a tired little sigh. "With the best of intentions," he said, "we make so many mistakes!"

Dubrovnik was delightful and the weather was just right for dining outdoors, and for swimming. There was a swimming competition and water polo in the harbor, with teams from Split and Dubrovnik competing, and I noticed that the women's teams made just about as good time as the men's in similar competition. After this there was a wonderful folk play given in the town square. The stage was the entrance to an old church but the actors spread out in the square, used the archways and even the balcony of an old monastery, while the audience was in the square. The entire performance was much as it must have been years ago.

I was astonished to discover that this town of about nineteen thousand inhabitants has a theater company that runs summer and winter. Amateurs are called in from among the citizens to take certain parts, although the principal actors are professionals and very good ones. I have never spent a more delightful evening or felt myself in a more medieval atmosphere.

I kept finding out more about the changing industrial system. At Zagreb we visited the Rade Koncar factory, named for a factory worker who was a guerrilla leader during the war and was killed by Italian troops. The plant was making electrical transformers and other machinery needed for the development of power plants. Like others I had visited, it was operated by a workers' council and technical experts.

"Our experts are new at this kind of thing and they have made some mistakes," the manager told me. "But last year we ran at a profit."

"A profit?" I said.

"Oh, yes, that is one of the incentives for high production. After taxes have been deducted, the workers' council divides the profits, half going to pay interest and amortization on borrowed money or to improve the plant. The other half of the profits is divided among all the workers."

"Do you think that arrangement has increased production?" I asked.

The manager looked at the head of the workers' council and smiled. "Of course it has," he said.

The head of the council expressed his appreciation for the aid that had been received from the United States since the Yugoslav break with the Comintern. In fact, almost everywhere I went in the country I saw signs of the benefits of American aid and was told many times that the people were grateful.

Speaking in a general way, I found Yugoslavia a delightful place to visit and an interesting country in which to study the changing industrial, social and political system. The people were well fed, but their diet is mainly meat, fish, fats and bread. It was like asking for the moon to ask for a glass of orange juice or lemon for your tea—unless you were at the American Embassy. The prices in the shops I visited seemed high. Friends later explained that both wool and cotton have to be imported and paid for in foreign currency, which was difficult for the government to arrange, so that the prices for those goods naturally were higher than one might expect. The price of foodstuffs seemed reasonable, but I could not understand why there was so little variety. Here was a country in which 70 per cent of the population was engaged in agriculture, yet there were only a few vegetables and a few fruits in the markets. Officials estimated that the average family had to spend from 50 to 80 per cent of its budget on food.

I talked to a number of farmers and decided that they were perhaps the least satisfied people in Yugoslavia. This was partly because the Tito regime originally followed the Soviet pattern of collective farms. But after a few years it was recognized that this system was not a success in Yugoslavia and it was gradually changed to permit small private farms and to encourage co-operative farming. Some collective farms continued, however, in the best farming areas. The government provided all farmers with certain tools and with fertilizers and made available machinery such as they never had had before. But of all people, the farmers the world over are the most individualistic, and the Yugoslav farmers have been slow to accept new ways.

Industrially, the country has certainly made progress and important social security measures have been instituted. Medical care is provided on a universal basis and the hospitals I saw were equipped with modern laboratory and research facilities, most of which came from the United Nations or the United States. Typhoid and malaria have been largely wiped out except in a few rural areas. Generally, the medical services are better than one would expect in a country that calls itself as yet undeveloped. There are unemployment benefits and old-age pensions under the social security system, as well as payments for all children. Considering the economy of the country, these payments are generous and make a great difference in the life of the people.

Changes have also been made in the school system, and in rural areas four years of school, from the ages of seven to eleven, are obligatory. Then the child can go to technical school or to a factory school for several years. In the cities, high school training is free and so is instruction at the universities, which are crowded.

These are all important changes in the basic structure of the country and are in considerable contrast to conditions that existed before the war. The greatest difference in postwar Yugoslavia, however, probably is at the head of the government and I was eager to talk to President Tito.

XV

A DAY WITH TITO
AT BRIONI

I have said that I found much in Yugoslavia that was interesting and delightful and I think our trip from Zagreb to Brioni to call on President Tito was one of the most delightful days I spent there. The July weather continued good and, although the trip was not what we would call a long one, we used four modes of transportation—airplane, automobile, boat and a lovely carriage with horses—before we reached our destination.

We took the plane at Zagreb in mid-morning and within a few minutes, it seemed to me, we had landed and were driving by automobile into Rijeka with Mayor Eda Jardas. He took us around the port, explaining that it was a big harbor which accommodated not only the coastwise ships but big steamers, and we continued on to Opatija, where we had luncheon outdoors at the Hotel Kvarner. Later we drove on down the Istrian coast and through lovely mountain country to a point opposite the island of Brioni, where the President's boat was waiting for us.

The trip across about two miles of water to Brioni was quickly completed and we were on a wonderfully wooded island which makes a perfect summer residence for a busy President. There was a hotel for guests and villas to which the Marshal invited special guests. We —Miss Corr, Dr. Gurewitsch and I—were driven in an old-fashioned victoria from the landing stage to a guest villa on the water, with a fine view of the sea. There are no powered vehicles on the island, incidentally, except jeeps used by the military or police units guarding the President, and perhaps the absence of noisy motors and gas fumes added to the feeling of peaceful quiet all around us.

Mrs. Vilfan had been waiting on the dock for us and accompanied us to the villa where, after tea, she left us to our own devices. We had a swim and then dined under a grape arbor and finally went for a walk. The sun set in splendor and a new moon drifted across the sky; and it was so wonderfully peaceful that we could hardly believe that there had been fighting here during the war and that the villa in which we were staying was so badly damaged it had to be rebuilt.

In the midst of all this contentment, I received a week's delayed copies of the Paris *Herald Tribune* and, of course, I felt I had to catch up immediately on the world's news. It destroyed some of the evening's peacefulness, because there was much about testimony before Senator McCarthy's congressional investigating committee, including an attack on the American clergy which was entirely unjustified and which backfired on the Senator and his cohorts. I read that the State Department had taken a sensible position in regard to proposals for getting rid of all Communist books in our Information Service libraries and it gave me hope that the fear which Senator McCarthy had created was wearing off. That raised my spirits again, since I hate to see the American people afraid of anything.

I was up early the next morning and arrived at the President's villa alone promptly at ten o'clock, riding in a victoria. There were no obvious signs of guards or police near the villa, although no doubt the Marshal was thoroughly protected in an unobtrusive way, as our White House is protected by the Secret Service men. There was a huge German shepherd dog outside the villa which I'd been told was a favorite pet of Marshal Tito. I was ushered inside and to a large room that the Marshal uses as an office. At the door I could see Mr. Vilfan and another man at a desk far across the room and it made me think of the accounts of the office of Premier Benito Mussolini in Rome, where visitors had to walk across a huge, bare space of floor to reach the desk behind which stood the stern-faced Italian dictator.

As I entered, however, a young-looking man came across the room to greet me. For a few moments I could not believe that this was Marshal Tito because he seemed far too youthful. It was only after he had greeted me warmly and I had seated myself on a sofa beside him that I was able to observe that his hair was graying and that there were deep lines of experience in his strongly molded face. He has great charm and a strong personality. His jaw juts out and he speaks in the manner of a man who gives orders and expects them to be obeyed. But he demonstrated a good sense of humor, he was certainly very pleasant to me and, most important perhaps, he conveyed the impression of speaking frankly and honestly.

Tito spoke a little English and some German, but most of the time we spoke through our translator, Mr. Vilfan, in order to be sure that there was no misunderstanding. Not long after I arrived, the President's youthful wife and Mrs. Vilfan came into the room. Mrs. Broz had been a Partisan who had fought in the army during the war. She is very beautiful and gave me the impression of having both intelligence and strong character. She told me she had arrived on Brioni only a couple of days earlier because she was taking her examinations in Belgrade.

"Examinations?" I said, puzzled.

"Yes," she replied, with Mrs. Vilfan translating for me. "You see I'm going to school. The war interrupted my education but now I have gone back and picked up where I left off, and I must complete my courses at the university."

The President, watching her, seemed to be proud of his wife's decision to complete her education so that she would be well fitted for her position as first lady of the land, and I felt he would encourage her in what must have been a difficult task under the circumstances.

Dr. Gurewitsch and Miss Corr arrived at the villa shortly afterward and all of us went down to the dock, where we got into a handsome speedboat to go to a small island that Marshall Tito uses as a retreat when he wants to be alone. The Marshal himself piloted one speedboat, taking me with him, and seemed to get a deal of fun out of it. He obviously enjoys life, and he dresses in handsome uniforms or in well-tailored jackets and slacks of bright but attractive colors. As a boy, he never owned a suit of clothes until he was old enough to earn the money for it by hard labor.

"Then," he said, "I had hardly had a chance to put on that fine new suit before it was stolen from me! It was a terrible blow to a young man."

Looking at him at the controls of the boat and thinking back over his boyhood, I felt he was right to be concerned about his dress and about the impression he made on visitors. He talked much about his vineyard on the little island we were approaching and showed a keen love of the land. He was at times almost boyish, as if he were enjoying his holiday from affairs of state, and later he romped enthusiastically with his big shepherd dog. That morning, however, he talked seriously for nearly three hours. He smoked feverishly but answered all my questions.

After luncheon on the island we went for a walk to inspect the vineyards and to visit his small stone cottage where the wine is tested. Like any small winegrower, he had samples of the vineyard produce stored in the walls of the cottage, and proudly asked us to sample the various wines. The cottage was conical in shape and we entered through a low stone door, but there was room to sit on benches and stools around a little table. Each of us was given a glass on which there was a figure of a man or a woman in Yugoslav costume.

"These glasses," the President remarked, "are used in almost every household in the country on festive occasions." He poured wine into our glasses. "You know, the real value of these wine storehouses," he went on, "lies in the good talk that goes on in them when the wine is being tested. When you are in an office, you feel the weight of accumulated problems on your back. But when you get out and talk to people the weight lifts."

We sipped our wine slowly and it was excellent. I thought that Marshal Tito was a man who knew how to face problems, but also that there was about him a kind of buoyancy that comes from courage, the sort of courage I saw both my husband and Winston Churchill show during the most trying times of World War II.

Later, the President showed us a little orchard and then a charming arbor with a table and seats overlooking the sea. On the stone table had been carved in the dialect of the President's native region an admonition to sit there and rest and eat grapes. The arbor had been the gift of his wife and friends on his last birthday and he was evidently proud of it. Later in the afternoon we took a short trip on the state yacht in the Adriatic. The security officers surrounding Marshal Tito were obviously nervous about the possibility of kidnaping, and the ship was accompanied by armed vessels while military airplanes were constantly overhead or nearby.

The President, however, was enjoying himself and completely unconcerned as we steamed along the coast, and he pointed out various landmarks. We returned to Brioni in time to dress and attend a formal dinner at his villa. It was altogether an enjoyable day.

At dinner I told the President a story I had heard about two Yugoslavs sitting in a Belgrade café. The first man was complaining loudly about conditions in the country under the Tito government.

"If Tito really knew what was going on," he concluded, "he would do something about it in a hurry."

The second man snorted scornfully. "Why that blankety-blank wouldn't do anything for us!"

The first man leaped to his feet and struck the critic of Tito on the chin, a fight ensued and the police finally carted both men off to jail.

When I told the story, the President seemed to be amused, so I asked him: "Well, Mr. President, was the man who defended you kept in jail?"

"I don't know," he replied with a chuckle, "but if both of them were put in jail that shows we have freedom of speech in Yugoslavia, doesn't it? You'll have to ask my Minister of Interior whether my defender was kept there."

After dinner I did talk to the Minister of Interior, who was one of the guests, about the number of political prisoners.

"There are not really many political prisoners," he asserted.

"Well, how many?" I persisted. "Would you say that as many as twenty-five political prisoners were arrested in a month? Or fifty? Or seventy-five?"

"Less than seventy-five," he finally replied.

"What is the reason for most of the arrests?"

"The major reason," he replied, "is for infiltrating Soviet ideas into Yugoslavia."

This answer struck me as amusing, because that seemed to be the main thing feared by anti-Communist investigators in the United States!

Like many men who have acquired power, the President evidently loves it and he has a certain vanity. But he is intelligent enough to recognize that in Yugoslavia he can have power in the long run only if the people give it to him voluntarily. It cannot be just a matter of what he wants or doesn't want done. There must be at least a willingness on the part of the people that he should have the power to act. As a result, I believe, he is concerned with providing a government that benefits the people, or at least enough of the people to maintain him in power.

"Do you believe the people are contented under your Socialist form of government?" I asked him.

He lit another cigarette and looked at me questioningly. "If you owned property," he remarked, "and the government nationalized your property would you be contented?"

I said that I would not be happy about it.

"Then," he replied, "I will say that I don't think everybody in Yugoslavia is content. But on the whole I believe the people realize that we are doing the things that will be best for our country in the long run."

"Mr. President," I continued, "you have been quoted as saying that the Western democracies should take advantage of any conciliatory gesture from the Soviet Union but not press too rigidly for settlement of world problems on strictly Western terms. Would you be more explicit?"

His reply covered some issues that were important then but have since lost their immediacy, but he said that there might be a chance of unifying Germany on a compromise basis. The Russians, he continued, sometimes seemed to be weakened by the internal rivalries of their leaders but nobody should fool himself by overestimating this weakness. At the time we had this talk there was no indication of the uprising that shook Soviet rule in Hungary in 1956, but Tito remarked that there was still a great army in Russia and that the Soviet Union would, under certain provocation, act firmly to maintain its influence in the satellite countries. "And any apparent threat to Russia itself," he added, "would unify the Russian people as they have always been united against a foreign threat."

I asked him about the working of Communism in Yugoslavia, where practically everything is nationalized, although citizens have the right to own private property such as a house or a small farm of not more than twenty acres. "I have seen something of your experiment in industry," I said. "I visited one steel plant which, I found, was actually run by two technical experts while the council merely passed on questions of wages and working conditions and the division of the surplus profits, if any. In some ways, this system seemed to me to be not so very different from the system in the United States."

"We have been rather disappointed," he replied, "that so many of the workers' councils have not allocated the surpluses for the good of the community as a whole but have merely divided the funds among the workers."

Human nature, I thought, does not change very much the world over, because that is about what would happen in our capitalistic system! But I asked him only if he really considered that his country was practicing Communism.

"Communism," he answered, "really exists nowhere, least of all in the Soviet Union. Communism is an ideal that can be achieved only when people cease to be selfish and greedy and when everyone receives according to his needs from communal production. But that is a long way off."

He said that Yugoslavia was developing a Socialist state that was one step toward this distant aim of Communism. "I suppose," he added, "that I might call myself a social democrat." Marshal Tito does not want what is being developed in Yugoslavia to be called Communism, and he also objects to the use of the term Titoism. Every country should develop according to its own needs, he continued, and he does not want Yugoslavia to be held up as an example for others, since Yugoslavia's system might not meet the needs of any other country.

"I am not a dictator," he insisted. "We have a group—all of us were Partisans during the war—that works closely together and prepares for each step to be taken." When a law has been prepared it is published in the newspapers; then various organizations, especially the trade unions, send the government large numbers of letters containing criticisms and suggestions for changes. These criticisms are carefully analyzed, Tito said, and the law is redrafted and again published in the newspapers so that the people will again have an opportunity to express themselves about it before it is sent to Parliament for consideration.

"But you have a one-party political system," I said.

"Yes, but there is virtually always more than one candidate for a nomination so that the people have a choice." Then, with a smile, he added: "There is no great difference between our system and the American system. We have one party but you have only two—just one more!"

On the basis of our conversation, it seemed to me that the President conceived of the current government as a step forward in the education of the people. He was perhaps not sure what the final steps would be, but he hoped they would lead to development of a political body along socialistic lines with a social conscience that responds to the needs of the country rather than to individual needs. I concluded that he had a concept of self-government by the people—quite different from ours, because there it comes from the top down rather than from the bottom up, as in our country. But it did not seem impossible for our type of political philosophy to live and co-operate with the system that appeared to be developing in Yugoslavia.

I said that I understood that Yugoslavia had broken with the Cominform because the Cominform, controlled by Russia, tried to impose its will on the internal affairs of Yugoslavia. "But supposedly the Cominform was an instrument for spreading Communism through the world," I added, "and so far as I know you have never repudiated this idea."

Marshal Tito lit another cigarette and replied that the trend in the world was toward socialism but that he believed each nation should develop in its own way and that one country should not try to impose its will on any other. This, he made clear, applied to the great democracies of the West as well as to the Soviet Union.

I commented on the American aid that had come to Yugoslavia. "I have been very favorably impressed by the appreciation and gratitude of the people here for that assistance," I said. "But mere gratitude of the people, important as it is, does not necessarily convince us that the government will not swing back to the Russian system when it has reached a point where American help is no longer needed or no longer so important."

The President looked shocked, and he did not seem to care for my implication that I was not the only one in the United States who might be worried about this point. He declared emphatically that when Yugoslavia broke with the Cominform it had done away with Stalinist methods for good and all.

"I am ready to repeat what I told your Ambassador," he said. "Regardless of whether the United States gives us help or not, the attitude of Yugoslavia toward the United States will not change."

All progress is achieved by stages, he continued, and he believed that Yugoslavia was still at a point where certain measures had to be imposed by force—a law, for example, that had been passed forbidding any incitement to hatred or any kind of civil war such as had occurred in the past among the different nationalities and different religious groups in the country.

It occurred to me that we at home were inclined to think of Communism anywhere as an international movement trying to spread its domination everywhere by any means at its disposal. Whatever the attitude of the Yugoslav leaders toward this program was in the past, I found during my visit not the slightest evidence that anyone from Marshal Tito on down intends to return to world Communism. They were concentrating on rebuilding their own country and improving the standard of living and they keenly realized that peace was necessary for this purpose. Their attitude toward the United States at that time was warmer than in any other country I visited. This, of course, does not mean that we will always agree with them on methods. They are a socialist state and we are a capitalist state, but if the Yugoslav brand of Communism were the only kind we had to face in the world we would probably revise our attitude toward it.

I doubt that many people will agree when Marshal Tito describes himself as a social democrat. He acknowledged that the use of force by the government was necessary in his country. I felt, too, that as yet there were inconsistencies in the development of his theories of government. But I left him with the opinion that this was a powerful leader and an honest one, with some kind of long-range concept of self-government by the people. And I thought that much of the future would depend on the United States and how well we could prove that our democracy is concerned about and benefits the people as a whole.

Since I was in Yugoslavia, Tito has accepted overtures from Russia, and our government and our people have not always been sure where his real allegiance lies. But I still think he wants independence for Yugoslavia, although he believes in Communism.

XVI

CAMPAIGNING FOR STEVENSON

One of the best things about long trips to foreign countries is coming home again. I suppose I am one of those persons who like to be on the go much of the time, but when I returned from my second trip around the world I told myself that I really was not a very good traveler any more. I had had some wonderful experiences and seen many fascinating places and I had talked with a number of remarkable persons. I am sure I shall always like to go to new places and, if I am traveling with pleasant companions, I have no objections to the discomforts that are a necessary part of travel in distant lands.

But when I landed once again in the United States I had a feeling of great satisfaction at being home. When I am alone, I thought, I really want to be among familiar surroundings—my apartment and friends in New York, my cottage and neighbors in Hyde Park. It was true that my foreign travels were by no means ended, but for a while I was far more interested in what was going on in my own country and in catching up with everything I had missed while abroad. I wanted to see old friends, too, like Mrs. Lewis Thompson, who was once the Republican national committeewoman from New Jersey and whom I had known for many enjoyable years. Mrs. Thompson has long been interested in many charities and she occasionally brought several women to my apartment for luncheon or tea to talk about one of her pet projects.

One day she called me and said she would like to bring eight women to luncheon and I said that would be fine. A little later she called back.

"I have more than eight now," she said.

"Oh, dear!" I exclaimed. "I just can't serve more than eight."

"All right," she replied. "Don't worry about it."

So I didn't worry until she arrived at one o'clock with her eight guests and four other women. I must have looked horrified.

"It's all right," Mrs. Thompson said gaily. "There are only eight for luncheon. I had the other four bring their own buns."

And sure enough, each of them carried a little sack that contained a sweet roll and, while we talked and the rest of us had luncheon, these four ate their buns and drank the coffee that my maid provided for them. They didn't seem to mind and Mrs. Thompson assured me that everything was all right, so I suppose it was. Mrs. Thompson knew how to manage almost anything.

Coming home meant seeing people like Mrs. Thompson and her friends and getting into the swing of things again and, especially, finding out what was happening in political affairs in the United States. The next presidential election was still two years away and I had no intention of taking any important part in the campaign, but I was much interested in what the Democratic party leaders were doing and saying.

I had been concerned with political affairs most of my adult life, from the time of the Republican Bull Moosers to the day of the Democratic Eggheads, as the men around Governor Stevenson were sometimes called, and I had always enjoyed studying at first hand the successful as well as the unsuccessful campaigns in which my husband and many close friends took part.

My own participation in political campaigns was interrupted after Franklin's death in 1945, partly because I became a member of the delegation to the United Nations and took great pains not to mix political affairs with my official duties. I believed that the questions we were dealing with at the United Nations were of the greatest importance to our country's position in the world and that they should not be approached from a partisan point of view. In 1952, it was my opinion that Governor Stevenson would probably make one of the best Presidents we ever had had, but I also believed that it was practically impossible for the Democrats to win the election because of the hero worship surrounding General Eisenhower. I did make a speech on the United Nations at the Democratic National Convention that year at the request of President Truman, and I came out for Governor Stevenson; but I did not intend to be active in that campaign, and I was not.

Why then did I re-enter politics in 1956? For one thing, I was out of the United Nations delegation by that time and, as a private citizen, I had no feeling that I was barred from taking part in a political campaign. In addition, I believed as strongly as before that Adlai Stevenson would make a good President. For another thing, I had not been much impressed by the progress of what President Eisenhower called Modern Republicanism.

The Eisenhower brand of Republicanism seemed to me to be an acceptance of certain social advances that some of the younger Republicans regarded as important to the party's status in our changing domestic picture. These things usually had their origin in the New Deal days but had become so much a part of the people's thinking that Republicans who had not solidified in the old mold were willing to accept them and had more or less persuaded the President to think along the same lines. President Eisenhower had seen much of the international scene and was keenly aware of the vital importance of our role in world affairs, but the net result of his administration had not been impressive, because there were enough old-line Republicans in powerful positions to keep the party, on the whole, a conservative, businessmen's party.

Of course, the Democratic party had many conservatives in powerful positions, too, but in general it was more progressive. Some of us have long hoped for a political realignment that would result in major parties that more truly represented the conservative and progressive thinking of the people. But it is difficult to say whether that will ever be possible.

Still another thing that influenced me in getting back into politics as the 1956 campaign approached was Governor Stevenson's high standing among statesmen of other countries which are our allies or which we want to have on our side in the world struggle against Communism. After his defeat in 1952, Governor Stevenson had taken a trip around the world to study conditions in other countries and, during my own world travels, I had been greatly interested in the impression he had made on foreign statesmen. Again and again, they told me that Mr. Stevenson was the kind of man who listened, who wanted to learn all the facts. I came to the conclusion that it might be a good thing if more of us did more listening and did not try to ram our own ideas down other people's throats.

After Governor Stevenson had traveled around the world and had made a special journey to study African problems, he came to call on me one day to talk about whether he should again seek the Democratic nomination for President. He is a very intelligent man but he is also a humble man, and there were questions that he was trying to resolve in his own mind.

"Don't you feel," he asked in reference to the coming national convention, "that there are others who would do better than I as leader of the party?"

I pointed out that perhaps the most difficult problems of the day were in the field of international relations and I added: "I cannot think of anyone else who has the ability to do the job you could do in meeting the most vital needs of today."

But I could tell that there was some other question he really wanted to ask me. And finally he said: "Will you tell me something? You and Franklin had very much the same kind of background when you were growing up that I had. Yet both of you were always very much more at home in talking with the people than I am. What is it that makes this difference?"

It seemed to me that Governor Stevenson, in his humility, had put his finger on a problem in his own political career. It was the intelligent kind of self-criticism that would never have been possible for most politicians. I answered as best I could. I said that Franklin had grown up in Dutchess County as a member of a long-established family, just as Governor Stevenson had in Illinois. But Franklin had the advantage of getting to know all of the people of the area at an early age. He rode his pony everywhere with or without his father, and he talked with all kinds of neighbors and friends. Later, as a young man, he drove his automobile all over the district in political campaigns. He listened to the people and, most important of all, he got the "feel" of the people. You might say that he "felt" their attitudes.

This, however, was a knowledge and a feeling of country people. Later, he had to make an effort to achieve the same relationship to city people and their problems. I remember when, before we were married, I was working at the Rivington Street settlement house in New York City and Franklin called for me there late one afternoon. I wasn't ready to go with him because there was a sick child in my class, and I had to see that she was taken home. Franklin said he would go with me. We took the child to a slum area not far away, and Franklin went with me up the three flights to the tenement rooms in which the family lived. It was not a pleasant place and Franklin looked around in surprise and horror. It was the first time, I think, that he had ever really seen a slum and when he got back to the street he drew a deep breath of fresh air.

"My God," he whispered, "I didn't know people lived like that!"

I told Governor Stevenson that I thought he would not be making an error if he got a small automobile and traveled leisurely in various sections of the country. I suggested that in each area he should be accompanied by a man who knew the local people and that he should talk to them and find out how they were living and what they were thinking. "You should stay in each area," I added, "until you can 'feel' what they are feeling."

"Well," he replied, "I don't know whether I can ever do that."

As it turned out, he didn't try. Or perhaps his advisers didn't let him try. I suppose that in modern political campaigning it is becoming more and more difficult really to get to the people, to let them see their candidates face to face and to enable the candidates to draw strength and ideas from the people. In the future, there doubtless will be more and bigger television appearances by presidential candidates, and fewer whistle-stop train tours of the country. But my opinion is that nothing can really take the place of whistle-stop appearances, because voters will always want actually to see the men for whom they vote. Naturally, some candidates make more votes by whistle-stop appearances than others. Franklin enjoyed that kind of campaigning and, what was more important, he got a great deal out of it. Seeing the people, being close to large crowds, was important for him and gave him ideas. It did much to help him know the needs and the mood of the country. President Truman was much the same. But Governor Stevenson did not have the same easy feel of political crowds, and it seems to me that President Eisenhower gets nothing at all from such campaign appearances.

Of course, I urged Governor Stevenson to run, but I did not expect to take an important part in the campaign and decided to go to Europe with my two grandsons at the time of the Democratic National Convention. To my surprise, this horrified some of my friends. "If you fail to attend the convention," one of them said, "everybody will think you have changed your mind about supporting Adlai. You must be there."

So, finally, I sent my grandsons off alone on the boat and arranged to spend a couple of days at the Chicago convention before flying to Europe. When I arrived at the Chicago airport I was met by several supporters of Governor Stevenson. They were upset. They hurried me to an automobile and, instead of going directly to my hotel, said they would drive me around a bit while they explained what was going on. The most important thing going on was that, while I was en route to Chicago, former President Truman, who had begged Mr. Stevenson to run in 1952, had come out in favor of the nomination of Governor Averell Harriman of New York.

I certainly was not thrilled by this news for various reasons. President Truman had always been especially considerate toward me. I had reported to him personally after the various meetings of the United Nations and had learned that he had a remarkable understanding of the office and duties of the President. He was a student of the Constitution and it was important to our nation that he was a jealous guardian of the ideas of the founding fathers. I felt that he had to make more than his share of big decisions as President and that he made very few mistakes in times of crisis. The mistakes he did make were human mistakes in smaller things; the mistakes all of us make in our everyday lives. But one of the sad things about being in the White House is that not even these human mistakes are permitted to a President; even loyalty to friends is not permissible, because the Chief Executive must first be loyal to the country.

That morning in Chicago, however, I was thinking of President Truman's great ability as a campaigner, and I was dismayed by the idea of publicly pitting my political judgment against his. I could only reflect that sometimes one had to do things one does not like to do.

Finally I was told that I was going not to my hotel but to a press conference. When we drove to the hotel where the newspaper people were waiting I had to face more reporters and more cameras than I had ever seen before. I was fearful of the ordeal of justifying my judgment in opposition to President Truman but actually it turned out to be no ordeal at all. I said as simply and frankly as possible what I believed, and it was no more difficult than an ordinary press conference. The reporters, of course, made as much as possible of my opposition to President Truman because it is more interesting to write about disagreements than about routine agreement. But they hadn't counted on the fact that I had previously asked President and Mrs. Truman to luncheon that day. Mrs. Truman could not come but, immediately after my press conference, I met the former President in the grill of my hotel. The reporters scented another story. Were we going to make a deal? In no time at all, newspapermen had taken over a large table about three feet from my elbow and were more intent on my conversation with President Truman than they were on their food.

They didn't get much to write even if they had keen ears. We talked about everything except the convention until we had finished luncheon and then our differences were mentioned only indirectly.

"I hope you will understand that whatever action I take is because I think I am doing the right thing," President Truman said.

"Of course," I replied. "I know you will act as you believe is right and I know you will realize that I must do the same."

President Truman nodded and grinned. "What I want to do is make this convention do some real thinking about issues," he said.

Later, when I had gone to my hotel room, I felt that I was a fish out of water and that I really had nothing to do at this convention. But I did attend a reception Governor Stevenson gave in my honor and I accompanied him on visits to various state delegations to seek their support. I saw many persons in my room, attended a luncheon for women delegates and went before the Platform Committee twice to speak on civil rights and education. Paul Butler, the Democratic National Chairman, also asked me to speak briefly to the convention. When I got there the pandemonium was so great that I don't believe any speaker could have been heard with the possible exception of Governor Frank Clement of Tennessee, whose keynote address proved that he had a strong voice. However, what I said could be heard over radio and television, and later many persons were kind enough to say that my words gained considerable attention in the contest for delegates. In any event, I was pleased when Governor Stevenson won the nomination.

During the lively contest for the Vice-Presidential nomination between Senator Estes Kefauver and Senator John Kennedy, a friend of Senator Kennedy came to me with a request for support. I replied that I did not feel I could support him because Senator Kennedy had avoided taking a position during the controversy over Senator Joseph

McCarthy's methods of investigation. Senator Kennedy was in the hospital when the Senate voted censure of Senator McCarthy and, of course, could not record his position. But later, when he returned to the Senate, reporters asked him how he would have voted and he failed to answer directly.

"Oh, that was a long time ago," the Senator's friend told me. "He was unable to vote and it is all a thing of the past. It should not have anything to do with the present situation."

I replied that I thought it did. "I think McCarthyism is a question on which public officials must stand up and be counted," I added. "I still have not heard Senator Kennedy express his convictions. And I cannot be sure of the political future of anyone who does not willingly state where he stands on that issue."

Senator Kennedy came to see me in Chicago and I told him exactly the same thing. He replied in about the words he had previously used in talking to reporters, saying that the McCarthy censure vote was "so long ago" that it did not enter the current situation. But he did not say where he stood on the issue and I did not support him.*

I did not stay in Chicago for the balloting on the Vice-Presidential nominee but flew back to New York the day before my plane left for Europe. That evening I had for dinner several young people who had come from Nottingham, England, on an annual scholarship established in honor of Franklin. It was a confused evening because the fight on civil rights was still going on at the convention and I talked on the telephone with various persons in Chicago at frequent intervals. It all seemed utterly unrealistic because I felt that I had no influence and why people consulted me was beyond my understanding, but my young English guests were deeply interested.

---

* In 1958 after I had written about the above question in one of my articles in the *Saturday Evening Post* I began to be visited by a number of people who told me that the Senator felt I had misquoted him or incorrectly understood his position. I certainly had not intended to misquote him and I usually understand people and at least am able to gather what they mean, but in this case I may well have misunderstood the Senator. He has recently said that he had made statements upholding the vote of the Senate but this is not exactly what I think is called for. I believe that a public servant must clearly indicate that he understands the harm that McCarthyism did to our country and that he opposes it actively, so that one would feel sure he would always do so in the future. This is, however, of minor importance as what I have said is purely a record of the past which the Senator himself can correct.

On the day I flew to Europe I felt a sense of great relief at leaving politics behind. I would be away three weeks and then, I thought, I would return to keep a number of lecture engagements and perhaps take some quiet role in the Presidential campaign. It didn't work out that way. The two months after my return proved to be among the most hectic in my life because I ended up doing far more than I had expected in the campaign, and I had to keep my lecture dates at the same time.

In connection with the campaign, I should like to make clear that I do not believe I qualify as an Egghead. I always remember a young man who made a study of American columnists for his college thesis and concluded that a reader should have at least two years of college to understand the columns of Walter Lippmann and Arthur Krock. But, he added, you need only a fifth-grade education to understand Mrs. Roosevelt's column! So I am not an Egghead, but I am in favor of Eggheads if that means the application of our best intellects to the problems of government. I believe most voters feel the same way and I do not think that the description of Governor Stevenson's advisers— or some of them—as Eggheads was detrimental to his campaign. I don't believe the voters want their candidates to be dumb.

Let me cite a couple of Egghead ideas that were bitterly attacked by the Republicans during the campaign. First, there was the question of abolishing the draft. Since 1956 it has become more and more obvious that drafting young men for a big standing army is unwise and unfair. The draft takes too long a time out of a young man's life at an important period. A big standing army is obsolete, costly and not what we want. We need a well-paid, well-trained professional atomic army with a big reserve of trained citizens. If young men received four months of intensive training at eighteen and then two weeks of training each year for the next ten years our system would be more in keeping with the times. And I think girls should receive similar periods of training in civil defense and other emergency duties.

During the 1956 campaign I always got a warm response from audiences when I discussed this problem. Governor Stevenson did not generally get a good reaction when he spoke on the same subject, but it is noteworthy that since then the Republican administration has been forced to move more and more toward consideration of adjustments in the draft system.

Another Democratic issue in the campaign was the continued test explosion of atomic bombs. This was derided by the Republican leaders as just an Egghead idea, but, as everybody knows, it has since become a problem of great concern to people everywhere.

Of course, I believed there were numerous other reasons why Governor Stevenson should have been elected or why the Eisenhower administration should not have been re-elected. I thought and I still think that a good business executive does not necessarily make a good government administrator, nor does an administration of businessmen necessarily make for good government. A businessman needs certain qualities for success; a government official needs a wide variety of qualities and some quite different ones. He cannot really be successful unless he has a knowledge of people and politics, and there is no doubt that a number of Eisenhower appointees had to learn this in a slow, difficult manner. Often businessmen go into government with the idea that they will be the men at the top and that their orders will be carried out. That is probably the correct approach in business but in government, as they soon find, it is necessary to persuade others that what they want to do is the best course. Unless Congress goes along with them, they can't get results. President Eisenhower evidently felt that he could establish an administration in the pattern of big business, but such an approach to the complexities of government is not necessarily either democratic or successful—as I believe he has discovered.

In the same way, I don't believe that because a man is a successful corporation lawyer he will necessarily be the best person to direct the Department of State. Outsiders like myself, of course, do not have all the facts at their command in regard to international affairs, but surely it was blundering that carried us into the mess in which we found ourselves in 1956—and still find ourselves—in the Middle East.

Secretary Dulles served in all but two of the United Nations Assemblies in which I served, but he was then the ranking Republican or minority member. I often observed that he was rarely inclined to take a stand, to say that this was right or that was wrong. I thought little of it at that time because I supposed it was due to the fact that he represented the minority party and thus felt he was not in a position to enforce his views. Since then I have changed my mind about why he shied away from decisions. Now I feel he just doesn't like to make himself responsible for a definite position, right or wrong. This is a quality in his character. It is, I believe, also the reason he has not come to the defense of loyal public servants in his department when they were under bitter and often unfair attack. And naturally it has led to low morale in the State Department.

I might add here that I don't believe there is much question that Vice-President Richard Nixon will succeed Mr. Eisenhower as party leader, regardless of the opposition of some Republicans. I regard Mr. Nixon as a very able and dangerous opportunist, but since 1952 he has learned a great deal. He now knows the importance of gaining the confidence of the people and he has worked hard at it and made progress. This still does not make me believe that he has any strong convictions, although my son John, who is a Republican, tells me that I am unfair to Mr. Nixon. That, however, is John's opinion.

I remarked earlier that I did not believe that President Eisenhower profits from what contacts he has with crowds. I believe that he also misses a great deal because of his disinclination, frequently reported in the press, to read the daily newspapers. As I understand it, he prefers to have the news digested for him or to be briefed orally on the news. That, I suppose, is a military habit. But it cannot be an effective system for the Chief Executive of a great and diverse country to form opinions on the basis of what his assistants think is the important part of the news.

I remember when Louis Howe was an adviser at the White House he was ill for a long period, but he received daily newspapers from all parts of the country and read them carefully in bed. He not only knew what was important news but he knew the different points of view held in various sections of the country or by people in different economic circumstances. Almost always when I was starting on a trip, Louis would ask me to come and see him. He would look over my itinerary and say: "Now in this city you will find people are thinking about flood control." Or in some other city about something else. He could tell me in advance how each audience I might face would react to various subjects. And he was always right because he had trained himself to read the newspapers intelligently.

It seems to me that such knowledge is of great importance to the President because it enables him to understand the issues of the day in terms of how they affect the people. One of the important duties of the President—and one that the Republican administration neglects—is to be the educator of the public on national problems. Most people do not have the time or inclination to inform themselves fully on the complex and perhaps seemingly remote problems that must be settled by government. But, if he knows the issues and explains them clearly, the President is in a position to make the people aware of what must be decided and to make them feel their responsibility as citizens in reaching a decision. Without such "education" of the public, democracy can become a dangerous kind of government because voters are called upon to make decisions or to support decisions without having sufficient knowledge of the factors involved.

I have said a great deal here about the Republicans and not much about the Democrats. I think there are many able young men in the Democratic party and that there will be no difficulty in selecting a strong Presidential nominee in 1960, but the next national convention will be guided by much that is still to happen and I would hesitate now to try to guess who might emerge as its candidate.

In fact, I hope very much that next time I will have no particular preference, or feeling that some one person must be supported, because my enthusiasm for Governor Stevenson in 1956 led me into a period of such intense activity that I have no desire to try it again. To get back to the subject of that campaign, I had gone late in September to Oregon to do anything I could in behalf of Senator Wayne Morse's race for re-election to the Senate—this time as a Democrat instead of on the Republican ticket. I had to work my political appearances into a tight schedule so that I could also keep my lecture engagements, which were often in distant cities. It was hectic and I will cite my schedule for a few days on the Pacific Coast just to show what I mean by that word.

I arrived in Portland about 9 A.M., September 26, after an all-night flight from New York. I went to the home of former Congresswoman Nan Honeyman and took advantage of the chance to sleep a little before lunch. That afternoon I went to a television studio for a fifteen-minute interview and then to a cocktail party of a political character and then to a dinner in my honor attended by a thousand persons. I don't remember, but the record shows I talked on conservation and several other issues. At 9:30 P.M., Senator Morse and I went on the radio for fifteen minutes and then rushed to a reception at the Masonic Temple. At 11 P.M., I made a recording to be broadcast later with four high-school students. When I got back to Mrs. Honeyman's I talked for a while with her guests but I soon had to go to bed.

The next morning, not long after eight o'clock, I got on a plane and flew to San Francisco. There I borrowed a stenographer and wrote two newspaper columns before going to Oakland for a half-hour speech. I was then guest of honor at a dinner at the Athens Club, where my dinner partners changed every ten minutes because the people giving the dinner wanted me to talk politics to as many guests as possible. I got back to San Francisco late that night and was up at seven o'clock next morning to catch a plane for Los Angeles. The plane had internal difficulties and the trip was delayed two hours, throwing my schedule into confusion.

It had been planned for me (speaking from Los Angeles) to introduce Governor Stevenson over the television for a speech he was making that night in Milwaukee, but I also was scheduled to speak at a luncheon, hold a news conference, attend a reception, and then go on to San Diego to appear on another television program. Despite the delay in my schedule, the political managers awaiting me at Los Angeles were planning to carry out the program somehow, but I got a little tired and temperamental.

"It is impossible!" I cried. "The delay in getting here has mixed up the schedule so badly that something will have to be changed. I just will not try to make the television introduction of Governor Stevenson. They'll have to arrange for someone else."

I got into the waiting automobile and, far behind time, was whisked to a luncheon for four hundred persons. I made a half-hour speech and then went to a press conference, from which I dashed away to attend a reception for at least a thousand persons on somebody's lawn. I had hardly shaken a hundred hands and was only well started across the lawn when a breathless messenger from the political managers arrived and stopped me.

"We've got everything fixed up," he said. "You have time to get to the studio and go over the script and make the television introduction of Governor Stevenson!"

At that point, I accepted my fate and left the lawn party. We got into an automobile and, with the sirens of a police escort making a great deal of noise, rushed to the television studio. There all was confusion, nervousness and a kind of breathless suspense because the studio directors were fearful there would not be enough time to get ready. But I looked at the clock and saw that there was half an hour to spare.

"Here's the script," one of the directors said, trying to rush me.

"Now if you'll just go over it while . . ."

"No," I said firmly. "I have to write two newspaper columns first. Get me a stenographer, please."

"But, Mrs. Roosevelt . . . !"

I insisted and one of the office stenographers was produced. While the directors and the political managers bit their fingernails, I took the stenographer into a dressing room and began dictating. The studio directors paced the floor and kept looking at the door of the dressing room, convinced that we would never be ready for the 5:30 P.M. television appearance. To their surprise, I got through much of my work and emerged from the dressing room at 4:45 P.M. They all sprang into action, bringing me the script and leading me to the make-up room. While the make-up was being applied I studied the script, made some changes in the brief introduction of Governor Stevenson, and was ready to go on at 5:30 P.M. as scheduled.

I fear the studio was left in a kind of shambles and goodness knows what happened to the nervous systems of the directors. I was happy that I had learned long before the kind of discipline that enabled me to avoid sitting on the edge of my chair and chewing my fingernails in such a situation.

After I introduced Governor Stevenson, I had time to hear only the first sentences of his speech before speeding out to the airport to get aboard a private plane that had been hurriedly chartered for the trip to San Diego. We did not arrive there until approximately the time I was supposed to be appearing on my second television program of the day—a debate with Senator Thomas H. Kuchel of California.

"Maybe we can make it yet," the local political representative said as I scrambled into his automobile. We raced to the television studio but it was already past the hour for the program when we arrived. I kept watching the minutes slip by and observed that I was six minutes late as we went in the studio door. Senator Kuchel was speaking and at that moment he concluded his remarks. The announcer looked up at me with astonishment and a great sigh of relief. He motioned me to a chair and, without pausing, introduced me to the television audience. I had no idea what Senator Kuchel had said but I knew what I wanted to say about the presidential race and I said it for the next seven minutes. I don't suppose the audience had any idea how close I had come to missing the program entirely.

From the studio I went straight to a press conference and then to a haphazardly-managed reception where about two thousand persons went through the receiving line. The confusion was so great that the crowd almost crushed me against a stand before the police leaped to my rescue. At 10:30 P.M. I was at the airport again and caught a plane to Los Angeles. An hour later, I was happy to lie back in the reclining seat of still another airplane—headed for New York with my shoes off!

That was just a sample of what happened to me during the 1956 campaign. There were a good many other days just as crowded later, but I did have a couple of days' interlude after reaching New York on Friday. I had made an appointment months before to speak to the West Point Cadets on the following Sunday evening in a series of lectures on "World Affairs." So on Saturday I did a few recordings to be used in Mayor Robert Wagner's campaign in New York City and loafed around until dinnertime, when I had twelve people at my apartment for the evening. Sunday was still peaceful and the jaunt to West Point and back was really rather pleasant. But on Monday, which was October 1, I had to fly to Clarksburg, West Virginia, to resume campaigning.

That night at Clarksburg, where I was welcomed by Governor Marland, Mrs. Nunley Snedegar, the national committeewoman, and Ben Stout, I discovered that vanity was a mistake during a campaign. I had brought some rather nice-looking shoes. They were not comfortable but I decided to wear them anyway. We attended a dinner for about a thousand persons and later I stood up and shook hands with most of them. By the time I finished, my left foot was hurting me so badly that I thought the affair would never end. When I got my shoes off at last, my foot was badly swollen and the next few days it was so uncomfortable that I had great difficulty keeping a smile on my face and not limping around like an old lady with the gout.

The next morning I drove to Beckley for luncheon. This was country I knew well—beautiful country, but a mining area that had not always brought happiness to the people. The campaign managers there were raising money by the "Dollar-for-Stevenson" method. They had a big truck in front of the hotel and some of us stood on it to speak and to receive dollars handed up from the crowd.

I also stopped at a mine that day when the shifts were changing and talked to some of the miners, something I had not done since the early days of the depression in the 1930's. The miners were better off than in those days and I was happy to see the changes. I also met Congressman Joe L. Smith, who was the only Democrat to beat an incumbent Republican anywhere in the United States in 1928. Somehow I felt at home in this mining environment. It took me back to the depression period when I spent much time trying to see what could be done for the people, particularly the children, in this area.

Later, we drove to Charleston for a dinner, after which I was scheduled to take a plane to Detroit, but fog had settled down and there was no possibility of a flight. So I had to wait until the next morning and, of course, that disrupted my campaign schedule in Detroit. From Detroit I was supposed to take an evening plane to Marquette, in the upper Wisconsin peninsula, to keep a lecture appointment the next day, but I missed my connection and had to go by private plane, arriving at one o'clock in the morning.

I managed to keep my dates the next day, including an unscheduled Democratic reception. I also ran into Senator Alexander Wiley, the Republican incumbent, who was on his own campaign tour. Senator Wiley was having his troubles and there were those who believed that he would be defeated because of the opposition of his Republican colleague from Wisconsin, Senator McCarthy. President Eisenhower had not come very strongly to Senator Wiley's support, although the Senator had been a staunch administration man in Congress. But I admired the way in which Senator Wiley had fought for a sound foreign policy and I greeted him warmly when I saw him in Marquette. I was later told that he felt this had done him no harm in his winning campaign.

Again I had to take a private plane to Chicago, where I caught an air liner for New York for perhaps the worst phase of the campaign as far as I was concerned. I barely had time in New York to get a bite to eat before—without even changing my dress—I had to go to a rally in the downtown section where I was to join Governor Stevenson. The rally was held just where the cars come off one of the bridges going from Manhattan to Brooklyn. A loudspeaker had been set up and big spotlights were turned on to attract the late-afternoon crowds. There were a number of speakers who were supposed to warm up the crowd before Governor Stevenson and his party arrived, but when they started speaking the public address system did not work. In the noise of automobiles and trucks, nobody could hear what they were saying.

I urged some of the party officials to do something about it but, although they presumably tried, the public address system had not gone on when Governor Stevenson arrived with Senator Herbert

Lehman and Mayor Wagner. The Senator started speaking but his voice was lost in the roar of confusion around the busy corner. I sat there praying that the mike would come on but it didn't and both Mayor Wagner and I spoke without anybody hearing a word. Then Governor Stevenson struggled valiantly but with no more success. The whole affair was a complete failure and waste of time.

I was very angry and convinced that the Tammany Hall organization, which had arranged the meeting, could not have done so poorly unless it had deliberately tried to. I was told later that this was not true, but I felt nevertheless that the whole evening tour of the city was poorly arranged. We went to the Yorkville area on the upper East Side but there were comparatively few people there. A meeting in Harlem was even less satisfactory. I was very discouraged and I had no doubt where the blame lay.

New York City is in the hands of the Tammany organization, which can arrange what it wishes to arrange, turn out big crowds when it wants big crowds and, I feel sure, have properly working loudspeakers when it wants its candidates to be heard. I knew that Tammany had no enthusiasm for Governor Stevenson and I believed that the tour of New York City was deliberately sabotaged.

I left New York that night on an eleven o'clock plane to continue campaigning in the Middle West and West, moving rather rapidly from one area to another on a tight schedule. Looking back on it, I wonder how the schedule ever worked out; and I think I managed it only by taking every opportunity to snatch some sleep—sitting in a plane or an automobile or resting a few minutes in a chair. I am sure that my companions in some of the cities where I spoke thought I slept in very odd places indeed!

Once, in Chicago, I went to the airport at ten o'clock in the evening after a busy day and was told that my plane would be slightly delayed. I was just looking around for some place to sleep for a few minutes when a young man spoke to me.

"There's a young couple in the next room who are on their honeymoon," he said. "They've both worked very hard for Governor Stevenson and they would like very much to meet you."

So instead of sleeping I talked to the young couple, who had been married that day. Then there was word of further delay and we waited there until we got the horrid news that our plane would not leave until 3 A.M. When we finally did get aboard I collapsed in the seat until we reached New York at dawn, which was fortunately a Sunday and I was able to get some rest at my apartment.

This kind of thing went on for weeks. I never fooled myself about the difficulties of defeating the incumbent administration at a time when there were no great and compelling reasons for the public to make a change. If the people are fairly comfortable and there is no great unrest, they prefer to let well enough alone, and it is seldom possible to stir them up by pointing out that there are grave problems ahead—in this case, in the international field. You can't expect the voters generally to respond very strongly in such a situation. But in a campaign you have to feel that you may be able to overcome your handicaps, for otherwise you will not be able to give your speeches with any conviction. So I kept telling myself that we had a chance to win and that it was worth while to make the strongest possible fight.

I did, however, get awfully, awfully tired of motorcades. I have no idea how many times I rode through the streets of various cities in a procession of open-top automobiles carrying candidates for national and local office. Most of these were rather silly performances. There are only two people who really become well known to the people during a campaign. In this case, one was the President whom they knew and the other was the head of the opposition ticket who was trying to become President. Of course, there are some local candidates for office whom they recognize, but as far as I was concerned the motorcade always seemed ridiculous because there was no reason for anyone to bother to come out on the street to look at me.

In mid-October, I was joined on my campaigning trips by Earl Banner of the Boston *Globe*, whose editor had given him an unusual assignment.

"He happened to see a copy of your schedule sent out by the Democratic National Committee," Mr. Banner told me. "After he read it, he said it was impossible for anyone to keep up with such a schedule. So he sent me to accompany you for the next few days and to expose that schedule as an exaggeration."

Mr. Banner strung along with me for a few days, but with some difficulty. He did, however, acknowledge that I was keeping up with my schedule of meetings in various towns and he wrote a story for his newspaper certifying that fact. He also wrote about something that had happened almost without my realizing it. In Minnesota, I was riding with the wife of Governor Orville Freeman by automobile near

Shakopee and several other automobiles were following in our little procession, including one carrying Mr. Banner. At one point we were speeding past a fork in the road when it seemed for an instant that we might collide with a truck. Our driver, Wally Olson, was excellent and I did not feel that we were in any real danger. He avoided the collision and I really hardly noticed the incident, but Mr. Banner wrote in his story that day that it came very near to being a serious accident, and perhaps it did.

The last days of the campaign were really strenuous and I was getting mighty tired of the sound of my own voice, as I told my son James one evening when he was driving me to the airport at Los Angeles. My final appearances were in Washington, where I was on a television program with Senator Margaret Chase Smith at five-thirty in the afternoon, and in St. Louis the same evening, where I spoke at the Kiel auditorium. Early the next morning I took a plane back to New York. I got to Hyde Park in time to cast my vote, which was the last if not least important thing I could do in behalf of Governor Stevenson.

That night I went with some friends to hear the election returns in a room that my son, Franklin, Jr., and his partner had taken at a hotel. The returns, of course, were unhappy from my point of view, but perhaps others present were really more disappointed than I. I suppose that a long time spent in politics has inured me to disappointments. I felt sad because I am a strong admirer of Governor Stevenson and I believed his abilities were needed to meet the problems that would arise in the next four years. But I knew that somehow those problems would be met and I was pleased that I could at least say to myself that I had done all I had been asked to do, and all I could do.

When it was all over, I was glad to be out of politics. I couldn't forget that sometimes my feet hurt during that campaign and that I seldom got enough sleep. Later, my children told me that I had tried to do too much. "You're going to have to slow down," they warned. "You're going to have to stop working one of these days and you certainly should never get involved in another such job of campaigning."

They may have been right. But I noticed that I could often keep going longer than they, and I thought that it was never easy to know what one would do or not do at some time in the future. I was seventy-two in 1956 and sometimes I felt very old and sometimes I felt very young!

XVII

ON THE ISLAND OF BALI

Most of my journeys abroad have been in connection with official or semiofficial business of some kind, but I have been fortunate in being able to combine work with a great deal of sight-seeing and sometimes I have been able simply to take off on my own for a short time, as I did when I visited the famous island of Bali in 1955.

I had been asked to be a delegate to the World Federation of United Nations Associations, which was meeting that summer in Bangkok, the capital of Thailand, and I was happy to accept, partly because it would give me a chance for another look at the Far East en route. I did not feel that I was very well acquainted with the problems and people of Indonesia, which was long in the Dutch colonial domain but is now a federation of independent republics. And I had always wanted to see Bali, which I had read so much about and which usually was pictured as the loveliest and most peaceful of the fabled South Sea islands.

The Dutch, I knew, were not popular in the islands after the war and apparently were becoming still less popular. Yet I had known Queen Juliana for some years and felt that she had worked hard to further a better spiritual understanding among peoples. I should like to tell a little about the Queen, because before I went to Indonesia one of the royal families of Europe I enjoyed visiting was that of Holland. I had always admired the former Queen, Wilhelmina, for her staunch courage and her insistence upon being a good Dutch housewife as well as a capable ruler. Even when she was on the throne, she often went by herself to a small cottage that she owned and, for a week or so at a time, did her own housekeeping, cooked her own meals and, I suppose, even made her own bed. I must confess that I have never understood the Dutch manner of making up a bed. When I stayed at one of the Dutch summer places I was given a historic suite, built several centuries ago and usually reserved for distinguished guests. The rooms were delightful and I enjoyed staying there—except when I tried to sleep. There were wonderful linens on the bed but I can never escape the feeling that the Dutch go out of their way to make themselves uncomfortable at night. There usually is a long bolster placed at the head of the bed and it is tucked in so firmly when the bed is made that I can never find a way to remove it. Then, in addition to the bolster, there are big pillows. This makes such a mass of things at the head of the bed that you do not have room to lie down and stretch out unless you are a short person, which I am not.

Struggling with this problem on one occasion, I tried sitting up to sleep but that is not satisfactory for me. About all I could do was to curl up as comfortably as possible with my feet against the footboard. Perhaps I just don't understand the sleeping habits of the Dutch.

I have a very special feeling about Queen Juliana because, like Princess Martha of Norway, she came a number of times to stay with us at Hyde Park with her husband and children. Franklin was godfather to their third daughter. She and her husband have brought up their children in a democratic way and part of the time they have attended the public schools. Once when two of the children and some small friends were walking home they passed an orchard where they picked up some apples that had fallen outside the fence but which, of course, did not belong to them. The owner called the police and a little later the police telephoned the palace and informed the then Princess Juliana that her children were more or less in custody.

"Very well," she replied, "you must deal with them just as with the others. Then telephone me again and we will come get them."

All of the children were reprimanded by the police and at least a couple of them received additional punishment at the hands of their parents when they got back to the royal palace.

I was the guest of Juliana before she became Queen at the time the University of Utrecht awarded me a degree of Doctor of Laws. It was a colorful ceremony and at the end of it the Princess and I drove in a carriage drawn by four horses, with great pomp and ceremony, to the women's house of the University. The women were very proud because it was not often that a woman was given a degree, and on this occasion they not only participated in the ceremony but served as out-riders accompanying our carriage. The Princess was at the students' house with me and I look back upon this particular incident with a great deal of pleasure.

As Queen, Juliana has worked vigorously to help develop under-standing among Europeans. She has sought with other Continental powers to awaken the peoples of Europe to their responsibilities. Her government has been influential in the Council of Europe and she has led in the humanitarian efforts of her country to help refugees. The pages of history will record that she was a woman who loved her fellow human beings.

So, feeling as I did about the Queen, I decided in 1955 to take advantage of my journey to Bangkok and visit the islands that in past years had been so strongly under Dutch influence. Dr. Gurewitsch also was a delegate to the Bangkok sessions and we planned our travel schedule with plenty of spare time. We stopped at the ranch of my son Elliott in Colorado and then continued across the Pacific to Japan and the Philippine Islands en route to the South Seas.

I should mention that during the week we spent in Japan I revisited many of the places and people I had seen in 1953 and, incidentally, I wore a pair of shoes that I did not have to untie but could easily slip off whenever we went into a shrine or a house. This is a fine idea when visiting Japan and it saved me all the tying and untying that I had gone through on my first visit. The standard of living in Japan was still poor when seen through Western eyes, but I felt that condi-tions were improving since I had been there in 1953 and that the peo-ple looked happier. One thing that had distressed me on my first trip was the number of difficult problems that would have to be overcome to establish democratic government firmly in that country. Yet when I returned there after two years I thought that the people were accept-ing more and more of the important aspects of democracy. They had gradually begun to want to take part and have a say in their govern-ment. Of course, the habits and customs developed during centuries of feudalism had not been eliminated overnight, but I thought a great change was taking place in the thinking of the people.

We flew from Japan to Hong Kong and then to Manila and touched down at Djakarta, where we were delayed two hours at the airport by some fault in the fuel tank. I was interested to see how many Indonesian families, father, mother and the children, were sitting at the airport, sipping cold drinks, watching the planes come and go and enjoying life fully although they obviously were not going anywhere themselves. I thought that the tempo of life was quite different here and perhaps in a pleasant way. There were, too, many persons at the airport who had come to meet friends arriving or to say good-by to friends departing. It made me realize that in our busy lives at home we should take time out more often to meet people when they come to our country from distant lands. We are usually content if we have flowers or a note of welcome awaiting them at their hotel, but it was wonderful at Djakarta to see the flowers and their donors at the airport; nothing is too much trouble for these people if it will add to your comfort and pleasure.

While we waited our pilot stopped to chat and said: "If you want to go out of the way a bit, I'll show you some volcanoes on the way to Bali." We agreed, and took off on a trip over green rice paddies and mountains and—true to the pilot's promise—six volcanoes. He circled low over the craters and in several we could see fires burning because they had been active not long before. It reminded me of the time when I was a child and, with considerable fear, looked down into the crater of Mount Vesuvius in Italy, with my father holding on to me and reassuring me.

It was almost dark when we arrived in Bali and were met by Mrs. Bagoes Oka, the charming wife of an assistant to the Governor of the province. She was a very tiny, black-haired woman wearing a simple cotton print tied at the waist with a broad belt.

"I am to be your guide," Mrs. Oka said. "You are invited to dine with the Governor and tomorrow morning I will take you to the village where you will be able to live in a Balinese house while you are here."

Mrs. Oka had been on a trip several years earlier to the United States at the invitation of our State Department, and had visited several other countries. She had six sons, ranging in age from two to twelve, she taught English and biology in a high school, she had lectured to women in all of the islands and was a great help to us during our visit to Bali.

The next day we drove to the village of Ubud through country that was green and seemed to have plenty of water. We stopped at a large compound with mud walls. There was an open market at the gate with all kinds of foods and handwork on display.

"This is the local Rajah's house," Mrs. Oka told us. "You will stay here in one of the guest houses." The Rajah, it turned out, was a plump little man in a sacklike gown tied at the middle with a broad sash. For economic reasons, he had converted his compound into a kind of hotel. We went into an outer court where there were guest houses and then into the inner court, where there were others. These guest houses each had one room, with mud and wood walls and thatched roofs. There was little in the way of modern plumbing. The washing facilities were in a small separate room which one reached by going through an archway. There also was a wide veranda with chairs and tables.

The third and final courtyard contained the Rajah's own house and behind it were the cooking facilities for the entire establishment. All the cooking was done over an open wood fire. There were no set hours for meals; food was produced at any hour the various guests asked for it and was produced in a remarkably short time. But I regret to say that the meals generally were very poor for my taste, and the accommodations were not much better.

"The most important part of the house is where you sleep," Mrs. Oka told me. "Then comes the kitchen."

On this basis, I wondered what the rest of the Rajah's house might be like. I shared my guest house in the compound with an American woman who was traveling by herself and who had wanted to visit Ubud, which is well known as the residence of various foreign painters who live in Bali. We were allotted a high ceremonial stand where we had our meals in the middle of the inner court. There were at least three one-room cottages in the court and probably more, in addition to the Rajah's house. To reach the little dining place, one climbed up six steep stone steps. The thatched roof was woven over bamboo poles and shaped into a high peak. It was supported by wooden posts and framework, all of which were beautifully carved and, I suppose, looked very romantic in the moonlight.

I must say that I did not find my one-room cottage so romantic. I shall never forget waking up in the morning and looking up through the mosquito netting at the thatched roof. There I saw a number of very colorful and pretty little objects hanging down. As I watched they moved—and then I saw that they were the tails of lizards clinging to the ceiling! I could only hope they stayed there until I managed to get up and dress, which fortunately they did. The lizards were decorative as they scurried across the thatched roof, but they were not exactly what I looked for or wanted in my bedroom.

The basic food of the people is rice for every meal, usually with vegetables, but there is a feast about once a week when they eat chicken and pork and make up for the lack of variety in their daily diet. We did not have to eat rice all the time, but I must say that later when I moved to a little Dutch hotel overlooking the water the meals were good and I was so much more comfortable that it seemed like heaven.

Nevertheless, I was glad to have had the experience of staying in the Rajah's compound. He invited us one evening to listen to his private orchestra playing in the courtyard for a dancing class for little boys and girls. Only a rajah would be rich enough to afford an orchestra of his own. The instruments are expensive so usually a whole village joins in providing an orchestra for the Balinese dancing. The Rajah's orchestra was made up of villagers who worked during the daytime at a variety of occupations, but he provided the instruments for them. The music was simple and sweet and very pleasant to my ears.

One of the most interesting things was to go in the evening to another courtyard and watch the older women making up the dancers, most of whom were from seven to ten years old. The dances are really a kind of religious ceremony and all the girls who dance in the temples must be virgins. The ceremony of preparing the young girls for the dance at the Rajah's compound took place at one side of the courtyard under flickering lights put up for the occasion. The older women rouged the cheeks and drew dark lines around the eyes of the tiny dancers so that all the faces assumed a formal masklike appearance. Flowers were arranged in their hair and all of them were very lovely-looking by the time the dance started, even though they had lost some of their childlike appearance.

Just to sit on our porch and watch the endless flow of people through and past the compound walls was interesting. Some came into the compound to seek the advice of the Rajah or to sell sarongs, paintings or beads. They would place their wares on the floor for inspection and stand silently by, never urging anyone to buy. And if you did not want to buy anything they left in silence.

I do not want to try to describe Bali and its people because they have been written about so often and so skillfully by many noted authors. But I do want to remark that I never saw so many dancers or so much dancing day after day, and most of it very interesting. The whole population seems to learn to dance at an early age, and by the time a girl is thirteen years old she is generally regarded as old enough to stop dancing and get married. Before she is much older, she is expected to work in the rice fields or even help build houses or carry heavy burdens, including stones, on her head.

One afternoon we were invited to visit a nearby group of dancers who had been to the United States and had had a great success there. One would have thought they would have been considered very important citizens since they had traveled far and appeared on the New York stage. But that was not exactly the case.

"Before they went away," I was told, "everybody knew them and they were like all other young girls in the village. They could dance, but so could all the other girls and nobody thought anything about it. But then they went to the United States and were showered with praise and adulation. For almost a year they lived a quite different existence than they had known and when they returned here perhaps they thought that this admiration and praise would be continued. But here they were again just some girl dancers who had been away and it proved difficult for them to adjust to village life. In fact, they are now too old to dance and younger girls are taking their places."

We saw all kinds of dancing. Very small children took part in some of the dances but most of those we saw were in their early teens. Usually the dance enacted a story. One was the dance of self-defense, in which young men move with great beauty and swing swords with furious enthusiasm. Another is the dance done only at dawn or sunset known as the struggle between good and evil. The dancers, all men, work themselves into a frenzy and, near the end, draw knives which they brandish wildly. The idea is that if they have made themselves spiritually strong enough the knives will not penetrate their skin. One young dancer we saw worked himself up to such a pitch that when the dance ended he would not give up his knife and it took three men to get it away from him and bring him back to normal.

The people, however, are quiet and peace-loving and most of the dances are less strenuous or dangerous. One night the dancers of Ubud put on for us a special dance that is usually done in preparation for the period in which burials take place. When a person dies the body is wrapped and laid away but the cremation may not take place for some time, since the priest must be consulted and must set an auspicious date. Or a poor family may have to wait until they have accumulated enough for the feast and other festivities in honor of the dead. Death is not an occasion for sorrow and there is no mourning, for if the dead person has lived well on this earth the people believe that he or she will progress to something better.

For this dance the whole village gathered in the outer courtyard of the Rajah's compound. At the back, little portable shops selling food were set up, each with an oil lamp burning. The crowd sat around the cleared central space facing a shrine which was outlined by lamps to the very top, where an agile little boy had to climb to put a lamp so high that it looked like a twinkling star. The orchestra sat on the ground at one side and the musical pipes made a lovely sound.

The dancers came slowly down the steps of the shrine, one at a time. They spoke the lines of the old story, based on religious themes of India, and the people listened intently although they knew the lines by heart. The actors also interpolated jokes on current political or other affairs into their lines and the crowd laughed wildly. The play or dance moved very slowly, the steps sedate and drawn out so that one could watch each movement and enjoy its beauty. Every flutter of a finger, every motion of a fan had some special meaning.

Almost everywhere we went there was some kind of dancing, on street corners or in homes or in public halls. We even went to a dance held in connection with a tooth-filing ceremony for one of the children of the house. The teeth are filed when the children near the age of maturity. On this occasion the actual filing had already been done and the dance was more like a social occasion. There was a professional dancing girl who first danced alone. Then she singled out a boy in the crowd, touched him with her fan and he had to come out, put on a ceremonial overskirt and dance with her. The boy she picked was very shy and reluctant. He finally got on the dance floor, but a moment later his overskirt fell off and he ran away, apparently with great relief. The girl then picked out another boy to dance. Such parties often go on all night, we were told.

By the time we left Bali for Djakarta and Bangkok I felt I had seen enough dancing to last me the rest of my life, but it was the kind of dancing that goes with the island and its people and we thoroughly enjoyed our visit.

The meeting of the World Federation of United Nations Associations in Bangkok was interesting but not particularly newsworthy. We were greeted upon arrival by the Prime Minister, Field Marshal P. Pibul Songgram, and his wife as well as people from the United States Embassy. I found the city unusual and interesting despite the fact that it was the rainy season and sheets of water fell during the afternoons.

Thanks to a hospitable government, a number of us were able to make a trip to see Angkor Wat, the famous temple of the ancient Khmer Empire of Cambodia. We went by plane over a fertile valley where, in the rainy season, there was water everywhere. While still aloft we could see the temples at Angkor Thom and Angkor Wat. I thought they were the most impressive monuments I had ever seen.

We approached through the outer gate of Angkor Wat, which is some distance from the temple. The temple itself is built of huge stones fitted together without cement. There are five high acorn-shaped towers that rise some two hundred feet and form a kind of central pyramid. The walls are elaborately carved, and by studying them one could get a good idea of the whole history of this part of Asia. As we climbed the steps at one corner we passed statues of Buddha on each level, and on two levels at the very center is the shrine of Vishnu with a central figure and several smaller statues.

We climbed to the top of the temple, up narrow and well-worn steps, some of which were blocks of stone two feet high. Our guide was most considerate, leading us to the steps that he thought we would find easiest to climb, but none was easy and one surmised that this climb had been intended to be a test for the faithful. From the top, the view was magnificent and we could see the plain stretching out below for many miles.

I had a warming experience in this ancient and faraway part of the world. An officer of the Thai Air Force offered us some tea at one of our stops, and then spoke to me.

"I have long wanted to meet you to thank you for your husband's kindness," he said. "He made it possible for me to attend West Point. I was the first from my country to be educated there and it was your husband who signed a special bill enabling me to attend. I have always been grateful."

XVIII

KING MOHAMMED

There is another journey to a new and developing country which I want to describe before I come to what was to me the most important experience in recent years. But to do it I shall have to switch back to Hyde Park to a time not long after Morocco had achieved its independence from French colonial rule. One day Archie Roosevelt, one of the State Department's experts on the Arab world, telephoned me and asked if an old friend of his could come to my house for tea. I said I should be delighted but was later amazed when a huge limousine arrived. A small girl got out, then an American woman, then a Moroccan woman and finally two Moroccan men carrying a huge box of flowers.

I had not been expecting such a delegation but it turned out that one of the men was the chief adviser to Sultan Mohammed V of Morocco, who later became King Mohammed V. They had come to place flowers on my husband's grave and I had thought they were just coming for tea. They explained that they had expected to meet two officials from the State Department when they reached Hyde Park, but something had gone wrong and they did not show up until later.

After we had had tea, the adviser to the Sultan arose rather mysteriously and said: "Mrs. Roosevelt, I would like to speak to you alone."

After the others had left the room, he continued: "We Moroccans never forget a kindness. The Sultan asked me to say to you that he recalls your husband as one foreign head of state who gave him disinterested advice. He wants me to say that he believes there would have been no secret treaty between France and the United States in connection with the establishment of United States air bases in Morocco if your husband had lived. But we do not blame the United States for making the treaty and we will raise no difficulties now in the negotiations on the bases between your government and ours.

"The Sultan also extends an invitation for you to visit Morocco."

"I am grateful for the Sultan's invitation and message," I replied. "But at the present time I do not believe there is much possibility of arranging for a visit to Morocco, although I should like to go there sometime." They then left, accompanied by the head of the Memorial Library, Herman Kahn, to place flowers on my husband's grave.

I thought no more about the invitation, but a few months later some friends of mine in New York told me that a problem had arisen in connection with a large group of Jews in Morocco who wanted to migrate to Israel. They had been granted visas by the French government and were all prepared to go but, at the last minute, the Moroccan officials raised various obstacles to their departure.

"The French constabulary has been withdrawn and there is a good deal of Arab hostility toward the Jews," I was told. "They are now in temporary camps which are crowded and unsanitary, and there is fear of an epidemic. We have tried to get something done to bring about their release but with no success and we have not been able to get any word from the Sultan. Do you think you might appeal to him?"

"I will write him a letter," I said. I wrote it at once, saying that the Jews apparently were in considerable danger and also that there was fear of an epidemic that might endanger everybody in that area. I said I knew that he was interested in all people and I hoped he could do something to relieve the situation. I did not receive any reply to my letter. But not long afterward I learned that the necessary permission for the Jewish group to leave Morocco had been issued and that they had gone to Israel about two weeks after I wrote to the Sultan.

In 1957, the Crown Prince of Morocco and his sister visited the United States and the Crown Princess came to call on me. She was accompanied by the wife of the Moroccan ambassador and several other ladies, and by the Moroccan Minister to the United Nations. As they were leaving, the Princess spoke briefly with the Minister and he turned to me.

"My Princess says that her father, the Sultan, extends an invitation for you to visit our country," he said.

I expressed my appreciation and my hopes that I could make the trip sometime, but said I had no idea when. Then, late in the winter of 1957, Dr. Gurewitsch told me that he was planning to take his daughter Grania to North Africa for a vacation and, finally, we decided to go as a party and visit Morocco. My son Elliott and his wife joined us, as did their friends Mr. and Mrs. Cummings Catherwood and their daughter and Mrs. Mildred Morton. So at last I was able to accept the Sultan's invitation.

We left New York when the first signs of spring were visible in March, flew through snow and then on to a foggy Lisbon, where we had to circle for some time until the sun burned through and revealed the lovely green hills of the seacoast and a fairylike castle surrounded by charming white houses with red roofs. The air was soft when we landed and the orange zinnias were in bloom. In Madrid the next day, we were joined by Mrs. Catherwood and her young daughter for the three-hour flight from Spain to Casablanca, where we arrived after dark.

The white-robed Governor of Casablanca and a representative of the Sultan were at the airport to greet us. With them was Kenneth Pendar, whom Elliott and Dr. Gurewitsch greeted joyfully and persuaded to help us plan our visit. Elliott was in Morocco with the Air Force during the war and was assigned to his father when Franklin and Winston Churchill held their historic conference in Casablanca, so he knows the area well. The hotel where we stopped was the Anfa, where the conferences had been held. The house in which Mr. Churchill had stayed was now the United States Consulate, and we went there after dinner to call on Consul General Henry H. Ford.

The next morning I awoke early and went for a walk before breakfast. As the sun burned through the early-morning fog the flowers were lovely in the bright light. I walked among palms, cedars and eucalyptus trees, the latter having been imported to this area from Australia. The peaches were ripening, as were huge grapefruits, but the orange season was almost over. We spent only a day in Casablanca before driving to the capital, Rabat.

I was much interested in the country we drove through and in the people. I have never felt that the French were the best colonizers in the world, but, for that matter, no country can give another everything that it needs. The French had left in Morocco good roads and hospitals. Under Marshal Lyautey, they also had kept something of the old flavor of the country; instead of permitting ancient Arab towns to be torn down for new buildings they had seen to it that the new construction was outside the old sections. But the French residents of Morocco had almost a monopoly on power and irrigation and the Arab fields that we drove through were burned up by a severe drought. This naturally did not make the Arabs friendly toward the French colonizers. The Arab schools were poor and the country has a low literacy rate and, as usual, the masses have a very low standard of living. The Moroccans value their independence but the government had had to start almost from scratch and there was so very much to be done.

Under the expert guidance of Mr. and Mrs. Kenneth Pendar, we visited the Hassan Tower at Rabat—a beautiful tower that seems to change color in the twilight and in the dawn. Then we went to the walled Oudaïa Gardens, a peaceful spot with storks nesting all along the high walls. I had noticed that day the contrast of well-kept houses and dingy little huts in the same areas. People from the parched rural areas had flooded into the cities in the hope of earning a living, and this had created a serious problem. The government had done some building on the outskirts of Casablanca and Rabat to house the new arrivals but there were many who had had to erect shelters out of any materials they could get their hands on.

I was, as usual, curious about living conditions, so when we were at the Oudaïa Gardens I wandered along the top of the wall and looked down into the little alleyways between the crowded houses. At one point I could see into one of the houses and I was staring intently if impolitely into the establishment when one of the occupants saw me. She promptly began shouting and gesturing, soundly denouncing me for my impertinence in invading the privacy of her home, and I hurriedly turned away in some confusion!

Generally speaking, I thought that it was remarkable that the Moroccan people, who for the most part live in great insecurity, had not been lured into Communism. I later visited the home of an unemployed man who had come with his family from a farming area in a vain effort to find work in Rabat. Since there is not much industry in Morocco, he was probably worse off than before coming to the city. He was a thin, pleasant man of about forty, wearing tan cotton pants and shirt (with the tail outside) that had been washed so many times that they were almost colorless.

There were five tiny huts in a cluster and this man was one of fifteen persons who lived there, all of them cooking their meals over the same outdoor stove. The man's family included his wife, mother, married sister, a little girl and a baby. The establishment was clean and well-swept, but they had almost nothing in the way of furnishings and the children were obviously suffering from malnutrition.

"They get bread and mint tea," the man told me, "and once a week they get a piece of meat."

The little girl, wearing a clean but worn white cotton dress, came back from school while I was there. Following the custom of the country, she kissed everyone's hand from her grandmother's to the tiny baby's. It seemed to me a good custom and I was impressed that even in such difficult conditions the habits of family life were so carefully preserved. Before we departed, the man and his wife offered us tea with a wonderful gesture of hospitality, although they certainly did not have enough for themselves. This respect for customs I was to observe later in quite a different setting when we visited the Sultan's palace.

The Sultan had been in the hospital for an operation but only a couple of days afterward he invited our whole group to the palace. We drove to the palace late in the afternoon and were immediately ushered into the large reception room. Chairs were placed around the room in a semicircle. There were beautiful rugs on the floor. Mohammed V awaited us in a big chair on a raised platform. Despite his recent operation, he rose to greet me and I introduced the other members of our party to him. We were served refreshments as we chatted, and he politely asked the various members of the group about their interests and occupations. After a short time, the others left but he asked Elliott and me to remain for a less formal talk.

It was at this point that I witnessed a repetition of the little scene that had impressed me earlier. The Sultan's son, who had been with us, wished to leave on affairs of his own. So he whispered something to his father and then kissed his hand twice and walked to the door, where he turned and bowed. The same family courtesy and affection,

I thought, are shown in both the most insignificant and the most influential families in the land.

The Sultan was young and handsome, with a sensitive and kindly face. There was humor in his eyes and his slender hands were expressive as he passed the usual string of beads through his fingers. He wore long white robes—white over some delicate color—and a small cap. His conversation made it clear that he was alert and deeply concerned about the welfare of the people, their need for economic security and for aid in developing social services. But he was also well aware of the international complications affecting the Arab world. From his remarks, I felt that he hoped the three North African countries of Morocco, Tunisia and Algeria might become a kind of bridge between the East and West, helping to ease the tensions created by extremist Arab nationalism in such countries as Egypt and Syria and to bring about a better understanding among nations.

I had felt since our arrival that there was on the part of the Moroccans a greater warmth toward the United States than in other Arab countries but perhaps I did not fully understand it until we had talked with the Sultan. This attitude of friendship went back to the time during World War II when Franklin and Prime Minister Winston Churchill met at Casablanca. The French officials then ruling Morocco paid them a formal call, and when they departed Franklin said:

"Now we must see the Sultan."

Mr. Churchill looked at him without much enthusiasm.

"Why should we do that?" he asked. "We have seen the French."

"We must see the Sultan," my husband replied, "because this is his country."

So Franklin wrote a note in longhand to the Sultan, inviting him and the Crown Prince and members of the Sultan's household to dinner. The Sultan and Franklin talked with great enthusiasm about what might be done to improve conditions in Morocco after the war. My husband always had a horror of seeing unproductive land anywhere, and he believed that proper methods could do much to restore the fertility of desert areas in Morocco.

"You will doubtless find oil in your desert," he told the Sultan. "But when you do you must never turn all the concessions over to any foreign country. Keep control of a part of the oil, for I feel sure there are underground rivers under the Sahara. Once this area was the bread basket of the Mediterranean. It can be again if you keep control of some of your oil and have the power to pump the water to the surface."

It was this that the Sultan was thinking about when he said my husband gave him disinterested advice that convinced him of the friendship of the United States. His attitude of helpfulness had become known everywhere in Morocco and many persons told me that the assurance of the friendship of the United States was a kind of milestone in the Moroccan campaign for independence.

A few days after our talk with the Sultan I witnessed another and unusual demonstration of the friendship of the people when we visited Marrakech and the area in the foothills of the Atlas Mountains. Shortly before noon one day we started out from Marrakech in three automobiles. The countryside was parched and dusty and the roads were sometimes mere tracks of dirt. We passed a great assemblage of perhaps two hundred camels as we left the city and later came upon a well where a bullock walked slowly around and around in a circle, drawing water for irrigation of the desert fields. As we bounced across the hills we came upon a wonderful view of the little village of Demnat, which lay on a hilltop beyond a dry, brown plain with the mountains rising up behind.

There were a few travelers on the road, some driving little flocks of sheep through swirling clouds of dust as we drove to the residence of the Caid, some distance from Demnat. The leading officials of the town were there to greet us and the Caid had prepared the usual Arab feast, great platters of rice and mutton and sweets that must be eaten with the fingers. These feasts, I am sure, are never eaten as everyday meals. They are too elaborate and they keep one too long at table, but they symbolize the Moroccan's desire to give you his best. It was not always possible for us to enjoy the feasts because we ate too much and the food seemed to us to be very heavy, with a good deal of grease, for warm weather. My daughter-in-law Minnewa finally rebelled and exclaimed: "I just won't eat it again! I just won't!" I was a bit frightened that she would create an international incident by her attitude, but our hosts were kind and friendly people, and probably did not understand her.

After the feast, the officials of Demnat accompanied us on across the plain to their ancient walled town, one of the oldest in Morocco, dating back to the tenth century. The road was a rough dirt track and the dust was thick and the sun was hot, but a large and very enthusiastic crowd had gathered outside the main gate to the town.

"Welcome!" they shouted as our automobiles drew up. "Welcome!"

Even more impressive to me was the fact that they had made a crude American flag, which was hung over the gate, and a sign saying: "We always remember President Roosevelt!"

I got out of the car and walked with the officials through the crowd and into the old city, where we were greeted warmly and followed along the narrow, twisting streets by many of the citizens. I was very happy that I had come to Morocco and especially that I had visited dusty little Demnat, because I felt there could have been no better demonstration of the friendly feelings of the people for my country.

The more I traveled throughout the world, the more I realized how important it is for Americans to see with understanding eyes the other peoples of the world whom modern means of communication and transportation are constantly making closer neighbors. Yet, the more I traveled, the happier I was that I happened to have been born in the United States, where there exist the concept of freedom and opportunities of advancement for individuals of every status. I felt, too, the great responsibility that has come, with our good fortune, to us as a people. The world is looking to us for leadership in almost every phase of development of the life of peoples everywhere. We had— we still have—the opportunity to live up to that call for leadership of a free world, and there has never been any doubt in my mind that we will live up to it.

But leadership is a stern, demanding role and no person or state can lead without earning that right. On my visit to the Soviet Union in 1957 I was strongly impressed—I was almost frightened—by many things that showed how hard we must strive if we are to maintain our position of world leadership.

XIX

IN THE LAND OF
THE SOVIETS

I have written frequently in this book about my enjoyment from visiting many delightful places around the world, including the police-run state of Yugoslavia. I would not want to live in Yugoslavia, nor would anyone who values personal freedom. But I think I should die if I had to live in Soviet Russia. I traveled there extensively for almost a month in 1957. When I went to Moscow, the Stalinist dictatorship had been replaced by the less fearful—in theory, at least—dictatorship of Nikita S. Khrushchev, but the people still existed under a system of surveillance that must cause anxiety and the power over them still seemed to me a hand of steel.

I make these observations because my trip to the Soviet Union was certainly, to me, one of the most important, the most interesting and the most informative that I ever made. I tried to understand what was happening in Russia by looking at the country through Russian eyes, and unless all of us in the free world approach the Soviet Union from that point of view we are going to deceive ourselves in a catastrophic manner. I remembered that only forty years ago this great mass of people was largely made up of peasants living in houses with mud floors and, perhaps, with a farm animal or two in the kitchen in wintry weather. They were illiterate. They were oppressed. They were, as I well remembered, frightened of conquest by the Germans and, for many years, were bound together by a readiness to defend their homeland no matter how hard their lives might be.

We must never forget these things when we look at what Russia is today. I looked and was rather frightened. My fear was not of the Communist power or philosophy, not of awesome missiles or hydrogen bombs. What I feared was that we would not understand the nature of the Russian Revolution that is still going on and what it means to the world. If we fail to understand, then we shall fail to protect world democracy no matter what missiles or earth satellites or atomic warships we produce. So I want to explain carefully why I was frightened.

I must start my explanation back in the spring of 1957 when Dorothy Schiff, the publisher and owner of the New York *Post,* invited me to luncheon and posed a question:

"Would you like to go to China and write a series of articles for the *Post?*"

"I certainly would," I replied.

"Well, you make your application to the State Department for a visa and I will make the other arrangements."

I applied to the State Department and was refused a visa. I was quite irritated at the time. I believed that the Department was following a foolish policy in refusing to give visas to newspapermen to go to the biggest Communist country in the world so that we might at least have information about what the Communist regime was doing.

"It seems to me," I told Mrs. Schiff, "that it would be of value to see and learn whatever we can. If anybody is going to refuse, I should expect it to be the Chinese Communists."

"Would you be willing to make a legal test in the courts of the Department's right to refuse a visa?" she asked. I said I wasn't sure. I thought it over for a couple of days, but finally declined.

"It would be better," I said, "to let the newspapers carry on the negotiations with the Department."

Later, some of my irritation with the State Department waned. The Department, of course, has a responsibility to stand behind its visas and to afford protection to citizens traveling abroad on its passports. So I felt they had a right to point out that it was impossible to provide any protection for our citizens traveling in Communist China. However, it seemed to me that the Department could say that if newspapermen wanted to go to China under those conditions they were free to go, provided the Chinese Government would permit them entry. In any event, I did not get a visa to China and Mrs. Schiff asked me if I would go to Russia instead.

"Yes," I replied, "but I can't go until September, and I would want to take my secretary, Miss Corr, and Dr. Gurewitsch. He can speak Russian and his medical knowledge would also be of great importance in connection with my investigation of conditions."

Mrs. Schiff agreed to my proposal and we began making arrangements. It took three months to get our visas approved by the Russians. Dr. Gurewitsch's parents were Russian. He had been born in Switzerland but his birth was registered with the Russian Consulate and he had later visited his grandparents in Russia when he was a boy. He put down his entire history in applying for a Russian visa, but some of his friends were fearful that the Communist officials might cause trouble or even hold him in Russia. I thought that idea was foolish but I wrote to the Russian Embassy about it and was informed that there would be no trouble.

At the end of August, the three of us flew to Frankfurt and Berlin, where I was surprised to see how much building had been done since my last visit and how rapid the German recovery had been. From Berlin we flew to Copenhagen early in the morning and there shifted to the Scandinavian airline to Moscow. The plane was crowded, mostly with American and British tourists, but there also were some Central Europeans from the Soviet satellite countries. We stopped at Riga for passport examination and luncheon but were not allowed to leave the airport. That afternoon we flew on across Russia. I was surprised that so much of the country we passed over was wooded, for I had always thought of Russia as rather treeless steppes. It was getting dark as we approached Moscow but we could see that much new construction was in progress in the city; in many places the cranes and skeletons of buildings stuck up against the skyline. There were a surprising number of airplanes, most of them two-engine craft, on the ground at the Moscow airport, about the number one would see upon landing at Idlewild or La Guardia airports in New York.

Two young men from the United States Embassy met us at the airport, and we were also greeted by representatives of Intourist, the Soviet travel bureau, which was arranging my schedule of travel. I was not a "guest of the government" but was traveling as a reporter, and the Russians correctly treated me as they would have treated any other tourist-reporter except perhaps for the fact that my interpreter was Anna Lavrova, a charming and intelligent young woman.

"I was interpreter for President Roosevelt when he met with Premier Stalin and Prime Minister Churchill at Yalta in 1945," she told me. "I also saw your granddaughter Kate, when she was on a trip to Russia last year. She was very pretty and we liked her very much."

I said I thought it was a wonderful compliment that she should remember Kate after so long a time. I spoke to some of the American newspaper correspondents at the field and then Mrs. Lavrova took us into the airport building and to the office of the Intourist people. They gave me books of tickets that had to be presented when you ate your meals, four meal tickets for each day, including one for tea.

"An automobile will be at your disposal," Mrs. Lavrova said. "When would you like to talk to the head of Intourist?"

"I tried to arrange through the Consulate in New York for appointments with various government officials," I replied. "They insisted that I should wait until I arrived in Moscow. So I would like to go over my schedule with Intourist tomorrow morning."

"I will arrange it," she replied.

Going from the airport into Moscow—it is about fifteen miles—we crept along in two automobiles at what seemed to me to be a snail's pace. I didn't like to say anything but finally Dr. Gurewitsch said: "Perhaps they are going so slowly because they are respectful of your age, Mrs. Roosevelt?"

"In that case," I said, "we had better find out."

So we asked what the speed limit was on that road and, since it was considerably more than our rate of speed, we suggested that we speed up. The driver did step up the pace and we rolled into the city at a reasonable clip. My first impression of Moscow was that there were buildings going up everywhere. We drove past the lower side of the Kremlin on the way to the National Hotel, and it was very impressive with its many lights and high walls.

At the hotel, Mrs. Lavrova accompanied me to my apartment—a sitting room, bedroom and bath. The furnishings were ornate and heavy, yellow damask, carved table legs and a generally old-fashioned atmosphere; and the plumbing, while all right, was far from modern.

"The furniture in this suite," Mrs. Lavrova told me, "was taken to

Yalta and was in the suite your husband stayed in there. Later it was brought back here."

So some effort had been made to be hospitable and thoughtful; I appreciated it and was very comfortable.

After dinner at the hotel (of course we had caviar) we got into our car and drove around Moscow. The width of the main streets astonished us. It had begun to rain but we stopped on one side of the Red Square and, while Dr. Gurewitsch took pictures of the Kremlin, we looked in the windows of the big department store called GUM. This store covers three blocks, but the variety of goods was limited and the prices very high. Our window shopping ended, we drove on to get the atmosphere of the city before going back to the hotel.

The next morning Miss Corr and Dr. Gurewitsch had breakfast with me in my room. I had orange juice, tea, toast and honey and they each had a boiled egg. The weather was good and my high-ceilinged room with its tall windows and a balcony overlooking the Kremlin's red sandstone walls was pleasant. In fact, we were fortunate in having good weather for most of our visit and it was only later in September that the air turned a little coldish, something like November at home.

The food was generally good at the hotel and we ate almost no place else, because prices were extremely high in the few restaurants that we might have patronized. There were borscht with big pieces of meat and much cabbage in it, and chicken and, of course, tea and caviar and cakes and lots of ice cream. The Russians seem to love ice cream, which is not expensive, and you see them eating it all the time. You are not supposed to tip waiters or chambermaids or anyone else, but service at the hotel was very good and the maids in their neat aprons and black dresses and the waiters in white coats were always pleasant, at least to us.

I might say now that the Russians generally do not dress well. The government has discouraged any display in dressing because it is not important to the economic welfare of the country. Prices of clothes are very high by American standards and there is little good to be said for quality or variety. As a result, the people, whether on the street or in offices or working at manual labor, are dressed warmly but monotonously, usually in dark colors and without distinction. The only exceptions I saw were some colorful native costumes in cities far from Moscow—or perhaps worn by a provincial visitor to the capital. It is expected that the fashion picture will change when more consumer goods come on the market, but it seemed to me then that about the only word for the dress of the people was "drab."

The day after our arrival I called at our Embassy and then went to the Intourist offices, where I talked with the head of the bureau. We went over my travel plans in detail.

"I want to go as far away from Moscow as possible," I said, "because I want to see all aspects of the country. I have always been fascinated by Tashkent and Samarkand. Perhaps I could go there unless it is too far off the beaten path."

The bureau director smiled. "We have a commercial jet airplane service to Tashkent every day," he replied, "and it will be very simple to arrange. The flight takes four hours."

So he put Tashkent on the schedule, and Stalingrad, and a boat trip on the Volga, and the Black Sea and Leningrad and Kiev. But once I started traveling I'm afraid I didn't stick very closely to the schedule—much to the dismay of Intourist—and in the end I had to cancel some of the trips because of lack of time. Whenever I decided that I needed more time in some place and changed the schedule, the Intourist people went into a polite tizzy. They weren't used to having schedules changed because most Russian travelers more or less go where they are told to go when they are told to go.

"You can't change it," I was told time and again. And when I said I was going to change it, they came back with: "It will cost extra."

I proved to be pretty good at arguing, through Mrs. Lavrova, and actually had to pay extra only once.

I had made requests for interviews with a number of government officials as soon as I arrived in Moscow but it proved as difficult for me as for any other reporter to get specific dates confirmed. For a while I thought I would never get to see any top officials, including Mr. Khrushchev, because I was told they were very busy or they were away on vacation or they just couldn't be reached. But I persisted, going back to Intourist day after day to insist, and eventually I made most of the appointments I wanted. Then, when I kept the appointments, I was received with graciousness and friendliness and was given every assistance, including permission to visit many institutes and projects under the various ministries.

We discovered another thing, too, which I suppose all foreign reporters in Russia know. If you want to get something done, go to the head man. When we wanted to visit certain projects, we were given evasive answers by numerous subordinates. They put us off or said they would have to ask higher authority. But when we went to the top official concerned, we always were immediately given permission and a guide to take us around.

After a few days of seeing the ballet, visiting museums and attending a very good one-ring circus, Miss Corr and I were driven to a state farm about twenty miles from Moscow. There are two kinds of farms in the Soviet Union—state farms owned by the government, which hires and pays the workers, who have no personal interest in production, and collective farms where the land is owned, worked collectively and managed by private owners who elect one of the group as their head. Both types of farms are under state supervision.

Workers on the farms are given a house and a small plot of land which they may cultivate for themselves. Of course, the workers on a state farm do not take the risks that a collective farmer does. The collective farmer is in difficulties in a poor year when the crops fail; in a good year, however, he is able to raise his income considerably.

The state farm I visited was called Lesnie Poljana, meaning Prairie Among the Forest. The state-appointed manager told me that they had two thousand acres under cultivation and that they had a breed of milk cows, called Holmogor, for which they raise food.

"There are 550 pedigreed cattle on the farm," he said, "and 226 of them are milk producers. The milk is all shipped in cans to institutions in Moscow."

Some 230 persons worked on the farm throughout the year and about 20 others were hired in the busy summer season. Women do what we think of as men's work all over Russia—street cleaning and section-hand work on the railroads—and they did much of the work in the cow barns at this farm. There were some milking machines but most of the milking was done by hand. The beef cattle did not look particularly well fattened and throughout Russia I found that the meat is not so tender as ours, apparently because it is not hung so long. Even the chickens are usually freshly killed and therefore not very tender, so that one rarely had roast chicken. It usually was boiled or minced in croquettes or used in soup.

"May I visit one of the workers' homes?" I asked at Lesnie Poljana.

"Certainly," my guide replied, "but we must wait until the lunch hour."

At that time, they led the way to what was obviously one of the newest homes on the farm. But just across the street I noticed several older houses.

"I would prefer to see the ones across the street," I said.

"Oh, no. They are not as good as these homes because the families living there do not have separate entrances."

There did seem to be a great many persons going and coming around the older houses. My guide steered me firmly into the new house, which had a good-sized plot of ground and was surrounded by a fence. We went in a little entry, where the walls were lined with winter coats hanging on nails. Down a short corridor on the right was a small kitchen, which had the traditional wood stove and a one-plate electric burner.

Our hostess, who was one of the workers in the cattle barns, led us into the only other room in the cottage—a dining and living and sleeping room. The dining table stood in the middle with chairs around it. There were two beds on opposite walls and a sofa bed on the third. There also were a couple of extra chairs, a radio set and a television set. It was very crowded.

"Do you have running water in the house?" I asked the woman.

"No, but I do not have to carry it very far. We hope that in another year we will have it piped into the house."

The house was immaculate and the woman seemed to feel that they were fairly well off. She earned about eight hundred rubles ($80) a month and her husband, working in a nearby factory, earned one thousand rubles.

Not long after visiting the state farm, we took the jet airliner for Tashkent, where I had a chance to visit a collective farm. Travel on Soviet airlines is casual. Our Intourist people checked our bags for us when we went to the Moscow airport early in the morning and we waited in a small room which, I believe, was reserved for special passengers. After a few minutes a young man came in and said:

"All who are going to Tashkent follow me."

So we followed him on a long walk to the airplane, a sleek and efficient-looking machine. Each of us had a seat number. There was a stewardess but she was not in uniform and nobody said anything about not smoking or about fastening your seat belts (which were there, but seldom used). There was an altimeter where we could see it on the front wall of the compartment and I noticed that we climbed very rapidly and flew very high. It was comfortable but I could see little or nothing of the countryside. After a while the stewardess served fruit and cookies and then, less than four hours after we left Moscow, we came down at Tashkent, some two thousand miles away.

There was more desert here than I had expected and the green areas were confined to the source of water or to irrigated sections. Part of Tashkent dates back to the twelfth century, and this old section was being slowly torn down, the streets were being widened and new, modern apartment houses were being built. We drove into the city over broad avenues with trolley cars and big cement homes and office buildings, but later we did have a chance to see some of the narrow streets that still remain in the old city. The contrast was very great, indeed.

The collective farm that we visited—Uzbekistan Farm—was owned by an organization of farmers. Out of the over-all income of the farm, 7 per cent goes to the government in taxes. Another 16 per cent goes for capital reserve, 1 per cent to amortization and the like. Thirteen per cent goes into the operation of services, of which there are many, and the remaining cash is divided among members of the collective. We were told that a man might get about eight thousand rubles a year in cash on this basis, plus shelter, services, food and so on, which means that he is fairly well off. If the crops fail, of course, he is in trouble.

Cotton was the main crop, but the farmers also raised cattle for meat and milk. There were 1,160 houses and 1,700 able workers, representing a dozen different nationalities brought together in this ancient area of Central Asia. Each farmer annually received about 30 pounds of meat, a considerable quantity of grain and 150 pounds of potatoes, in addition to which he might raise food for himself in his garden plot and keep a cow, for which the collective provided food.

"The manager is chosen by a board of directors," I was told. "He is like a chairman and serves for a year, after which he must report on the work done. If it is satisfactory, he may continue another year at the discretion of the board, which, in turn, is responsible to the members of the collective."

We walked around part of the farm. Not all the houses were new but some of the old ones had been made to look better by stuccoing the outside—although no changes seemed to have been made inside. There was no running water in any of the houses but they all had electricity, and inside I frequently saw a one-burner electric plate on top of an old wood range. Toilet and bathing facilities were old-fashioned—usually a privy and a bathhouse. One woman showed me her home with great pride because she had made or collected innumerable quilts, which seemed to be a mark of wealth in that part of the world.

In the middle of the central area was a recreation house where there were shower rooms and nearby a large pond with greenish water, which I was told was used for bathing. The recreation house was surrounded by a garden with benches where the workers could rest at noon time.

Walking past one of the cowsheds, which had no sides, I noticed a cot standing in the middle of the shed. I mentioned it to our guide, who said: "Oh, somebody sleeps there every night."

"With the cows?" I asked. "Why?"

"Just in case something happened," he replied. "A cow might be calving or any kind of emergency might occur."

Every inch of land seemed to be in use. Even where small fruit trees had been planted there were growing crops. The farm had a maternity hospital and a baby clinic but in case of serious illness the farm people go to hospitals in Tashkent. There was a nursery, a kindergarten and a school. Children were taken care of at these institutions while their parents worked in the fields, but nursing mothers could leave their work and go to the nursery at stated hours when feedings were given.

The manager of the farm said that there had been a steady increase in production in recent years, but this collective also had increased in size and it was difficult to know whether it was operating more efficiently and getting a greater yield from the land or had just acquired more acreage. Later, in Moscow, I talked about farm production with Senator Allen J. Ellender of Louisiana, who was making his third visit to Russia. He was very much interested in Russian agriculture and had been to the new area in Soviet Asia where a large region was being plowed up for the first time. The Senator felt that there was a serious danger that the new land might turn into a dust bowl as happened in parts of our Southwest after the protective grass had been stripped from the plains. He said he had written a letter to Mr. Khrushchev warning him of this danger, but that the Communist party chief had not seemed to pay any attention. Later, talking to a Deputy Minister of Agriculture, I asked him about this problem, but he said that a thorough investigation had been made before the land was plowed up and that the top soil was found to be more than three feet deep. So he was not worried either.

The Russians, incidentally, had imported some of the famous Santa Gertrudis beef cattle from the King Ranch in Texas for breeding purposes. They had been shipped to Russia several years earlier and I was told that they had "disappeared." I was curious about them and eventually inquired at the Ministry of Agriculture about what had happened to them.

"Oh, they are the special pets of the Minister," I was told. "They were shipped to the southern part of the Ukraine and they are still there and thriving. They have also had plenty of little ones!"

In visiting the Russian farmers, I realized that the officials were probably showing me agricultural projects that were better than the average. Agriculture is perhaps of greater importance in the Soviet Union than in most countries because there are so many people to be fed. The Communist rulers have had some of their greatest difficulties with the farmers and doubtless some farm communities have suffered greater hardships from political dictatorship than any other part of the population. Even with months of investigation, it would be difficult to know just how successful the government has been in its agricultural program. But the mere fact that the two farms I visited exist and are operating successfully means that more and more will be developed along the same lines or have been developed long since.

In Tashkent, it was arranged for the city architect to drive us around the newly constructed sections. I had noticed that the women working in the fields wore drab shirts and pants or one-piece cotton dresses, while in the city we often saw holiday crowds dressed in native costumes. The women wore brightly colored hats or caps on the back of their heads and dresses made of a kind of silk that is stiff and almost glazed when new but which becomes softer after it has been washed. Their dresses usually have a red base, shot with dark green, black and blue. The men, too, dressed up on Sundays or holidays and wore little black hats with white embroidery.

Our guide, the architect, insisted on showing us only the new buildings, mostly of cement, on the broad new avenues. Dr. Gurewitsch asked our driver to stop on a street where there were new buildings on one side but the houses of the old city on the other side. He got out and began taking photographs of the old houses, which bewildered and incensed our guide.

"Why do you snap all that old stuff?" he demanded. "Most of those houses are empty anyway. The people have moved out."

He could not see why we were interested in the old culture. At one point he had the driver stop in front of a large building.

"This is the College of Music," he said. "Don't you want to go in?"

I must say that I was doubtful, but we did go and were much interested. We discovered that there were actually nineteen musical colleges of one kind or another in the Republic of Uzbekistan, which is about twice the size of New York State, and that they have made strenuous efforts to preserve the old stringed instruments and songs of the people of the area.

The College of Music and similar institutions illustrate how the Communists operate. Forty years ago there were no music schools in the area and the songs of the region were handed down from generation to generation. Then Moscow decided that it was important to preserve the culture of each of its republics and this was an example of how they were doing it. The college in Tashkent has 350 students and 150 teachers, who constantly watch for gifted young people so that they can become teachers or enter on a musical career anywhere in the Soviet Union. The state provides six million rubles a year to operate the college, which also had sponsored some thirty theaters for students of drama in the Uzbek Republic.

On Sundays, Tashkent was alive with music. There were little squares where singers gathered on platforms to entertain whoever happened to stroll by. There were dancers and musicians, too, and the crowds wandered about from one place to another, listening to the music.

We made a quick trip by air to Samarkand, and were met by two women who were local officials and a historian, who told us much about this capital city of Tamerlane. The government has spent heavily to restore some of the old buildings in the "blue city" and there are wonderful old tombs with colored inlays on their façades, including the tomb of the first wife of the Mongol conqueror and the tomb of Mohammed's cousin. Earthquakes have destroyed many of the buildings but there were still two domes of an extraordinary blue color. There is also a large hospital here for bone tuberculosis, which we visited and where I was impressed by the docility of the children.

One of the wonderful things about Samarkand and Tashkent, too, was the quality of the melons grown in that area. At almost every meal we had three or four different kinds of melon and all of them were excellent. Some were small watermelons, some Persian melons and others were white melons with faintly yellow meat.

We left Samarkand after a strenuous visit with the feeling that Tamerlane was a real person and not just a vague figure from the remote past.

XX

THE MOST IMPORTANT THINGS
I LEARNED ABOUT THE
SOVIET UNION

The most important things I learned about the Soviet Union—
and the things that may be most difficult for democratic peoples
everywhere to comprehend—came to a focus when I visited the city
of Leningrad, formerly, of course, the St. Petersburg of the Czars. I
had been absorbing various ideas from the time I landed in Moscow
and was gradually approaching certain conclusions on the basis of
what I had seen and heard. But it was at the Leningrad medical school,
which puts great emphasis on pediatrics, that I believed I really saw
what was happening in Russia and what this may mean in the world-
wide struggle between Communism and democracy.

To make this clear, I must go back a little in my travels in Russia
and a little in history, too. In trying to understand Russian thinking,
we must remember the names of two men—Nikolai Lenin and Dr.
Ivan Petrovich Pavlov. The influence of these two men—one a revolu-
tionary and the other a physiologist and experimental psychologist—
on the Russians today is tremendous.

Lenin is the nearest thing to a saint that the Russian people have to worship. The Revolution of 1917 unified the country and led to a triumph over the ancient rule of the Czars. The people thought they were fighting against injustice and Lenin symbolized to them the beginning of a better world. Since then they have gone through great hardships, a new kind of tyranny and two wars in which some twelve million persons were killed, but they have also made enormous physical gains, and in the last five years the daily lives of the people have gradually become better. And Lenin is still the symbol.

The proof of how the people feel about Lenin can be seen every day in Moscow's Red Square. Dr. Gurewitsch, Miss Corr and I joined a long queue one day to visit the tomb in which Lenin and Joseph Stalin lie together. People who had come from all over Russia were in the line, inching slowly forward toward the steps leading up to the tomb. The line forms every day that the tomb is open and it is always a long one. I did not realize how long until I followed it one day from beginning to end and discovered that it wound back and forth three times in the garden along the Kremlin wall before it even began to climb the last half mile up the hill to the entrance of the tomb. In all it must have been a mile and a half long. To whom or to what, I wondered, do we in America give such devotion? So the symbol of Lenin became a more important part of my background study than it had ever been before.

Then I began to encounter the second historic figure, Dr. Pavlov. I knew vaguely that, before his death in 1936, he had conducted many experiments and made extensive studies of conditioned reflexes and that the Soviet Government had built a special laboratory for him. But I had not realized until I saw some of the results of his work at Leningrad and elsewhere that he may well prove to be far more famous in history as the father of a system that seems to be turning the masses of Russia into completely disciplined and amenable people.

I had been in my customary controversy with Intourist because I changed the date of my departure for Leningrad, but finally we got away late one evening on one of the best railroad trains in the country, accompanied by Mrs. Lavrova. Miss Corr and I had a compartment, but Dr. Gurewitsch shared his space with a Russian general who was a good talker and spent hours insisting that the United States was busy preparing to attack the Soviet Union. I did not know where Mrs. Lavrova was tucked away. In fact, I seldom knew during our trips where she spent the nights but assumed that some special arrangements were made for the Intourist guides and interpreters.

Leningrad seemed to me to be a much more sophisticated city than Moscow, with beautiful old buildings and an air reminiscent of the Victorian era. Our hotel was pleasant but old and ornate, and the city generally, with its wonderful museums, seemed more cosmopolitan than the capital.

Dr. Gurewitsch had arranged to see certain medical institutions and, after he had gone on his way, the Intourist people suggested several things that I might like to see. Fortunately, I picked the right one.

"I think I would prefer to go to the institute of medicine oriented toward pediatrics," I said. "I'd like to see their methods of handling children."

We drove to the institute. It was a cold, bleak day and the big buildings appeared old and a bit gloomy although some of them probably were comparatively new. We got out at the main door and went into one of the older buildings. Inside it was spotless and, even though there were many walls of wooden panels, everything was glisteningly clean. As usual on visits to such institutions, I was conducted first to the office of the director, who had assembled the heads of several departments to talk to me. After a brief discussion, they asked if I would like to see an experiment. Thirty-two children taken at birth from lying-in hospitals, whose parents had died or abandoned them, were being trained. The purpose of the training was to see whether they could develop in an institution and be as advanced, healthy and happy as in an ordinary home.

The nursery was well equipped. While the head teacher and several doctors watched with me, one of the nurses—a solid, friendly young woman in white uniform and cap—demonstrated the kind of training given the babies. It was here, I later realized, that the Pavlov theories were being put into practice. The same pattern is followed in all nurseries and also by mothers training their children at home.

A six-month-old baby was brought to the nurse for his daily "conditioning." The routine was simple—to hold two rings out to the baby and persuade him to pull on them as the first step in the exercises. But I immediately noticed that the baby already knew what was coming and what he was supposed to do. He held out his hands to grasp the rings as soon as he saw the nurse. Then, after holding tightly to the rings throughout the exercise, he dropped them without being given any signal and shifted to the next exercise. This was using his legs and he went through the routine without any direction from the nurse. Then he lay rigid, waiting to be picked up by his heels and exercised on his head! After that, the nurse picked him up and hugged and kissed him and spent some time playing with him as any mother might do with a small baby.

This attitude of affection and loving care was customary, I observed, with children of all ages at all the institutes that I visited. The next group I saw consisted of four children about a year and a half old who went through a more complicated routine. They came in, a little like a drill team, took off their shoes, put them neatly in a row and pulled out a bench from the wall. One after the other, they crawled along the bench, then walked on it and then crawled under it. Then they climbed up on exercise bars. They knew exactly what to do and when to do it—like clockwork—and when they had finished the routine each one walked over and sat on the lap of a nurse. The nurse lowered them down backward to the floor and pulled them up again in another exercise. Then the children put on their shoes, put the bench back in place and went out. This kind of training in behavior goes on year after year as the children grow up.

What, I asked myself, does this mean in ordinary life outside the nursery or schoolroom? And as I watched the children I knew that I had already seen some of the answers in the conduct of the Russian people, the generations that are growing up or have grown up since Dr. Pavlov conducted his experiments and drew his conclusions about the conditioning of reflex action. I remembered the day I had stood in the long line, moving four abreast, across Red Square to the tomb of Lenin. There were many children with their parents in the line but they were always quiet and orderly.

One little girl I had been observing could not have been more than three or four years old. She apparently asked her parents for some money and then stepped out of the line and walked over to an old woman who sold little packets of food for the passersby to distribute to the pigeons. The child bought a packet and solemnly scattered its contents and watched the birds rush to eat. Then she carefully folded the paper packet, returned it to the old woman's basket and walked back to stand beside her parents in the slow-moving line.

I thought that any American child would have crumpled the packet and doubtless thrown it in the street or, at best, into a trash basket. But the little Russian girl had been conditioned by the age of three to be neat, to save the paper (which is scarce in Russia) and to avoid littering the street. I felt sure that it never occurred to her to do otherwise. She had been trained to do certain things in certain situations and she did, just as Dr. Pavlov had said she would.

For somewhat similar reasons, no adult ever throws a burnt match on the sidewalk in a Russian city. He puts it back into the box. No cigarette stubs are ever seen in the gutters. I visited cities in many widely-separated parts of Russia and some in very remote areas, and it is my conviction that the cities of the Soviet Union are the cleanest in the world. There are, of course, machines that hose down the streets of Moscow in the night and there are crews of women with long-handled brooms who sweep the streets almost constantly by day. But it takes more than those measures to keep Moscow or any other city so clean. Perhaps the most important factor is that the people themselves co-operate in an astonishing fashion to avoid making any litter. There is doubtless an element of pride behind this co-operation, but it seemed to me that there also was the element of years of training—of conditioned reflexes.

Such things as cigarette stubs and bits of paper may seem trivial in studying the actions of a great nation's population, particularly when the world is worried about missiles and hydrogen bombs and the cold war. But I do not believe the acts and attitudes of the Soviet Government can be fully understood unless we are aware of the way in which the people have been prepared to carry on the Socialist philosophy on which the regime is based.

Because of life-long conditioning, the government can depend on the mass of the people—there will always be exceptions—to react in a certain way to certain stimuli. The Russians today are a disciplined, well-trained people; not a happy people perhaps, but not at all likely to rise up against their rulers.

But more than this—much more—Americans should never forget that by controlling the entire economy the Soviet dictatorship can use this disciplined people to do things that are difficult if not impossible in our free economy. The Communist leaders are well aware of this power and know how to use it. They put far more emphasis and far more money into scientific and research projects, for example, than we do. To take just one field of endeavor: in 1956 the Russian schools graduated about 26,000 doctors. In the United States, we graduated about 6,500.

In the Soviet Union free medical care appeared to be one of the things most highly valued by the people. The Health Ministry has agencies throughout the country but the rules are made in Moscow, with some adjustments for local conditions. To become a doctor, one must attend school for ten years and then study at medical school for six years and then give three years of work to the state. The emphasis at first was placed on public health doctors. After completing his work for the state a doctor may choose his specialty and have three more years of training. I was interested to discover that a doctor is not supposed to work more than a six-hour day.

The whole Soviet Union is divided into health districts. We visited one district center in Leningrad for the care of mothers and children. It deals only with healthy children. Those who are ill are sent to a hospital. The district has nineteen thousand children. There are three nurseries in the city and four outside where children are sent for a more healthy atmosphere. There are eighteen kindergartens and eleven schools in the district. The district medical staff of ninety-one persons includes fifty-one doctors, each of whom spends two hours in the center and four hours making calls. They told us that only one child under a year old had died in the district in 1956 and only four children under sixteen had died. There was no venereal disease and no prostitution in the district. It is significant to note that there are more than thirty-five such centers in Leningrad alone, with two thousand doctors devoting themselves purely to preventive medicine.

We later visited Sochi, far to the south on the Black Sea, where there are fifty sanitariums owned by government-run industries or by trade unions. If a doctor certifies the need for a worker to go to a sanitarium during his month's vacation, 70 per cent of the cost of his care is paid by the union. The worker pays for his transportation, at a specially low rate, and also pays 30 per cent of his expenses during this vacation period. In cases of serious illness, the time spent in a special hospital or sanitarium is not counted as vacation time.

At Sochi, there is a remarkable arrangement that permits either men or women workers going to the sanitariums to take along their spouse, but at extra cost. I saw many husbands and wives enjoying the beautiful beach at Sochi, lying in the sun or swimming. The people spend much time and thought preparing for their holidays; in fact, I never realized how important vacations were until I heard them discussed so fervently in the Soviet Union.

I have written mostly about agriculture and medicine in Russia, but the government is just as keenly aware of the need for research and for generous financing in other scientific fields. There was in Moscow with us an American, Seth Jackson, who was a member of a United Nations delegation visiting Russia to study problems of forestry, particularly logging. He was a technical expert from our Department of Forestry, and it was his opinion that Russia was ahead in forestry research.

"The Soviet Union has surveyed all of its forests through the efforts of the Institutes for Research in Forestry," he said. "There are twelve such institutes in this country and they have steadily improved the machinery used for logging and other purposes. The United States hasn't ever mapped all of its forests."

Of course, a dictatorship can do many things in the line of research that are difficult or slow in a free economy. The dictatorship controls all production and can concentrate on what seems to be most important at the moment—the launching of earth satellites, for example—without much regard for the cost. The dictatorship controls prices as well as production and it can decide to let the people live less comfortably —very uncomfortably, indeed, by our standards—while the research is carried on. The people pay for it in hard work and scarcity of consumer goods and a low living standard. But there was no question in my mind that this system had brought important material progress in Russia.

There was another thing that interested me in regard to the Soviet encouragement of scientific progress. Able students have been given every opportunity to work freely, but I wondered what right they had been given to think. So I asked one scientist about it.

"Oh, we are encouraged to think freely just as we are given every encouragement to work," he replied with a smile. "We are free to discuss, to challenge and to think whatever we please." But if you ask any of them a political question, they invariably reply: "We know nothing about politics."

While I am on the subject of freedoms, I should mention that I visited a Baptist church in Moscow and talked to its director. He said there were about 250,000 Baptists in Russia and that the number was growing at the rate of 15,000 to 20,000 a year. When I was there the church was crowded to capacity and there were many young men and young women in the congregation, although in Russian Orthodox churches I had visited earlier it seemed to me that most of the worshipers were middle-aged or old women and men with a few little children. This was true also of Roman Catholic churches and even of synagogues.

"They take a great interest in the services," I was told, "and the church is entirely supported by their contributions, but only older people attend."

Later in Moscow, I had an interesting meeting with the Committee of Soviet Women, who were trying to arrange for an invitation to the United States.

"Why is it so difficult," one of them asked, "for us to get visas to visit your country? We have been trying for two years to arrange a visit through the State Department but we have failed miserably."

"Are you sure," I asked, "that your own government would give you permission to leave Russia?"

"Certainly," she said. "We have been given unequivocal assurances from our own government."

I told them that I would try to get a group from the National Council of Women of the United States to look into the problem and possibly take some action at the State Department. These women had a great desire to see America and I felt sure that it would benefit us to have a greater interchange between the Russian people and our own people. We have completely different backgrounds and our lives are completely different. But we have to see to understand. Possibly after seeing America they would prefer their own ways of life but such interchanges might lead us to sufficient understanding to work out the kind of peaceful coexistence our leaders talk about but seem unable to achieve.

One member of the group I already knew—Ludmilla Pavlichenko, a great heroine of the Soviet Union's Red Army, famous as a sharp-shooter who had fought the Germans with great success. I had met her when she came to the United States in the early days of the war with two other Russian delegates to a student conference. Miss Pavlichenko at that time wore the uniform of the Red Army and was given a great deal of publicity in the newspapers. There was even a hillbilly song written about her feats with an army rifle. When I saw her again in Moscow she was getting a bit stout and her hair was graying and there was nothing about her to remind you of her sharp-shooting days except the star on her blouse denoting that she was a Hero of the Soviet Union.

She was retired on a pension because of wounds and was working as a volunteer with war veterans. I did not recognize her until she spoke to me but we talked about the days she had been in America and how the Russian and British and American students had spent a weekend with me at Hyde Park. She invited me to her home, a four-room apartment where she and her husband and her mother live. Her mother was sixty and retired but she was in charge of the social welfare for their group of apartment houses. The apartment was comfortable and one wall of the living room was lined with books.

"I manage the household finances," Ludmilla said, "and I always set aside something for buying books. We spend a lot of our income on food—perhaps 350 rubles a week—but we eat very well. There is plenty of fruit and enough meat and borscht and sometimes we have caviar or fancy cakes."

I was happy to see her and to know that she was getting along so well but, of course, a Hero of the Soviet Union is entitled to special considerations in the Communist scheme of things.

There was one other phase of the "conditioning" of the Russian people that I observed everywhere I went in the Soviet Union, and it is one of particular importance to Americans at present. The most familiar symbol in the country is the dove of peace. You see it wherever you go. I saw it painted on the sides of trucks in the streets; I looked down from the tower of Moscow University and saw a great white dove outlined in stone on the lawn. It was on posters in distant villages. The finale of a circus I attended featured the release of a flock of doves over the audience, following a patriotic speech.

One might think that this was a noble effort on the part of the government to keep the people reminded of their need for peace. Heaven knows, they don't need to be reminded! They suffered enough in the war, and a traveler in Russia is quickly aware that the mass of people want peace.

But that was not the purpose of the dove of peace campaign. It was launched to remind the people that they must sacrifice and work because, despite Russia's desire for peace, their great enemy, the United States, is trying to bring about a war against Russia. The dove of peace symbolizes the efforts of the Soviet Union to protect the people from an aggressive war such as our government is alleged to be planning.

We Americans and the people of the free world must never forget or ignore this kind of distorted "conditioning" of the Russian people, this kind of indoctrination with ideas that are false but that by repetition and repetition can be drilled into the minds not only of the Russian people but of peoples in underdeveloped countries whom the Communists seek to turn against the United States.

A totalitarian regime regulates all the news—or almost all—that is available to the great mass of people. None but a Communist newspaper can be bought in the Soviet Union, so the people get only the slanted Communist point of view on what is happening in the world. They have no other interpretation of the position of the United States and very little concept of world opinion other than that fed to them by the Kremlin.

For us merely to say that their beliefs are false is not enough, because they have been conditioned to believe that Washington is plotting a war and that Moscow is striving to protect them from our aggression; and they do believe it. Almost the only news about the United States that I saw in Russian newspapers was the story of school integration troubles at Little Rock, Arkansas. When I protested that the Russians were getting a completely distorted view of the United States and of the attitude of the American people, I was usually met with silence or obvious disbelief. Or, if the person I was talking with was educated and intelligent, the reply might be: "Oh, I know nothing about politics."

It may seem ironic to us that a dove of peace has become the symbol of an American plot to start a world war, but I was convinced that we are going to have to make far greater efforts than in the past if we hope to avoid the war that the Kremlin has told the people over and over and over again that we might start.

XXI

INTERVIEW WITH KHRUSHCHEV

The word "kremlin" means a citadel and there are citadels dating back to the Middle Ages in a number of Russian cities. But in recent years the world has come to speak only of "the Kremlin" and, in democratic countries, to give the word an ominous inflection because it is the seat of Communist power in Moscow. Actually, the Kremlin, while old and in spots a bit like a rabbit warren, is a very attractive triangular section of central Moscow, like a city within a city. It is surrounded by high crenelated walls of reddish sandstone topped by seven towers, one of which houses the famous chimes above the main gate. Inside are three cathedrals built about the sixteenth century and the 300-foot-high bell tower of Ivan the Great with a golden cupola. Here, too, is the former Grand Palace of the Czars which has been rebuilt to provide a home for the Soviet parliament, and other buildings which house the various departments and agencies of the Soviet government.

As soon as I arrived in Moscow, I had requested an interview with Nikita S. Khrushchev, the leader of the Communist party in Russia and the man who survived a bitter internecine struggle after the death of Stalin to emerge as the real power in the Soviet Union. He is now Premier and First Secretary of the Central Committee of the Soviet Communist party. I did not get any definite reply but I was told to write a letter in which I was to state the questions I would want to ask Mr. Khrushchev. I did so, adding that I wanted to record his answers and have photographs taken. Still I received no reply, no date for a meeting.

I worried about it and frequently asked the Intourist people to find out whether Mr. Khrushchev intended to talk to me. But I received evasive replies or no replies at all. I couldn't even find out whether he was going to be in Moscow. As the days flew along, I became discouraged about the possibility of seeing him, although that had been one of the main purposes of my visit to Russia. This silence, this mysteriousness, was more or less typical of the Kremlin, I learned later. About five days before I was to start home I happened to mention my problem to the chief of the United Press bureau in Moscow, Henry Shapiro,

"I shall be terribly disappointed if I don't get the interview," I said. "Do you think it would be wise to send a telegram directly to Mr. Khrushchev?"

Mr. Shapiro said he saw no reason for not sending a telegram and I did, saying that I had to leave on September 28 and that it would be a great disappointment to my newspapers if I did not get a chance to see him before that date. I added that I would be willing to go wherever he was, for I understood that he was taking a rest near Yalta. Still no reply.

I was ready to admit failure and, three days before my scheduled departure, I went around to various government offices to thank them for the assistance they had given me and to say good-by. That afternoon I was talking to one of the department heads when my interpreter, Mrs. Lavrova, suddenly turned to me and said:

"I forgot to tell you, but we go to Yalta early tomorrow morning."

I was so irritated I could hardly reply. "Well," I said, "I'm glad you finally remembered!"

I asked what hour we would leave Moscow, but she didn't know exactly. I went over my schedule mentally.

"We can fly down tomorrow morning and see Mr. Khrushchev in the afternoon and return to Moscow the next morning," I said. "That will let me catch my plane to Copenhagen on the twenty-eighth. How long does it take to fly to Yalta?"

"About four hours."

It would be a hurried trip but I decided we could make it. After we returned to my hotel, Mrs. Lavrova came to me with further details.

"The plane does not leave until ten o'clock in the morning," she said. "Also it is impossible to fly over the mountains, so we will have to drive by automobile for about two hours and a half in order to get to Yalta. I will not know until we get to Yalta the hour at which we will be received by Comrade Khrushchev. We will fly back to Moscow the next day, which is Friday. We will have to leave Yalta by automobile at one o'clock in the afternoon in order to catch the plane at four o'clock."

I was appalled. This meant that I would not get to Moscow until nine o'clock at night on the eve of my departure for home on Saturday morning. What if the weather was bad? I would miss connections and might be greatly delayed in getting another reservation.

"Well," I said, "I will just have to trust to Heaven that we can get back in time."

Mrs. Lavrova was pleased. "I'm glad you're going," she said, "because I can show you where the Yalta conference meetings were held and the rooms occupied by the heads of state."

So the next morning we departed for Yalta. The weather was good and the drive through the mountains on the final leg of the trip was beautiful. When we reached the hotel, we had to wait about an hour until word arrived that Mr. Khrushchev would send his car for us the next morning at nine-thirty.

"That means that if we are going to see the palace where the Yalta conference was held we will have to get up early," I decided. So we drove to the palace the next morning at eight-thirty. The big building had been converted into a sanitarium for persons under observation for heart ailments and there were many men and women occupying the rooms that had once been the summer home of the Czars. Mrs. Lavrova showed us the private dining room, bedroom and study that my husband had occupied and also the room in which my son Elliott had stayed during the conference. We also visited the conference rooms.

On leaving the palace I was surprised and much interested to see that a large crowd of patients had gathered around our automobile. They cheered and shouted warm expressions of welcome to me, which pleased me very much.

At nine-thirty Mr. Khrushchev's car was at the sanitarium. We drove downhill toward the Black Sea and finally came to a gate with a soldier on guard. We passed through the gate and, a few minutes later, through another similarly guarded gate, and then we approached a comfortable but not imposing house on a lovely site looking toward the city of Yalta. We had, I observed, arrived exactly on the minute set for our appointment.

We were led through the yard and to a garden, where Mr. Khrushchev was talking with another gentleman. He came to greet us and bid us welcome, a short, stocky man with a bald head and a wide smile on his round, mobile face. He was bareheaded and wore one of the white Russian blouses with beautiful embroidery around the open collar and on the sleeves. He was obviously on vacation and was most hospitable.

"This is a beautiful view you have from your home," I said.

He beamed and immediately walked me down to where we could get a complete panorama of the city.

"It is particularly beautiful at night when the lights go on in Yalta," he said, with Mrs. Lavrova interpreting.

He then invited us to sit on the porch where there was a big table. Dr. Gurewitsch, who had accompanied me, set up our portable tape recorder so there would not be any danger of misinterpreting what was said and we settled down to talk. Mr. Khrushchev emphasized to me that he had been a factory worker, but I quickly discovered that he talked easily and that he expressed his views with confidence and clarity.

"I have been very much interested in my travels in your country," I began, "and I appreciate that you are taking time to see me."

Mr. Khrushchev made a little gesture. "Politicians," he said, "never cast aside political obligations.

"I appreciate your coming here," he went on, "and I want to speak of President Franklin Roosevelt. We respect him and remember his activities because he was the first to establish diplomatic relations between the United States and the Soviet Union. President Roosevelt understood perfectly well the necessity of such relations. . . . He was a great man, a capable man who understood the interests of his own country and the interests of the Soviet Union. We had a common cause against Hitler and we appreciate very much that Franklin Roosevelt understood this task, which was a common task. . . . I am happy to greet you in our land. . . ."

My first question concerned disarmament. I pointed out that after World War II we reduced our army from twelve million to one million men, but then because of the Soviet Union's actions we were forced to rearm. In such circumstances, I said, the American people wonder how the Soviet Union could expect us to agree to disarmament without inspection.

"We do not agree with your conception," he replied. "We consider that demobilization took place in the U. S. and in the U. S. S. R. . . . . In our country men and women were all mobilized. In our country perished roughly the number of persons you mention as making up the army of your country, almost the same number. Mrs. Roosevelt, I do not want to offend you, but if you compare the losses of your country with the losses of ours, your losses just equal our losses in one big campaign. . . . You know what terrible ruins we got. . . . We lost our cities. That is why our country was so eager to establish . . . firm peace. No country wished it so eagerly. . . . When you consider demobilization, just some circles in your country wanted it. Others thought and believed that the Soviet country would perish as a Socialist state. So they just hope it will perish, that it will die. . . . But it has become even more powerful."

"I understand, Mr. Khrushchev, but the Soviets kept a much greater proportion of men under arms than we did at that time."

Dr. Gurewitsch broke in to say: "Not just the proportion but the absolute figures were much greater—six million under arms in the Soviet." He spoke in Russian.

Mr. Khrushchev looked at him coldly. "Dr. Gurewitsch, you may perfectly know the number of your army men, but don't feel so sure of the number of our army men." He turned back to me. "I do not reject that our army was bigger. . . . Take a map and look at the geographical . . . situation of our country. It is a colossal territory, Mrs. Roosevelt. If you take Germany or France, just small countries which keep their army to defend either their east or their west, that is easy; they may have a small army. But if we keep our army in the east it is difficult to reach the west, you see, to use this western army in the east, because our territory is so vast. . . . So, to be sure of our security . . . we have to keep a big army, which is not so easy for us."

I said I understood, but that after the war the Russians wanted a group of neutral countries between them and Germany—countries that were to be free but closely tied to the Soviet Union for its protection against another attack. I pointed out that Germany was no longer a military menace and that Great Britain could not be considered a military threat. Why then, I asked, was it not possible to do without an offensive army in Russia, since it frightened the rest of the world?

"What can I tell you in answer?" he began. "When we increase our arms it means we are afraid of each other. Russian troops, before the [1917] Revolution, never approached Great Britain and never entered America. . . . But the troops of the U. S. A. approached our far east [after World War I], Japanese troops were in our far east in Vladivostok, French troops in our city of Odessa. And that is why we must have an army. Your troops approach our territory, not we yours. . . . Until the time when troops will be drawn out of Europe and military bases [American] will be liquidated, of course, the disarmament will not succeed."

I said that after World War II we were not suspicious of Russia. "I know my husband and, I think, President Truman had a real hope we would be able to come to understandings," I continued. "But then we felt the Russians did not strictly keep agreements made at Yalta and we became more and more suspicious."

"We have different points of view as to who broke [the Yalta] agreement," he commented. "We cannot agree on the policy of the U. S. A. that they want to liberate the European and Eastern countries from Socialism. They not only announced it but they also gave money for it. They have established radio stations and have arranged propaganda. . . . You know, Mrs. Roosevelt, what happened in Greece— the will of the people [for Socialism or Communism] was destroyed by English tanks. Even Mr. Churchill himself went through the country in a tank, and so the will of the people was destroyed. After the English troops left, the American troops [a reference to the Marshall Plan] moved in."

"Would you mind my saying that we believed it was not the will of the people [to have Communism]?" I replied. "We believed that the majority wanted their King back. . . . Does the government of the Soviet Union still believe that a Communist world must be brought about? . . . We think the Soviet Union wishes to spread Communism throughout the world, not only through the use of soldiers but through other agents."

"Am I also an agent?"

"You may have been for all I know. But what would be believed at home would be that you had arranged for the agents."

"Arranged by whom?"

I replied that it was generally believed that there was a constant effort to persuade people that the world was going Communist. "Now," I added, "we don't believe that this is the way the world has to be. We can believe in our way and you in your way."

"That is why we brought our agents—the agents of different philosophies—into the United Nations."

I asked whether the threat of war was going to continue because Russia and the U.S. each think the other is trying to impose its own philosophy on the whole world.

"Two questions, Mrs. Roosevelt, two questions. The first one is about two philosophies which may live in peace. No doubt about it, Mrs. Roosevelt, we must live in peace, we must live, we must."

"Not only must we live in peace," Dr. Gurewitsch said, "but we want to live in peace and we strive to live in peace in the United States."

"We also want to have, you see, something common in our economic activity, in our cultural life," Mr. Khrushchev said.

I said that was all very good, but did he think that the Communist philosophy only must spread over the world. I pointed out the motto at the top of the newspaper *Pravda,* the official Soviet organ.

"Yes," he said. "We have a motto: Proletarians of all the world unite. That was not my idea. We differ about our foreign systems. I I have never hidden myself from such questions. This is my statement. . . . Communism will win in the whole world. This is scientifically based on the writings of Karl Marx, Engels and Lenin.

"Your people in the U.S. are cultured people, so you know that all kinds of changes take place in economics, and how relations between nations change—Feudalism, Capitalism, then Socialism. And the highest state will be Communism. It is well known this is the meaning of history."

Mr. Khrushchev had sat much of the time with his hands folded on the table but when he worked himself up to an eloquent point he lost his smile, he became somewhat excited and gestured with his hands.

"When a state changes its order," he continued, "this is the business of the people themselves. We are against any military attempt to introduce Communism or Socialism into any country, as well as we are against your interference to re-establish capitalism in our country through military intervention. That is why we stand firmly for co-existence and collaboration."

I said I would agree generally, but that the same rules should hold for Socialist countries and that when there was a drive to put over Communist ideas outside Russia it was difficult to live in a peaceful atmosphere.

"If we speak about interference, Mrs. Roosevelt, you know what your State Department does in this sphere. Let Mr. Dulles tell what Mr. Loy Henderson had in view when he visited Turkey and the rest of the countries of the Near East. Mr. Henderson had a rather dirty mission."

I replied that we believed the Soviet Union started trouble in the Near East by permitting Czechoslovakian arms to go to Cairo, where the Egyptians had been boasting they would destroy Israel. I said I thought the situation should have been corrected long before by both Russia and the United States, but that now Soviet arms were going to both Egypt and Syria and that the United States felt they had to help other Arab states when requested. Why, I asked, could not our two countries come to a reconsideration of our entire attitude toward the Near East?

"Mrs. Roosevelt, you don't know about the proposals that were made by the Soviet Union that no country should sell arms to any country in the Near East. The United States refused."

"That was only after arms had been sent by the Soviet Union to Egypt and Syria," Dr. Gurewitsch said, "so the balance had already been destroyed."

"Are you the head of military supply, Dr. Gurewitsch?" Mr. Khrushchev demanded. "I don't think you know the exact situation."

I said it would be a good idea to bring up the exact situation in the United Nations.

"I ask you: who first started selling arms to the countries—we or you?" Mr. Khrushchev said. "How about Pakistan?"

"I think you did," I replied. "Pakistan is not in the Near East."

"The question was who first sold arms?" Dr. Gurewitsch said.

"I think the only thing to do about the situation today is to bring it up in the United Nations and try to come to some agreement," I persisted.

"You haven't answered my question," Mr. Khrushchev said, getting excited and a bit red in the face. "You do not like Communists and I have nothing against this because I may not love the people who stand on other platforms. But people might be honest. That is why my question: who were the first to sell arms to other countries and not only sell but supply them free of charge? Who was the first?

"I respect you greatly and I appreciate the activities of your great husband, Franklin Roosevelt, but the whole world knows that the United States started first the supply of arms, so I hoped to have an honest talk. Otherwise we cannot be sure of the interpretation of this talk."

"Are we going back to the Marshall Plan?" I asked.

"It is no matter whether it is the Marshall Plan or any other plan. I know the United States supplied all our enemies with arms."

"The emphasis of the Marshall Plan was on economic development within the countries."

Mr. Khrushchev snapped: "Arms are also economic aid?"

I said I agreed that many countries in the West received arms from us and that I could see how the Soviet Union would feel that such arms were provided to be used against them, but I pointed out that we had been forced to fear that the Russians had military intentions against the West.

"What were the arms supplied for?" Mr. Khrushchev persisted. "We never had them for tea parties."

I recalled the Soviet actions at the time of the blockade of Berlin and said that they seemed to be trying to push us out of that city. I remarked that mistakes might have been made by our government but that the Russians, too, made mistakes. "Having been here," I added, "I realize that your people do not want war."

"If you say the people do not want war, who wants war—their representatives?"

"The government, perhaps," I said. "For they do things on both sides which they believe are for the defense of the people. This happens in our country and it probably happens in yours."

"It takes place in yours."

"If so," I replied hotly, "it also takes place in yours."

"Definitely not in my country," he exclaimed, gesturing angrily.

"Oh, it does," I said. "Governments are much the same."

"There are signs," Mr. Khrushchev said. "There is logic. There is experience, so we may check up. Whose troops approach the borderline? Do the Soviet troops approach the United States' border? Is it American troops who approach the border of the Soviet Union? Yes. They are there."

"We are not trying to enter the Soviet Union."

"They do try," he said emphatically.

"We are not trying. But it can be only a defensive attitude if we are to have any kind of amicable coexistence. . . . Could we work for a greater interchange of people on every level in order to get greater understanding?"

"I am surprised, Mrs. Roosevelt. Maybe you are not informed quite well what the situation is. We never refuse. We always allow people to come here, but you never give a visa to our citizens."

"We don't always allow Communists to come to the United States. Neither do you always allow people to leave your country, even if we manage to get visas for them. . . . Misunderstandings have grown between our countries and there is fear on both sides. We will have to do things to create confidence. One thing is a broader exchange of people."

"I fully agree, Mrs. Roosevelt," he said in a calmer voice.

I asked him if he had any suggestions to make or questions to ask me.

"We have stated many times our purposes," he replied. "But the United States is used to speaking, to dictating, so they only speak about conditions they will accept. I want to know what are the words and what are the deeds. Where are the troops and whose troops are they?"

I pointed out that the Russians had a big army that could move quickly across Europe and that Europeans could only be fearful.

"There was a time when there was no American army in Germany, England or France," he replied, "and our army was much bigger [than now]. But we did nothing. We are not so stupid to make tricks. We have never made any attempts against these countries."

I brought up the question of a free press and said that the Russian people were able to read very little about America and then usually only about such things as the conflict over integration, a problem that affected only about seven out of forty-eight states.

"We also have small republics," he replied. "They make up the whole state of the U.S.S.R. and they are equal in rights. . . . Every republic has its own rights. They are independent. But let us come back to the question of what you say about the U.S.S.R. Do you say anything good in your newspapers?"

"I think there has been improvement, and there is not quite the vilification that I find in your newspapers here. But I would like to say I don't find antagonism toward us among the people."

I asked him whether his government desired greater economic interchange with the United States.

"Yes," he said. "Not because we need it but because economic intercourse is the best way to improve relations. You don't want to trade with our country because you don't want to give us military secrets. But it doesn't matter because we have atomic weapons. We are not going to buy arms from you, but we shall be pleased to trade with you."

"What else is there to do to improve relations?" Dr. Gurewitsch asked.

"Yes," I added, "that is what I am most anxious to find out."

"Tell the truth to the people of the United States," he said. "Tell the truth about the Soviet Government and about our country. You hate Communists."

"I don't hate Communists as people," I replied. "I happen to believe that through a free democracy you actually develop a more independent and stronger people. . . . I can quite understand the Socialist belief, but that does not mean I want to see their belief spread by methods of propaganda that are not always open and aboveboard—by hidden methods."

Dr. Gurewitsch reminded Mr. Khrushchev that he had said he was convinced Communism would spread over the world and asked whether that could be achieved peacefully. "You either acknowledge that an opposite idea has a chance or you simply wipe out the opportunity for coexistence," he added. "You must accept that two things can go on even though they may not lead to a complete meeting of minds at any point."

"Many people," Mr. Khrushchev replied, "believe that Communism is better than the system that exists at present [in the democracies]."

"Isn't there a contradiction in what you are saying?"

"Oh, no," Mr. Khrushchev said. "There is no contradiction. What I said about the spread of Communism is like telling about the law of nature. I am firmly convinced this is the natural course of history and has nothing to do with our living peacefully together and stopping the threat of destroying each other."

"We both know then that the bombs can annihilate the world," I said.

"We are in favor of full disarmament," he commented. "We don't need any arms if you accept our existence and stop interfering wherever you can."

"We, too, are for disarmament but there has to be some international inspection."

"We are for international inspection but there first has to be confidence and then inspection. Mr. Dulles wants inspection without confidence."

I said I thought inspection and confidence had to come together and that we had to start and then gradually increase our plans.

"Quite right," he replied. "It can be done only gradually. . . . That is what we proposed. . . . But in answer to our proposal, Mr. Dulles makes a statement which sounds as though he was making propaganda for the atom bomb, trying to make it palatable. He talks of a clean bomb as if there were such a thing as a clean bomb. War is a dirty thing. . . . You know, those rockets [have] made the situation more frightful. Now we can destroy countries in a few minutes. How many bombs does it take to destroy West Germany? How many for France? How many for England? Just a few. We now have hydrogen bombs and rockets. We do not even have to send any bombers."

I said that soon the small countries also would have atomic bombs.

"Why not? Research goes on. They learn about it. Let's get together so there shall be no war. We are ready to sign such an agreement now."

"Your people certainly want peace," I said, "and I can assure you that our people want peace, too."

"Do you think we, the government, want war?" he asked.

"Not the people but the governments make war," I replied. "And then they persuade the people that it is in a good cause, the cause of their own defense. Those arguments can be made by both your government and by ours."

"That," Mr. Khrushchev replied, "is right."

At the end of two and a half hours of conversation, I felt fully convinced that Mr. Khrushchev knew the danger that any new war would bring to civilization. I did not believe that he was moved entirely by humanitarian considerations, but I believed that he was honest when he said that he did not want war. He was tough and he was shrewd and he was fluent but, like the peasant stock he sprang from, he was cautious more than anything else. He was, I decided, convinced that war would be a disadvantage to the Soviet Union and to Communism because he believed that the wave of the future was Socialism and that his cause would triumph without war. He believed it, I told myself, and he would try to make the future serve his purposes.

After our formal interview had been recorded, I asked Mr. Khrushchev about the Soviet Union's attitude toward Jews within its borders, toward the state of Israel and toward the Middle Eastern situation in general. He started out by emphasizing strongly that Communists could not be anti-Semitic, because they opposed all discrimination for reasons of race or religion. If a Communist were known to be anti-Semitic, he added, no one would shake hands with him. He said that his own son, who was killed in World War II, had been married to a Jewess and that Jews in Russia were given all opportunities for education and for careers.

The Russians, he said, had voted for creation of the state of Israel but he now felt that Israel must change its policies and be less aggressive.

"The fact that the Soviet Union has given arms to Syria," I replied, "may be one of the reasons that the Israelis feel a sense of insecurity and therefore show aggressive tendencies."

Mr. Khrushchev flared up quickly and replied that there were eighty million Arabs and about one million Israelis and that if Israel continued her present course she would be destroyed. It was, he added, Great Britain, France and Israel that attacked Egypt.

I said that he had to separate the attitude of Israel from that of Britain and France. Israel had been told again and again by Egypt that she would be destroyed, so that the Israelis were acting in self-defense by striking before the Egyptians were fully armed by the Soviets and ready to attack.

"The Egyptian buildup of arms was proved," I added, "when the Israelis captured more than $50,000,000 worth of military matériel provided by the Soviets or their satellites and in possession of the Egyptians in the Sinai desert."

Mr. Khrushchev dodged this but when I said the Israelis were not aggressive because they needed peace to strengthen their country, he snapped: "The United States is backing Israel with arms."

"But you remember," Dr. Gurewitsch said, "that the United States voted with the Soviet Union to stop the British-French-Israel attack on Egypt?"

Yes, he replied, he remembered it very well but the United States wanted to keep on good terms with both sides because they did not want to lose the Arab oil. Then he switched the subject to say how stupid he thought the assertion was that anti-Semitism existed in Russia. Didn't I know, he asked, that there were many Jews of high rank in the Soviet Army, including a general, and that there was a Jew buried inside the Kremlin wall?

"That may be," I replied, "but it is very difficult for any Jew to leave the Soviet Union to settle or even visit in Israel."

"I know," he replied quickly, "but the time will come when everyone who wants to go will be able to go."

"It seems to me," I said, "that the Soviet Union could help if they were willing to work with the United States to achieve an understanding between Israel and the Arab countries. The Israelis are willing to sit down with Arab representatives and try to work out their difficulties, but the Arabs have always refused."

"I know very well," Mr. Khrushchev replied, "that the Arabs have made mistakes. But you must remember that the Soviet Union is for Socialist people—not for a state. Israel has all sorts of classes. We are for the Socialists [Communists] in Israel, but not for the state."

While I was in Russia, I came to the conclusion that the government was trying to integrate the Jews completely. The Soviet leaders are proud of the fact that they have allowed the various republics to retain their own culture. But the Jews are scattered everywhere throughout the cities rather than having a separate soviet republic. The government wants to make good use of their brains but they want them to be Communists, not people with a separate culture. There is no longer a Jewish theater in Russia, for instance. The Jews can attend the synagogue and train a certain number of rabbis. But there is no Jewish school. Certainly, Jews occupy high positions of all kinds but their culture is discouraged and they are not even given permission to make visits to Israel. How soon such permission may be given—the time "when everyone who wants to go will be able to do so"—was not indicated by Mr. Khrushchev.

After our talk, Mrs. Khrushchev, their daughter and their tall, fair son-in-law joined us for a few minutes. Mrs. Khrushchev was a pleasant-looking woman in her forties with light hair that was turning to dark gray. She was neatly dressed in a simple dark frock such as most Russian women wear, the kind of dress that can only be called nondescript. She did not say much, but I got the impression that she was a woman of strong character.

I explained that I had to leave by one o'clock in order to get back to Moscow in time to catch my plane the next morning for home and, with expressions of friendship, we said good-by.

As I was leaving Mr. Khrushchev wished me a pleasant trip, and asked:

"Can I tell our papers that we have had a friendly conversation?"

"You can say," I replied, "that we had a friendly conversation but that we differ."

He grinned broadly. "Now!" he exclaimed. "At least we didn't shoot at each other!"

XXII

A CHALLENGE FOR THE WEST

I was oh! so happy when our airplane, flying out of Moscow, touched down at Copenhagen, the first stop in the non-Communist world on our way back to the United States. For three weeks in the Soviet Union, I had felt more than at any time in my life that I was cut off from all of the outside world. For three weeks, I do not believe I had heard anyone really laugh on the streets or in a crowd. I had been among hospitable people but they were people who worked hard, who lived under considerable strain and who were tired. It was only after I had landed at Copenhagen and heard laughter and gay talk and saw faces that were unafraid that I realized how different were our two worlds. Suddenly, I could breathe again!

But, as I remarked earlier, I was rather frightened, too, and after I reached home my nagging fear continued. I was—I still am—afraid that Americans and the peoples of the rest of the free world will not understand the nature of the struggle against Communism as exemplified by the Soviet Union. It is urgently important for the sake of our country and our people that we get rid of some of our great misunderstandings and that we see clearly the things that must be done.

We are in a great struggle between two vastly different ways of life. While we must have guns, atomic weapons and missiles for retaliation against aggression, they are not going to win this struggle or prevent a catastrophic world war. Nor is belief in the idea of democracy likely to have great effect in areas where democratic institutions are not established. To overemphasize the importance of military power or to propagate merely the abstract idea of democracy is to miss the point. There is much, much more to be done if Western leadership is to be accepted by the masses of the world's underdeveloped countries, if our way of life and our hard-won freedoms are to survive—or, perhaps, if anything is to survive in the Atomic Age—and flourish. We must provide leadership for free peoples, but we must never forget that in many countries, particularly in Asia and Africa, the freedom that is uppermost in the minds of the people is the freedom to eat.

I think it is time for us Americans to take a good look at ourselves and our shortcomings. We should remember how we achieved the aims of freedom and democracy. We should look back in an effort to gauge how we can best influence the peoples of the world. Perhaps we made the greatest impression on underdeveloped countries in the 1930's when we ourselves were making a tremendous effort to fight our way out of a great economic depression. In that period, we united behind bold ideas and vigorous programs and, as they watched us, many people in far countries of the world began to realize that a government could be intensely interested in the welfare of the individual. They saw what was happening and it gave them hope that it could happen to them, too. That was a generation ago, but again today, it seems to me that it is essential for us to examine carefully our actions as a nation and try to develop a program for the welfare of the individual.

In this connection, I was sometimes astonished during my visit to Russia to see what the Soviet Government had brought about during four decades of Communist dictatorship. Illiteracy, which was once 90 per cent, has been reduced until it is now probably less than 10 per cent. The people have been educated in every field—crafts, arts, professions, sciences—and the government has used the educational system for political purposes, to shape the people to the will of the leadership. Educators are sent where they are most important for the purposes of the government. Doctors are sent where they can be most useful. Workers are sent to distant areas of Asia because new fields must be plowed and crops planted. This is dictatorship and it is hateful; but the results achieved by the Soviet regime are obvious to anyone visiting Russia. The water is pure; the milk is clean; the food supply is increasing; industry has made mighty strides. The people are not free, but they are better off materially each year. They know very little of other countries and they are willing to accept a hard life because of the insidious Communist propaganda that unites them in fear of aggression by the United States. Furthermore most of them are sustained by a belief in communistic aims.

In this book I have tried to tell a few of the things I saw and learned in Russia and to show what they mean to the people if we look at the Soviet achievements through Russian eyes. They mean a great deal—hope for a better life—to the Russian masses, and Communist propaganda, deceptive though it is, may make them mean something to the peoples of underdeveloped countries that as yet are uncommitted in the struggle between democracy and Communism. This is why we must realize that we are involved in much more than a military struggle.

The Russians recognize that there are vast masses of people in Asia, Africa and parts of Latin America who are closer to the economic conditions that existed forty years ago in Russia than they are to the conditions that have existed for many years in the United States. The leaders of the Soviets can say to them: "We know your conditions. Our people were once hungry, too, not only for food but for health and education, for knowledge and for hope for the future. Look at what we have done in forty years! Take heart. We can help you."

This is the challenge to democracy. This is the real challenge, and it cannot be met by mere words. We have to show the world by our actions that we live up to the ideals we profess and demonstrate that we can provide all the people in this country with the basic decencies of life, spiritually as well as materially. In the United States we are the showcase for the possibilities inherent in a free world, in democracy. If the lives of our people are not better in terms of basic satisfactions as well as in material ways than the lives of people anywhere in the world, then the uncommitted peoples we need on our side will look for leadership elsewhere.

Perhaps we think we have spent a great deal in grants to our friends abroad but there is more than that to the struggle for the minds of men. Just for example, we have taken no trouble to invite delegations from other parts of the world to look at our system and to see what we are doing under government auspices. If we are to be leaders, we must offer needy countries technical knowhow to help them achieve the freedom to eat, and practical help in developing, step by step, a democratic way of life. It is not enough to say that we do not like the

Communist idea. We have to prove that our own idea is better and can accomplish more.

We *can* accomplish more. There is no reason for us to be frightened by the scientific achievements under direction of the Soviet Government, which has concentrated money and manpower on sputniks and rockets for obvious propaganda reasons. We have been complacent and given as little money and as few men as possible to work that we should have pressed vigorously. We were more interested in our comforts, in making money and in having all the luxuries possible in this comfortable world of ours. We have to change and we will change that approach. If we are to lead the free world, we must become a mature people—or we may one day wake up to find that fear and laziness have reduced us from a strong, vital nation to a people unable to lead other nations in the only way to win the struggle against Communism, the way of the mind and the heart.

I can think of nothing more foolish than looking at the Russian scientific achievements and saying that we must rush to catch up with them by resorting to their methods. We have always said that our objectives were those that could be achieved only by a free people. So why should we be content ourselves with meeting each Soviet challenge? Why should a free people slavishly follow a Communist lead? That is not what we want. We must develop all our resources in our own way. We want our people to decide whether their children shall go to school, whether they shall be scientists or playwrights or mechanics. We don't want to be told what to do. What the world wants today is leadership in the true sense, and we had better decide what we want to achieve and then go ahead and do it—do it as leaders and not as imitators.

The only thing that frightened me in Russia was that we might be apathetic and complacent in the face of this challenge. I can well understand why the Russian people welcome the good that has come to them. But I cannot understand or believe that anything that has to be preserved by fear will stand permanently against a system which offers love and trust among peoples and removes fear so that all feel free to think and express their ideas.

It seems to me that we must have the courage to face ourselves in this crisis. We must regain a vision of ourselves as leaders of the world. We must join in an effort to use all knowledge for the good of all human beings.

When we do that, we shall have nothing to fear.

INDEX

Set in Linotype Fairfield
Format by Nancy Etheredge
Manufactured by The Haddon Craftsmen, Inc.
Published by HARPER & BROTHERS, New York